London
March 2013

MANET

MANET

MANET

Portraying Life

Royal Academy of Arts

First published on the occasion of the exhibition
'Manet: Portraying Life'

Toledo Museum of Art
4 October 2012 – 1 January 2013

Royal Academy of Arts, London
26 January – 14 April 2013

Sponsored by

BNY MELLON

Partner of the Royal Academy of Arts

This exhibition has been made possible by the provision of insurance through the Government Indemnity Scheme. The Royal Academy of Arts would like to thank HM Government for providing Government Indemnity and the Department for Culture, Media and Sport and Arts Council England for arranging the indemnity.

EXHIBITION CURATORS
Royal Academy of Arts
MaryAnne Stevens
assisted by Sarah Lea

Toledo Museum of Art
Lawrence W. Nichols

EXHIBITION MANAGEMENT
Royal Academy of Arts
Nicole Ruegsegger
assisted by Emma Enderby

Toledo Museum of Art
Karen Serota
Andrea Mall

PHOTOGRAPHIC AND COPYRIGHT CO-ORDINATION
Kitty Corbet Milward

CATALOGUE
Royal Academy Publications
Beatrice Gullström
Alison Hissey
Elizabeth Horne
Carola Krueger
Sophie Oliver
Peter Sawbridge
Nick Tite

Design: Maggi Smith
Picture research: Sara Ayad
Colour origination and printing: Die Keure
Typeset in Granjon and Zurich

EDITOR'S NOTE
All works illustrated are by Edouard Manet unless otherwise stated. Widely used titles of works in French, such as *Déjeuner sur l'herbe*, have been retained to avoid confusion. Works are travelling to both venues unless otherwise stated in the catalogue entries. Dimensions are given in centimetres, height before width. The abbreviations RWI and RWII are used throughout to refer to the two volumes of the catalogue raisonné of Manet's *oeuvre* compiled by Denis Rouart and Daniel Wildenstein (*Edouard Manet: Catalogue raisonné*, Lausanne, 1975).

Illustration on page 2: cat. 65 (fig. 47).

British Library Cataloguing-in-Publication Data
A catalogue record for this book is available from the British Library

ISBN 978-1-905711-75-8 (RA paperback)
ISBN 978-1-905711-74-1 (RA hardback)
ISBN 978-1-907533-53-2 (Toledo paperback)
ISBN 978-1-907533-52-5 (Toledo hardback)

Distributed outside the United States and Canada by Thames & Hudson Ltd, London

Distributed in the United States and Canada by Harry N. Abrams, Inc., New York

Contents

Foreword

Edouard Manet towered over the art world in the second half of the nineteenth century. It is perhaps unsurprising, therefore, that many exhibitions have been devoted to his art in recent decades. These have encompassed the exemplary 1983–84 retrospective directed by the late Françoise Cachin, and a variety of smaller focused explorations of the range of his *oeuvre*, his engagement with specific genres, and the contexts of individual masterpieces. All have both drawn upon and contributed to the rich and important research that continues to be undertaken on the artist and the social and artistic milieus in which he worked.

'Manet: Portraying Life' builds upon this rich legacy by identifying an aspect of the artist's *oeuvre* that has not previously been presented in an exhibition: the straight portrait. Through a number of case studies, we have considered the ways in which Manet systematically and innovatively translated his sitters into actors in scenes of contemporary life as a means to authenticate the truthfulness of his subject-matter. Because Manet painted portraits and genre paintings throughout his career, the exhibition permits an almost-retrospective review of his stylistic journey, from his dialogue with the Old Masters to the impact of his consideration of Impressionism in *c.* 1870. Manet's untimely death and the significant number of works he left unresolved have enabled us to examine his sensibility to relative levels of finish.

This exhibition would not have been possible without the generosity of our many lenders. We are fully aware of the sacrifices they have made to permit their great examples of Manet's work to hang on the walls of our two institutions and we thank them all. We also extend our thanks to those whose names appear in the Acknowledgements: our colleagues who have engaged with the exhibition and generously provided advice, support and the fruits of their knowledge and research.

No exhibition of this scope would be possible without the support of our sponsor. The Royal Academy is extremely grateful to BNY Mellon for their long-term partnership. We thank them wholeheartedly for their involvement in the realisation of this exhibition.

The two key portraits by Manet owned by the Toledo Museum of Art will be joined by a profusion of other masterpieces by this remarkable artist. We hope our selection will introduce visitors to the rich cultural world that Manet inhabited and reveal him as both the 'father' of Impressionism and a leading figure in the evolution of Modernism.

Brian Kennedy
President, Director and CEO, Toledo Museum of Art

Christopher Le Brun PRA
President, Royal Academy of Arts

Detail of cat. 7
Mme Manet at the Piano, 1868

Sponsor's Preface

'You would hardly believe how difficult it is to place a figure alone on a canvas, and to concentrate all the interest on this single and unique figure and still keep it living and real,' said Edouard Manet in 1880. 'Manet: Portraying Life' is the first exhibition to examine in depth the artist's portraits and the way in which he transformed his sitters into actors in his scenes of everyday French life.

The art collector and philanthropist Paul Mellon and his wife bought a number of Manet's paintings, later bequeathing many of them to galleries and museums for future generations to enjoy. Indeed, one of the paintings featured in the present exhibition, *George Moore in the Artist's Garden* (*c*. 1879), took pride of place in the dining room of the Mellons' New York home for many years before it was bequeathed to the National Gallery of Art, Washington, in 2006.

BNY Mellon continues to be committed to the arts as part of our global philanthropic endeavours, and our enduring partnership with the Royal Academy of Arts has spanned many projects. As a champion of public access and education, the Royal Academy engages with a broad audience through its exhibitions, educational activities and publications – a key principle that also informs BNY Mellon's international programme of arts sponsorship. It is therefore a particular privilege for us to support 'Manet: Portraying Life' and we hope that you enjoy this fascinating exhibition.

Michael Cole-Fontayn
Chairman of Europe, Middle East and Africa, BNY Mellon

Detail of cat. 43
The Amazon, *c*. 1882

Acknowledgements

The curators and organisers of the exhibition wish to acknowledge the generous assistance of the following individuals in the making of this exhibition and its catalogue:

Lucy Adams, Kathy Adler, Mikael Ahlund, Scott Allan, Masanori Aoyagi, Taru Arayashiki, Carol M. Armstrong, Sylvie Aubénas, João Vicente de Azevedo, László Baán, Don Bacigalupi, Colin B. Bailey, Laurence Baron-Callegari, Christoph Becker, Guido Beltramini, Brent Benjamin, Pierre Bergé, Giovanna Bertazzoni, Laura Braun, Margit Brinkmann, Christopher Brown, Amy Bubb, David Bull, Lorna Burn, Caroline Campbell, Thomas Campbell, Olivier Camu, João Castel-Branco Pereira, Görel Cavalli-Björkman, Thomas Cazentre, Gilles Chazal, Therese Chen, Bruno Chenique, Alan Chong, Jay Clarke, Melanie Clore, José Teixeira Coelho Netto, Guy Cogeval, Michael Conforti, the late Philip Conisbee, James Cuno, Hannah Darvin, Philipp Demandt, Therese Dolan, Richard Dorment, Chloe Downe, Michel Draguet, Douglas Druick, Florence Ducharme, Ann Dumas, Inge Dupont, Audun Eckhoff, Alexander Eiling, Kaywin Feldman, Hartwig Fischer, David Franklin, Maria Fratelli, Flemming Friborg, Thomas Galifot, Helena Gasparian, Hubertus Gassner, Judit Geskó, Lukas Gloor, Yves De Greef, Vivien Greene, William M. Griswold, Gloria Groom, Stéphane Guégan, Thorsten Gunnarsson, Dorothee Hansen, Colin Harrison, Frode Haverkamp, Anne Hawley, Per Hedström, Françoise Heilbrun, Wulf Herzogenrath, Robert Holden, Max Hollein, Sigmar Holsten, the late John House, Diana Howard, Jens Howoldt, Géraldine Jaffre, His Excellency Roberto Jaguaribe, Ellen and Paul Josefowitz, Stephan Jost, Valérie Joxe, Joachim Kaak, Kyoko Kagawa, Franklin Kelly, Declan Kiely, Udo Kittelmann, Daniel Koep, Felix Krämer, Camille Kulig, Milko de Leeuw, Leah Lehmbeck, Heather Lemonedes, Richard Lingner, Daniel Lobstein, Adrian Locke, Nancy Locke, Mario-Andreas von Lüttichau, Bernhard Maaz, Anne McCauley, Eric McCauley Lee, Suzanne McCullagh, Heather Macdonald, Laurence Madeline, Ana B. Martínez, Caroline Mathieu, Alex Matson, Olivier Meslay, Marina Messina, Charles Moffett, Christopher Monkhouse, Yoshiko Mori, Mary G. Morton, Pia Müller-Tamm, Hiroya Murakami, Diane Nixon, Patrick Noon, Maureen O'Brien, Hiroaki Ohashi, Mina Oya, Hermann Parzinger, Sylvie Patry, Jean Penicault, Nicholas Penny, Lionel Pissarro, Katia Pisvin, Caroline Porter, Timothy Potts, Earl A. Powell III, Rebecca Rabinow, Richard Rand, Chris Riopelle, Joseph Rishel, William Robinson, Andrew Robison, Malcolm Rogers, Jane Mayo Roos, Norman Rosenthal, Yves Rouart, James Roundell, Timothy Rub, James Rubin, Jennifer Russell, Jean-Pierre De Rycke, Luísa Sampaio, Naoki Sato, Philippe Saunier, Scott Schaefer, Sandro Schiffini, Manuel Schmit, Klaus Schrenk, Yu Serizawa, George Shackelford, Norio Shimada, Karin Siden, Gereon Sievernich, Clare Simpson, John M. Smith, Guillermo Solana, Melanie Spinella, Claire Stoullig, Harriet Stratis, Ann Sumner, Deborah Swallow, Akiya Takahashi, Shuji Takashina, Martha Tedeschi, Gary Tinterow, Jennifer Tonkovich, Oliver Tostmann, Ernst van Vegelin, Malcolm Warner, Angelika Wesenberg, Ully Wille, Marc F. Wilson, Juliet Wilson-Bareau, Ann Woolsey, Paola Zatti, Julián Zugazagoitia.

Detail of cat. 30
Stéphane Mallarmé, 1876

Overleaf: detail of cat. 12
Interior at Arcachon, 1871

MARYANNE STEVENS

Manet: Portraying Life. Themes and Variations

The truth is that our only obligation should be to distil what we can from our epoch, though without belittling what earlier periods have achieved.

Edouard Manet, 1878–79[1]

Fig. 1
Henri Fantin-Latour
Atelier in Les Batignolles, 1870
Oil on canvas, 204 x 273.5 cm
Musée d'Orsay, Paris, RF 726

IN 1870 EDOUARD MANET had two works accepted by the Salon Jury: a portrait of Eva Gonzalès (cat. 15) and a genre scene, *The Music Lesson* (1869; Museum of Fine Arts, Boston), for which Zacharie Astruc and Victorine Meurent had posed. Leaving aside landscape and still-life, these two works represent the balance of subject-matter within the artist's not very extensive *oeuvre*. At the same Salon, Henri Fantin-Latour (1836–1904), the painter of still-lifes, mythological scenes and group portraits of artists, writers and musicians, exhibited *Atelier in Les Batignolles* (fig. 1), a work that encapsulated the key aspiration of Realist portraiture in the mid-nineteenth century: to represent the individual as a record of contemporary life.

Fantin-Latour shows Manet at his easel, making a portrait of Zacharie Astruc, who had in fact sat to him four years earlier, in 1866 (cat. 27). By 1870 Manet had already produced a number of portraits of family members and friends; he exhibited his *Portrait of M. and Mme Auguste Manet* (fig. 2) at the Salon of 1861 and showed others at subsequent Salons and other venues. Manet's work, 'recognised as being of a very pronounced realist tendency',[2] thus acknowledges Manet as a portraitist of note. In Fantin-Latour's canvas the artist is surrounded by a small coterie of friends, admirers and supporters, all of them identifiable.[3] A cast of the figure of Minerva and a Japoniste vase by the French ceramicist Bouvier on the table to the left imply Manet's commitment to the truthful depiction of the external world. *Atelier in Les Batignolles* therefore also contends that Manet is engaged with genre painting – the artist in his contemporary setting – using his known sitters as actors in order to guarantee a work's authenticity. This interchange between

Fig. 2
Portrait of M. and Mme Auguste Manet, 1860
Oil on canvas, 110 x 90 cm
Musée d'Orsay, Paris, RF 1977 12

portraiture and genre painting could be seen as the logical conclusion of the Realist programme, as the critic Castagnary put it in respect of Manet's *Eva Gonzalès* (cat. 15): '[The artist's] duty is to furnish according to his ability and temperament a reflection of the society in which we live', displaying 'extensive intellectual preoccupations' and using his 'powerful faculties of observation'.[4] But it also reflects a more general shift that was then taking place, in which the boundaries between genre painting and straight portraiture were being blurred in the face of the relative decline of the latter.[5] As the works selected here reveal, Manet was committed to the pictorial implications of the 'reflection of the society in which we live'. However, his relationship to the art of the past, his receptiveness to contemporary art, his adherence to traditional pictorial genres, and his distinction between sketch and finish mean that the ways in which he realised this programme are complex and perverse, and often shot through with ambiguity.

MANET THE MAN

Edouard Manet was born in Paris in 1832 into a comfortable, property-owning middle-class family. His father Auguste (1797–1862) was a senior civil servant in the Ministry of Justice, and his mother, Eugénie-Désirée (1811–1895), the daughter of a diplomat. Edouard had two younger brothers: Eugène (1833–1892), who married the artist Berthe Morisot in 1874, and Gustave (1835–1884), who became a lawyer and a politician. Having failed to enter the Navy, Manet enlisted in the merchant marine and travelled to South America in 1848. A year after his return to Paris in 1849, he entered the studio of the successful salon artist Thomas Couture; for the next six years, he pursued a training within and beyond Couture's studio, combining a somewhat argumentative relationship with his teacher with study of the Old Masters in the Louvre, in the salerooms of Paris and abroad, in the Netherlands (1852; see the text by Lawrence W. Nichols on pages 66–71), Germany, Austria (1853), Italy (1853 and 1857) and, belatedly but very importantly, Spain (1865). Exposure to contemporary art came through the Paris Salon, independent exhibitions such as Courbet's Pavillon du Réalisme (1855) and at the 1855 Exposition Universelle. Manet failed to gain acceptance at the Salon of 1859, but succeeded at the following one, held in 1861, with his portrait of his parents. Two years later he married Suzanne Leenhoff (1829–1906), a talented pianist and the mother of Léon Koëlla Leenhoff (1852–1927) (fig. 3), who became part of the Manet family but whose paternity remains uncertain.

Manet was the quintessential urban figure. He lived in Paris, moving from his natal home on the left bank to Les Batignolles in the north of the city, before settling in 1866 in the Quartier de l'Europe, immediately to the northwest of the Gare Saint-Lazare, an area recently constructed as part of Baron Haussmann's extensive programme for the modernisation of Paris (see cat. 53). He moved his studio to the same quartier in 1870, and his subsequent apartments and studios were all located in the area.[6] Like his fellow Parisians, he left the metropolis for leisure and relaxation,

Fig. 3
Young Man Peeling a Pear (Portrait of Léon Leenhoff), c. 1869
Oil on canvas, 85 x 71 cm
Nationalmuseum, Stockholm, NM 1498

although he wrote to Astruc: 'The countryside only has its charms for those who are not obliged to live there.'[7] He spent holidays on the Normandy coast, visited friends at their country properties, sought respite from the privations of the 1870–71 Siege of Paris at Arcachon on the Bay of Biscay, and suffered 'enforced' sojourns in the semi-rural retreats of Bellevue, Versailles and Reuil for health reasons in his last years.

Throughout his life, Manet surrounded himself with a wide circle of friends, admirers and supporters from the artistic, literary and musical communities. All professed leanings towards the more radical movements of the day, including adherence to republican politics, and encompassed Baudelaire, Zola, Mallarmé, the younger Impressionists and the critics Duret and Duranty.[8] Social gatherings infused with critical discussion and debate took place in the cafés that Manet frequented, from the fashionable Café Tortoni and Café de Bade on the Boulevard des Italiens in the early 1860s, to the more bohemian Café Guerbois on the Grande Rue des Batignolles (now the Avenue de Clichy) and the Café Nouvelle Athènes on the Place Pigalle from *c.* 1866 and *c.* 1872 respectively.[9] These gatherings were complemented by visits to his studio, and the Tuesday and Thursday soirées at the Manet family's home, where the cultural world mingled with men of politics, such as Georges Clemenceau, Léon Gambetta and Manet's lifelong friend the Député Antonin Proust; journalists and editors such as Georges Charpentier; and patrons and collectors, including Albert Hecht and Ernest Hoschedé. Many of these personalities were to find their way onto Manet's canvases, in straight portraits, group portraits or as actors in scenes from contemporary life.

THE ARTIST

Manet's career as a professional artist lasted less than three decades, cut short by his premature death in 1883 at the age of 51. The 1975 catalogue raisonné compiled by Denis Rouart and Daniel Wildenstein contains 430 oil paintings, 89 pastels and over 400 works on paper. Some works are known to have been destroyed,[10] slashed,[11]cut down,[12] scraped down and unfinished, abandoned as sketches or lost. Of the surviving *oeuvre* of both finished and unresolved oil paintings, approximately half could be categorised as straight portraits and genre paintings, including costume and modern-history paintings.

Despite being branded the 'famous Naturalist revolutionary'[13] and being consistently accused of violating the conventions of colour and technique,[14] Manet was a serious and dedicated artist, committed to the process of making art. He accepted and challenged the art of the past; he embraced and denied, through privileging technique, the direct recording of nature; and, as Carol M. Armstrong (pp. 42–49) has proposed, he responded to – and produced 'boldly strange' painted alternatives to – the portrait photograph. He was both alert to academic and avant-garde practice, from Léon Bonnat and Carolus-Duran to Gustave Courbet and the Impressionists (see Colin B. Bailey, pp. 58–65), and defiantly individual. Most importantly, he was not averse to risk: 'Each time [one] begins a picture … [one] plunges headlong into it, and feels like a man who knows that his surest plan to learn to swim safely is, dangerous as it may seem, to throw himself into the water.'[15] He threw himself into the challenge of finding subjects, compositional formats and techniques that would provide a new language of art suitable for the representation of modernity. This entailed extensive study of the Old Masters, notably those of seventeenth-century Holland and Spain, with special reference to Frans Hals and Diego Velázquez, and of eighteenth-century France[16] and, to a degree, England (see below). In addition, the potential of Japanese art to provide a model for the representation of contemporary life was complemented by Manet's awareness of the relationship between direct observation of the subject and its environment. This led him after *c.* 1870 to a tempered consideration of Impressionism, which included working to a limited degree out of doors in front of the motif.[17]

Although critics deplored the unpredictability that Manet's determination to craft a modern idiom seemed to generate, he recognised the absolute imperative and strength of this approach: 'It has always been my ambition not to remain the same, not to repeat the next day what I had made the day before, to constantly be inspired by something new, to register a new note.'[18] Abandoning the constraints of tradition and convention, each new work represented a break with all that had preceded it, whether his own work or those of earlier artists. To contemporary critics and viewers, the resultant range of his *oeuvre* and the variety of his approach to subject and execution consistently defied categorisation. However, it endowed Manet with a position among his younger contemporaries, such as the Impressionists, as the 'founding father' of modern art. This label, with its problematic and contested meaning, has ensured that his art has been studied, analysed and interrogated by subsequent artists, critics and art historians, each generation adding layers of interpretation to an ever-growing body of literature.

Manet was ambitious and craved public recognition and success; he never doubted the importance of exhibiting at the Paris Salon. Between 1859, when his first submission, *The Absinthe Drinker* (fig. 4), was rejected, and the year of his death, despite a barrage of negative criticism he submitted work to each of the 21 Salons that took place, with the exception of 1867 and 1878. He was rejected four times,[19] had two of four submissions refused on one occasion,[20] and chose to show *Nana* (1877; Kunsthalle, Hamburg) after its rejection from the Salon of 1877 in a shop window in the Rue des Capucines. Away from the Salon, he recognised the potential of the growing diversification of exhibition venues, from commercial galleries and exhibitions outside Paris[21] to independent artists' associations and self-financed solo shows. Although he did not directly associate himself with the Impressionists' initiative to hold independent exhibitions from 1874, Manet joined Legros, Fantin-Latour and the more established artists Puvis de Chavannes and Carrier-Belleuse as a member of the Société Nationale des Beaux-Arts. Founded by Louis Martinet in 1861, the Société exhibited at Martinet's luxurious gallery at 26 Boulevard des Italiens; Manet participated in the exhibitions of 1864 and 1865.[22] Manet also used Martinet's gallery to show individual works in 1861 and, two years later, for one of his three solo exhibitions. Beyond the presentation of his works in his studio – as occurred in 1876, following the rejection from the Salon of *The Artist* (cat. 20) and *The Laundry* (1875; Am Römerholz, Winterthur) – Manet had two further solo exhibitions: in May 1867 he showed 50 works in a temporary pavilion erected at his own expense on the Avenue de l'Alma, and in April 1880 he presented 25 paintings and pastels at the gallery of *La Vie moderne*.

Fig. 4
The Absinthe Drinker, 1859
Oil on canvas, 180.5 x 105.6 cm
Ny Carlsberg Glyptotek, Copenhagen

'VARIATIONS' ON STRAIGHT PORTRAITURE

By the mid-nineteenth century the straight portrait was required to give the physical and psychological likeness of a sitter. A characteristic pose, dress and appropriate attribute might also provide additional information about the sitter's intellectual, professional or social standing. Most importantly, as Frédéric Chevalier noted in 1877, a work's individual constituents should not detract from its pictorial unity.[23] As might be expected, Manet's concern to tackle each subject anew meant that his engagement with straight portraiture was not without its ambiguities and complexities, as we shall see below.

Fig. 5
***George Moore at the Café*, 1878/79**
Oil on canvas, 65.4 x 81.3 cm
The Metropolitan Museum of Art, New York, 55.193.
Gift of Mrs Ralph J. Hines, 1955

A certain number of his works more or less fulfil the requirements of straight portraiture, such as his portraits of women (as Leah Lehmbeck discusses on pp. 50–57) and his representations of politicians and some writers, artists (cat. 15) and children (see cat. 49, fig. 8).

The majority of these straight portraits in both oil and pastel came about through an invitation from the artist rather than by commission. He drafted in friends, supporters and members of his family to submit to his direct scrutiny, writing: 'The eye should forget all else it has seen, and learn anew the lessons set before it. It should abstract itself from memory, seeing only that which it looks upon, and that, as for the first time.'[24]

This 'tyranny' of the eye is determined by Manet's understanding of the Realist programme. Categorised by critics such as Champfleury and Castagnary, and given pictorial form by Gustave Courbet, Realism was grounded in the need to describe the modern world rather than the desire to create scenes informed by myth and history. As Stéphane Guégan has succinctly shown, for Manet, Realism had its roots in Romanticism, and was developed by two of the artist's friends and supporters, Gautier and Baudelaire. Manet's determination to conform to the Realist programme in his practice led him to claim that he created his portraits directly from the sitter in a single session. The reality, as Monet reported, was rather different: 'Manet made things very difficult for himself: he had a laborious and careful method. He always wanted his paintings to look as if done at the first attempt; but often, in the evening, he scraped down with his palette knife everything that he had done during the day.'[25] Monet's observation is substantiated by the fact that, with a small number of exceptions, such as the *Portrait of M. Arnaud (The Rider)* (cat. 41),[26] Manet appears to have made few preliminary studies on paper or small-scale oil sketches. Rather, he worked directly onto the support in oil, building up his sitter's characteristic features and establishing the pose, as can be seen in the several portraits abandoned at a very early stage, such as those of Proust,[27] Faure[28] and Moore (fig. 5). To push a portrait towards greater resolution, Manet needed his sitter constantly in sight: 'That has always been my principal concern, to make sure of getting regular sittings. Whenever I start something, I am always afraid the model will let me down, that I will not see them as often nor in the conditions that I would like. They come, they pose, then they go, telling themselves that he can finish it off on his own. Well, no, one cannot finish anything on one's own, even less so since one only finishes on one day what one starts on that day, and that means starting again and having plenty of days.'[29] Several of his sitters, from Eva Gonzalès and Berthe Morisot[30] to Georges Clemenceau and Antonin Proust, recorded the agony of protracted sessions, while Manet's reference to 'starting again' is upheld in both Proust's and Albert Wolff's accounts of their experiences, the latter recalling in 1884: 'After the fifteenth sitting, my portrait was no further advanced than on the first day; the model was discouraged and also the painter.'[31] Wolff's portrait (fig. 6) remained unfinished; for that of the actor Philibert Rouvière (cat. 33), who died before the work was completed, Manet was forced to call upon his friends Proust and Roudier to stand in as models for the hands and legs respectively.[32] In the case of Manet's portraits in pastel, of which 75 are recorded, the majority made after *c.* 1878, the medium enabled him to deliver a brilliantly executed likeness in one sitting, as he recorded in 1879: 'Take the portrait of the poet Moore. As far as I was concerned, it was finished, in just one sitting.'[33]

Fig. 6
Portrait of Albert Wolff, 1877
Oil on canvas, 92 x 73 cm
Kunsthaus, Zurich

Manet's handling of his sitters was more personal than conventional. He actively set the pose, such that Desboutin is shown recently returned from an urban stroll (cat. 20), and Eva Gonzalès serves as a commentary upon a model derived from Goya (cat. 15). In the case of *Portrait of Georges Clemenceau* (cat. 44), the pose was probably inspired by a carte de visite of the sitter. As regards his sitters' dress, Manet could also be interventionist, using it as the vehicle for articulating aesthetic and artistic preoccupations. He adopted Baudelaire's contention that fashionable dress was the appropriate means for expressing the heroism of modern life.

A smart dresser himself and acutely alert to trends in high fashion, he advised one of his female sitters, Mme Guillemet's sister Marguerite, to bring 'the light-coloured summer dress you told me about, and if you have a pretty garden hat do not leave it behind'.[34] He noted with pleasure Méry Laurent's 1881 autumn outfit in which she posed for *Autumn* (cat. 55),[35] and suggested a set of clothes to Albert Wolff: 'Would you wear your blue frock coat with the velvet collar and your brown trousers tomorrow?'[36] Likewise, in the billowing white muslin summer dresses worn by Jeanne Duval (cat. 31) or Eva Gonzalès (cat. 15) he explored both the aesthetic implications of Whistler's radical imposition of a single colour note throughout a composition, as in his *Symphonies in White 1–3* (1862, 1864 and 1865–67 respectively; fig. 7), and pursued his own investigations into the relationship between the rendering of light and the colour white (see cat. 31).

Fig. 7
James McNeill Whistler
***Symphony in White No. 1: The White Girl*, 1862**
Oil on canvas, 213 x 107.9 cm
National Gallery of Art, Washington. Harris Whittemore Collection, 1943.6.2

Manet's career as a portraitist coincided with the coming of age of the photographic portrait in the form of the daguerreotype and the carte de visite. Their advent presented artists with both an aid and a challenge. As Carol M. Armstrong (pp. 42–49) and others have observed, the impact of photography on Manet's practice cannot be ignored. On a practical level, he embraced the new medium: he sat for his own portrait (figs 45, 47, 48);[37] he had a carte-de-visite album of family and friends;[38] he used photographs as direct and indirect sources for his work;[39] and from the late 1860s onwards he maintained a photographic record of his paintings commissioned from Godet.[40] The degree to which photographs had a wider impact on his art has been extensively studied,[41] and as Carol M. Armstrong argues, in certain portraits Manet may have taken pose, setting or lighting effects from photographers' practices. However, she also notes that the precise relationship between his art and photography should be understood within the context of the contemporary debate surrounding the relative aesthetic merits of the two disciplines and the already sophisticated practices of photography. Critics and artists were divided on the relative merits of the photograph. Within the context of the Realist debate, which called for an objective record of the external world, they recognised that photography could provide a faithful mechanical reproduction of a subject. Once aesthetic criteria were applied, however, the relative values of the two media had to be confronted. For some, the photograph was welcomed as a substitute for the sketch.[42] For others, such as Manet, it presented the artist with a new range of poses and compositions that had not previously been related to portraiture and which could be usefully manipulated but not adhered to rigorously.[43]

Although the question of finish and unfinish has been addressed in the work of his younger contemporary Paul Cézanne,[44] the comparable situation in Manet's portrait *oeuvre* has received little attention. Manet's portraits appear to range from the highly finished to the seemingly sketchy and unresolved. As a point of departure, it has been suggested that works that had entered the public domain, through exhibition, commission, sale (as in the case of the 24 paintings sold to Durand-Ruel in 1872) or gift to a friend or supporter, could be deemed finished, whereas those that remained in the private domains of the studio and the artist's home might be considered unfinished or unresolved. This distinction can generally be applied to the highly resolved *The*

Fig. 8
Portrait of a Child (The Little Lange), 1862
Oil on canvas, 115 x 72 cm
Staatliche Kunsthalle, Karlsruhe

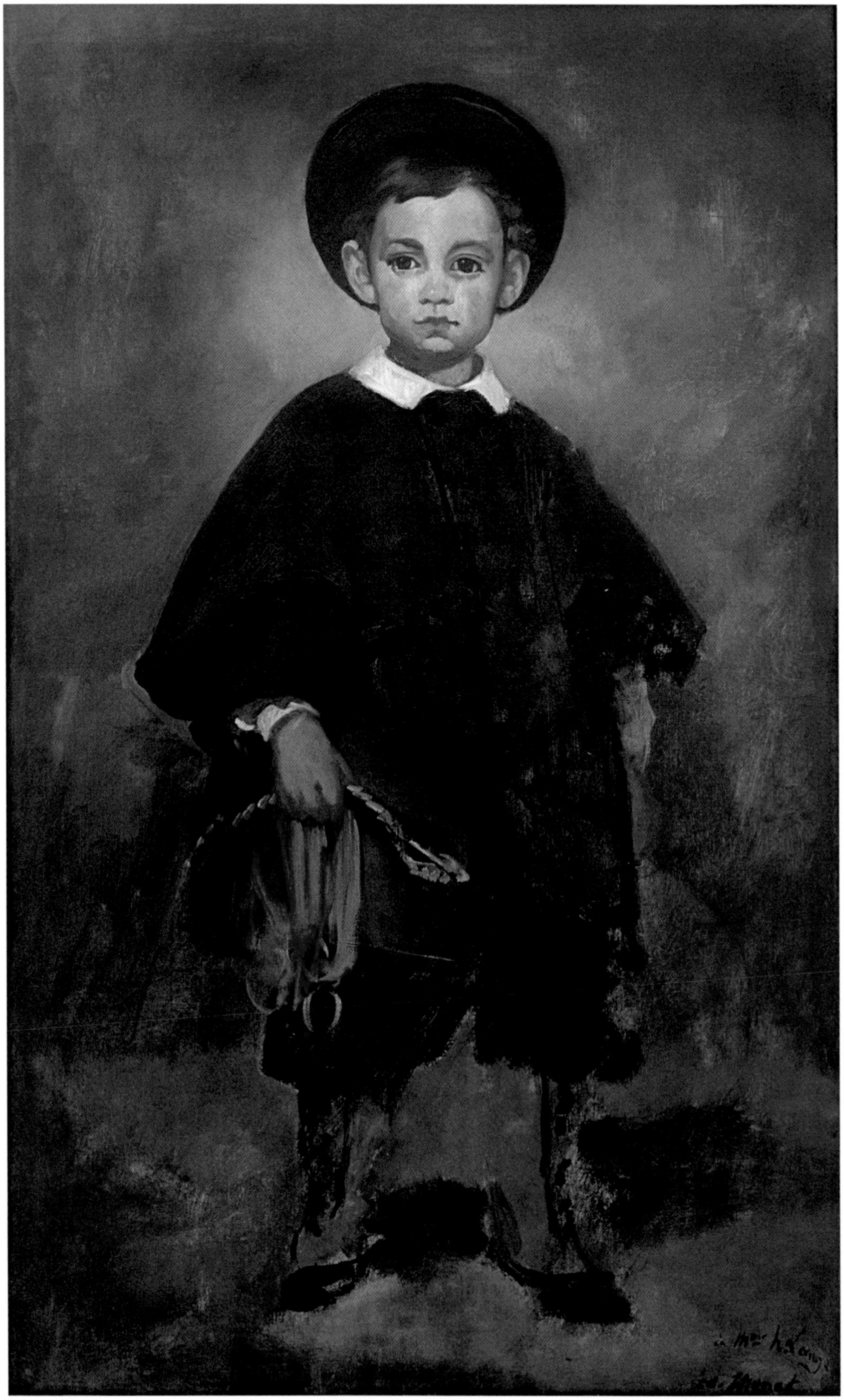

Luncheon (cat. 10), exhibited at the 1869 Salon, when compared to the more freely handled *The Velocipede* (cat. 11), which was cut down and remained in the studio, and *Woman with a Cat (Portrait of Mme Manet)* (cat. 5), which hung in the Manets' apartment. Furthermore, as has been noted, portraits were left unfinished either because of the artist's or the sitter's dissatisfaction or the sitter's unavailability. Such works remained in the studio, often unframed,[45] some to be completed by another hand prior to exhibition, as is recorded in the case of *Autumn* (cat. 55),[46] or prior to a posthumous sale, as in the case of *Portrait of M. Arnaud (The Rider)* (cat. 41).[47] A number of examples, however, complicate this neat categorisation. *The Repose*, the 'portrait' of Berthe Morisot (cat. 18) exhibited at the Salon of 1873, is executed with a greater degree of technical licence than the 1879 Salon piece *In the Conservatory* (cat. 39), a freedom that caused it to be seen as 'a study' by the contemporary critic Paul Mantz[48] and by Duvergier de Hauranne as 'a confusion defying all descriptions; one must have faith to try to disentangle the good intentions which could be hiding under this indecent and barbarous smear.'[49] A similar ambiguity arises with the commissioned portraits of children, *Portrait of a Child (The Little Lange)* (fig. 8) and *Henry Bernstein as a Child* (cat. 49). Both portraits are freely handled and leave visible traces of changes in their poses, and yet they entered the collections of the sitters' families, and must have been deemed sufficiently resolved for Manet to have allowed them to enter the public domain.

'VARIATIONS' ON GENRE PAINTING

Whereas portraiture is primarily concerned with the particular and the distinctive, the external physical likeness and the internal or spiritual condition, genre painting addresses the circumstantial, the social character and the environment. A development of seventeenth-century Dutch art, genre paintings are scenes from contemporary life executed on a relatively small scale. Although their narratives ranged from moral subjects to conversation pieces, their domestic scale and concern with local particularities contrasted with large-scale history paintings, the noblest form of art within the academic tradition, whose subjects gave generalised representations of the passions and the intellect. Manet's genre paintings initially appear to conform to this traditional definition: they comprise single- and multi-figure compositions, and they address scenes from contemporary life. They are generally on a domestic scale, such as *Music in the Tuileries Gardens* (cat. 26). However, Manet also subverted this norm; for example, he presents *Déjeuner sur l'herbe* (1863; Musée d'Orsay, Paris) and *Street Singer* (cat. 51) on a monumental scale. Furthermore, as we shall see, his determination to reinvent both subject and technique in his search for an authentic representation of modernity led him frequently to collapse the distinction between genre painting and straight portraiture.

Manet came to genre painting initially through costume pieces that drew their inspiration either explicitly from specific examples of the art of the past, for example *Spanish Cavaliers* (1859; Musée des Beaux-Arts, Lyons), or implicitly to provide the source for subjects taken from contemporary life. Posed by models, the roles that the sitters performed provided a commentary on contemporary social conditions and taste: *The Absinthe Drinker* (fig. 4) and *Street Singer* dealt with social marginalisation as a result of the modernisation of Paris,[50] and *The Spanish Singer* (fig. 18) and *The Spanish Ballet* (1862; Phillips Collection, Washington) addressed the taste for Spanish art and culture.[51] Yet Manet also employed his Old Master sources to inform both his technique and his reading of subject-matter in order to address contemporary moral and aesthetic conventions: the *fête champêtre* of the Italian Renaissance and eighteenth-century French art is adopted to challenge contemporary criteria of beauty and morality in *Déjeuner sur l'herbe* and *Olympia* (fig. 9), while seventeenth- and eighteenth-century images of the transience of life are translated into Léon Leenhoff blowing bubbles (cat. 9).[52] From the early 1870s, although he generally divested himself of overt references to older prototypes, Manet maintained his commitment to genre painting, fully recognising that its capacity to reflect modernity lay in the conjunction of subject-matter – the railway, bourgeois leisure – and innovative composition.

Complexity and ambiguity begin to arise in Manet's manipulation of genre painting with his use of models who are identifiable both through repeated use and through the absolute emphasis upon them as real individuals rather than generalised types. Suzanne Manet in *Mme Manet at the Piano* (cat. 7) is both the artist's wife and a talented pianist, the actor who illustrates the act of music-making. Marcellin Desboutin, the sitter for *The Artist* (cat. 20), has no conventional attributes; instead he carries a furled

Fig. 9
***Olympia*, 1863**
Oil on canvas, 130.5 x 191 cm
Musee d'Orsay, Paris, RF 644

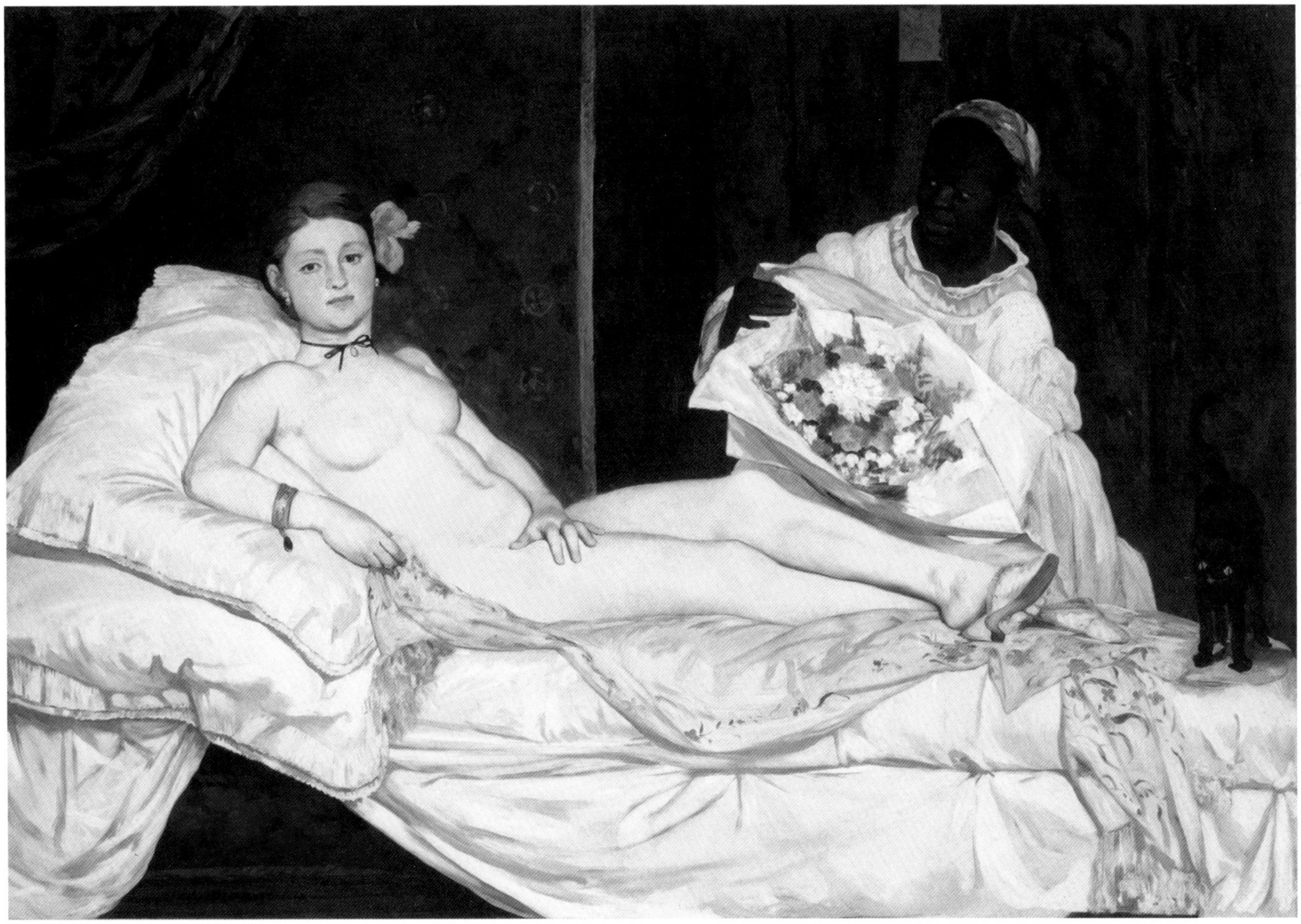

Fig. 10
***Young Lady in 1866*, 1866**
Oil on canvas, 185.1 x 128.6 cm
The Metropolitan Museum of Art, New York, 89.21.3.
Gift of Erwin Davis, 1889

umbrella, prepares to light a pipe and is accompanied by his dog in order to present 'the most extraordinary character in the neighbourhood'.[53] And Claude Monet is both the Impressionist artist and the father enjoying bourgeois leisure with his family (cat. 25). This transfer even occurs when Manet uses a known professional model. Victorine Meurent sat to him for a straight portrait in 1862 (cat. 50) before becoming the immediately recognisable model of such transgressive works as *Déjeuner sur l'herbe* and *Olympia* or the more subtly suggestive paintings *Young Lady in 1866* (fig. 10) and *The Railway* (cat. 53). Manet was well aware of the ease with which he could move his sitters from one category to another. When Nina de Callias's estranged husband objected to *Woman with Fans* (1873; Musée d'Orsay, Paris) being exhibited as her portrait, Manet

Fig. 11
The Balcony, 1868–69
Oil on canvas, 170 x 125 cm
Musée d'Orsay, Paris, RF 2772

reassured him that: '[It is] a fantasy figure based on Madame de Villars [*sic*] and not a portrait.'[54] To these cross-transfers should be added another strategy that complicates the distinction between genre painting and portraiture. Whereas in *The Balcony* (fig. 11), Manet employs a clearly identifiable Berthe Morisot in a scene from contemporary life, and in the straight portrait *Berthe Morisot with a Bouquet of Violets* (cat. 16) he shows her in a pose that is both frontal and static, his *Berthe Morisot* (cat. 19) presents his future sister-in-law moving through the picture space with hardly a glance towards the viewer, a passer-by on the streets of Paris. As with his somewhat comparable treatment of Isabelle Lemonnier (cats 61, 62), the identifiable sitter inhabits an indeterminate zone between genre and the portrait.

MANET AND THE CRITICS

Manet's lack of respect for the traditional distinctions between genre and portraiture, taken with his manipulation of Old Master sources, his disregard for the representation of three-dimensional space and his distaste for working within an identifiable and consistent style, provoked unrelenting critical abuse whenever he entered the public domain. As Hamilton has shown,[55] the critics, that ever-growing phalanx of writers who served to mediate between a rapidly expanding art scene and a public craving instruction and aesthetic direction, expressed dislike and incomprehension. They decried the fact that his scenes of contemporary life were also portraits; and they deplored his portraits for their attacks on convention, that his figures were not anatomically sound, and that his technique, whether derived from seventeenth-century models or informed by Impressionist procedures, appeared either incompetent or perversely sketchy.

In his *Les Peintres Impressionnistes* (1878) Duret encapsulated the position succinctly: 'And Manet! One could say that criticism has gathered up all the insults which it has poured on his precursors for half a century, to throw them at his head all at one time.'[56] And Manet himself expressed his sense of hurt, as in correspondence with Baudelaire following the furore provoked by the exhibition at the Salon of 1865 of *Olympia* and *Christ Mocked by the Soldiers* (1865; Art Institute of Chicago)[57] and in an outburst of 1882 recorded by Proust: 'I have suffered cruelly [from the critics' attacks], they have been like the lashes of a whip. I would not wish for any artist to be subjected to such things at the beginning of his career. It would be an annihilation of his personality.'[58]

MANET'S EXEMPLARS FOR PORTRAIT-GENRE

Thus far Manet's artistic procedures for his straight portraits and genre scenes have been focused on his own practice. However it is important to consider how far he was to find precedents for his singular approach to both types of subject and their hybridisation in the art of his predecessors and contemporaries. Or does he remain exceptional? Among his immediate predecessors, the example of Gustave Courbet, already noted, calls for closer scrutiny, as does the relatively less analysed study of certain models of the eighteenth century. In both cases, as will be seen, Manet was provided with important precedents for his particular treatment of portraiture and genre that he could both follow and challenge.

Manet's actors in his genre scenes tend to be predominantly identifiable. They engage with each other and are generally presented on relatively modest-scaled formats. This approach recalls not the generalised presentation of types in Dutch seventeenth-century genre but rather the eighteenth-century conversation piece, a domestic-sized group portrait in which identifiable sitters engage in social intercourse. Manet's enthusiasm for the art of the eighteenth century, especially that of Watteau, Chardin and Boucher, whom he admired for their 'feeling of truth', was informed by study of their work in the Louvre, through exhibitions, in the salerooms and in engravings and publications. Although much attention has been given to his reliance upon these sources for individual figures, and compositional formulae such as the *fête champêtre*,[59] less has been devoted to the model of the conversation piece. As a hybrid of portraiture and genre, as in the work of Jean-Baptiste Charpentier and Charles Lepeintre, this may have influenced Manet's own integration of a known sitter, for example, Léon Leenhoff, into genre scenes such as *The Luncheon* (cat. 10). Manet shared an interest in eighteenth-century French art with his literary friends. Tellingly, several of these, including Gautier and Duret, also had knowledge of eighteenth-century English art and wrote about the subject. Together with Ernest Chesnau, whose comparative study *Les Arts et les artistes en France et en Angleterre* was published in 1864, they called attention to the work of William Hogarth, the English artist who had established a sophisticated formula for the conversation piece. Typically, however, Manet both adheres to and disrupts this model: in *Chez le Père Lathuille – en plein air* (cat. 60), he uses the criterion of social engagement between the two protagonists, but in *The Luncheon* and *The Railway* the social interchange has been wilfully disregarded: Léon and Victorine Meurent disengage with both their companions and the viewer as they gaze passively out of the pictorial space.

Fig. 12
Gustave Courbet
Burial at Ornans, 1849–50
Oil on canvas, 315 x 668 cm
Musée d'Orsay, Paris, RF 325

Fig. 13
Carolus-Duran
Mme Ernest Feydeau (Lady with a Dog), 1870
Oil on canvas, 230 x 164 cm
Palais des Beaux-Arts, Lille, P.595

Throughout Manet's formative years, Gustave Courbet consistently assailed the academic tradition in Paris. Breaking with accepted practice, he used family members, friends and associates as the staffage in his scenes from everyday life, such as *After Dinner at Ornans* (1849; Palais des Beaux-Arts, Lille), *Burial at Ornans* (fig. 12) and *The Studio: A Real Allegory of Seven Years of My Life as a Painter* (1855; Musée d'Orsay, Paris), but presented them on a grand scale normally reserved for history painting. Shown at the Salon from 1849 and at the artist's own Pavillon du Réalisme at the 1855 Exposition Universelle, these works demonstrated Courbet's programme to elevate the mundane to the level of the heroic, to achieve 'the representation of real and existing things'.[60] These works provided a benchmark for critics such as Duranty, for what was variously termed 'realist' or 'naturalist' art: 'a frank and total expression of an individuality that attacks precisely the conventions and imitation of any kind of school'.[61] Like Courbet, Manet selected his actors in his genre paintings from a similar group of associates in order to represent 'real and existing things'. It is therefore important to gauge the degree to which the older artist provided a model for Manet's own artistic practice.

Manet certainly admired Courbet. He wrote enthusiastically about *Burial at Ornans*, declaring: 'Yes, the Burial is very good. It cannot be said often enough that it is very good, because it is better than anything else.'[62] Manet drew upon Courbet's portraiture for his *Portrait of Mme Brunet* (cat. 36). He may have modelled his 1867 Avenue de l'Alma pavilion on the older artist's 1855 Pavillon du Réalisme. Courbet's *Young Woman with a Parrot* (1865; Metropolitan Museum of Art, New York), shown at the Salon of 1866, may have provoked Manet's inclusion of a parrot in his *Young Lady in 1866* (fig. 10), and an echo of Courbet's *Woman in a Riding Habit (Amazon)* (1856; Metropolitan Museum of Art, New York) might be found in Manet's late *The Amazon* (cat. 43).[63] Yet, as with Manet and the conversation piece, the relationship is not straightforward. Why did Manet revisit Courbet late in his career after he had moved so far beyond the Realism of the 1860s? More tellingly, although they both shared a common starting point for their genre paintings, Manet converts Courbet's strategy for making scenes of modern life from the generalised to the particular. Courbet used known models to populate large-scale scenes from rural life in which they became representatives of local types. Manet used his family and friends as actors in scenes from urban life, generally on a smaller scale and, despite having appropriated them into a genre narrative, he insisted that they retain their individuality. Even when he refers to them collectively as examples of a type, for example women of the Third Republic, Manet emphasised that his examples – Mme de Callias, Ellen Andrée – still had 'their own particular character'.[64]

Fig. 14
Léon Bonnat
***Président Jules Grévy*, 1880**
Oil on canvas, 152 x 116 cm
Musée d'Orsay, Paris, DO1986-15

Equally, there is the question of Manet's position in relation to his contemporaries. Did he lead the way towards this new approach to genre painting and its relationship to portraiture? Did his approach to portraiture echo developments within and outside academic conventions?

Given Manet's consistent attempts to present works at the Salon, we must consider paintings such as the portraits of Mme Brunet, Mme Gamby or Antonin Proust alongside the work of such successful practitioners of the genre within the Salon as Carolus-Duran (fig. 13), Tollemache, Gervex and Léon Bonnat. Although such an extensive topic is beyond the scope of this text, it can be observed that whereas the pose of the *Portrait of M. Antonin Proust* (cat. 45) resembles that of, for example, Léon Bonnat's *Président Jules Grévy* (fig. 14), Manet's disregard for finish and his delight in focusing upon detail contrasts with the sombre, unified presentation of Bonnat's president, revealing Manet's indifference to the

Fig. 15
Edgar Degas
Sulking, *c.* 1870
Oil on canvas, 32.4 x 46.4 cm
The Metropolitan Museum of Art, New York, 29.100.43.
H. O. Havemeyer Collection, Bequest of Mrs H. O. Havemeyer, 1929

accepted norms of portraiture. These were the transgressions so readily and regularly commented upon by the critics.

In the case of his younger contemporaries Whistler, Fantin-Latour and the Impressionists, the situation is more fluid. Manet's handling of the single figure in his or her environment has much in common with Whistler and Degas: Whistler paints his mother (1871; Musée d'Orsay, Paris) within an austere grey-toned interior, and Degas presents his sister Thérèse de Gas (1863; Musée d'Orsay, Paris) statuesquely immobile in an interior, just as Manet does Mme Brunet (cat. 36) against her generalised landscape. Affinities also exist where genre paintings are concerned: Whistler's *Symphony in White No. 1: The White Girl* (fig. 7), a single figure devoid of narrative, presages Manet's equally enigmatic *Young Lady in 1866*; and Manet's evocation of a psychological state in his depiction of Berthe Morisot in *The Repose* (cat. 18) responds to Whistler and parallels Degas, as in *Sulking* (fig. 15).

Looking further afield, the appearance of identifiable sitters in genre scenes by Renoir and Monet, especially in the 1860s, suggests a certain communality of approach. And yet, comparison of such works as Renoir's *The Couple* (fig. 17) or Monet's *The Luncheon* (fig. 16) with Manet's genre painting *Street Singer* (cat. 51) reveals that the identity of the sitters or models in the younger artists' works is of secondary importance to the need to project the subject of each work and the characteristic environments in which they appear. Perhaps it is only in Degas's *Place de la Concorde* (1875; State Hermitage Museum, St Petersburg), with its handling of the movement through urban space of Vicomte Lepic and his children, that a close parallel can be found with Manet's

Fig. 16
Claude Monet
The Luncheon, 1868
Oil on canvas, 231.5 x 151.5 cm
Städel Museum, Frankfurt

Fig. 17
Pierre-Auguste Renoir
The Couple, *c*. 1868
Oil on canvas, 105.4 x 75.2 cm
Wallraf-Richartz Museum, Cologne

fusion of genre and portraiture in the gently glancing figure of *Berthe Morisot* (cat. 19), as she slides in and out of her pictorial space.

Linda Nochlin identified the problematic territory of Impressionist portraits when she surmised that they 'should not on the whole be considered as portraits but rather should be seen as part of a broader attempt to reconfigure human identity by means of representational innovation, at times working within, at times transforming, and at times subverting the time-honoured and seemingly unproblematic, indeed self-explanatory, pictorial genre'.[65] She expands the proposition by identifying the permeability of portraiture and scenes from contemporary life.

As the Impressionists' immediate predecessor and acknowledged 'leader', Manet established the parameters for this new condition of portraiture and its collusion with genre painting. Simultaneously respectful of and yet able to disregard current conventions, past art and traditional categories, Manet determinedly questioned the mode of making and representation, resulting in an *oeuvre* that was stylistically unstable, compositionally experimental and iconographically ambiguous. His individual voice belies any form of categorisation, save that his struggle to portray modernity through his own hard-won and constantly questioning visual language entitles him to his undoubted position as one of the key exponents of modern art.

STÉPHANE GUÉGAN

Théophile Gautier, Militant of Modernity

The Romantic School had within it some partisans of absolute truth, who rejected verse as unnatural... Being of one's own time, nothing seems simpler and yet nothing is harder.

Théophile Gautier, 1859[1]

IN 1861, WHEN HE PARTICIPATED in the Salon for the first time, Manet was completely unknown.[2] The two works he showed that year, *The Spanish Singer* (fig. 18) and the portrait of his parents (fig. 2), did not impress the art critics at all, even those most sensitive to the 'new wave' of the late 1850s. Théodore de Banville and Albert de la Fizelière, for example, overlooked them entirely.[3] But there were one or two exceptions: Manet's talent was spotted by Hector de Callias, and more importantly by Théophile Gautier, a prominent figure in the arts since the mid-1830s, a leading reviewer of the Paris Salon exhibitions and a major contributor to *Le Moniteur universel*, the official journal of the Second Empire.[4] Gautier wrote:

> Caramba! Here is a *Guitarrero* who has not stepped out of a comic opera, and who would cut a poor figure in a romantic lithograph; but Velázquez would give him a friendly wink, and Goya would ask him for a light for his papelito. – How heartily he sings as he plucks away at his guitar! – We can almost hear him. – This bold Spaniard in his *sombrero calañés* and his coat from Marseilles wears a pair of trousers. Alas! Figaro's knee-breeches are now worn only by the *espadas* and the *banderilleros*. But this concession to fashion is redeemed by the alpargatas. There is a great deal of talent in this life-sized figure, broadly painted in true colour and with a bold brush.[5]

One might wonder why Gautier, who had provocatively worn a red vest to attend the premiere of Victor Hugo's *Hernani* on 25 February 1830 in support of its Romantic manifesto, was one of the only commentators to show some prescience in welcoming Manet. It may also seem strange that Gautier's thoughts on *The Spanish Singer* highlighted how the young Manet both relied upon and yet simultaneously rejected the accepted stereotypes of Velázquez and Goya. Instead of disdaining the hybrid clothes

Fig. 18
***The Spanish Singer*, 1860**
Oil on canvas, 147.3 x 114.3 cm
The Metropolitan Museum of Art, New York.
Gift of William Church Osborn, 1949, 49.58.2

of its main figure, Gautier insisted on their importance, identifying the mixed impression that the image raised. The painting definitely records a modern performance, one that might have taken place as much in Madrid as in Paris. So, what was its peculiar appeal to Gautier? Was he not the writer most hostile to the contemporary world and to any form of Realism? In this short text, I will explore the misunderstanding that continues to result in his being discounted as one of the actors of modernity.

Fig. 19
Nadar
Théophile Gautier in a White Smock, 1854–55
Albumen photograph, 23.5 x 18.6 cm
Musée d'Orsay, Paris, PHO1991-2-74

GAVARNI OR COURBET?

First, it would be a mistake to reduce Romanticism to a form of nostalgic subjectivity that rejected modern society and its arrogant materialism. The nineteenth century was eager to show that it was radically breaking new ground. Both past and present were analysed according to the same historical relativism. An age in which society was in flux challenged the idea of human permanence and consequently the legitimacy of values derived from the classical past. Thus an urgent need arose to describe the contemporary world as it was, albeit from a personal perspective.

During the Bourbon Restoration and the July Monarchy in the first half of the nineteenth century, French painting had experienced its own revolution; it sought to give an account of the entirety of reality, unconstrained by taboos and received aesthetic programmes. Moreover, artists were eager to adapt their output to new modes of exhibition and innovative uses for their images. A survey of Gautier's earliest critical writings on art – he was active from 1832 – reveals the degree to which the young poet was receptive to the debate around the representation of the 'present time', the new Spanish taste and the emergence of Realism.[6] Throughout the July Monarchy, Gautier supported all those writers (from Alexandre Dumas to Honoré de Balzac) and painters (from Paul Chenavard to Thomas Couture, whose studio Manet entered in 1850) who were determined to confront – and depict – reality no matter how it looked. In 1836, long before Baudelaire addressed the challenges of such an approach, Gautier had identified the 'black male dress' as the symbol of modern society and its paradoxical beauty. On the one hand he could declare that: 'For better or for worse, we have to lock ourselves in sordid black shrouds, in which we seem to be in mourning for our cheerfulness.'[7] On the other, Gautier enthusiastically eulogised such artists as Paul Gavarni or Vincent Vidal, whom he recognised as being able to express 'the elegance, the taste, the refined understanding of modern beauty which is equal to that of the Antique, but from which our artists, too preoccupied with Greece and Rome, do not know how to extract the ideal'.[8] Hence, after the 1848 Revolution, he was already primed to examine carefully Gustave Courbet's early artistic achievements. Although his views are generally disregarded, Gautier's initial reaction in 1849, when Courbet showed seven works, including *After Dinner at Ornans* (Palais des Beaux-Arts, Lille), was very positive. Courbet confirmed Gautier's belief that history painting should abandon its outdated codes and adopt a certain realism derived from objective observation. However, *Burial at Ornans* (fig. 12), presented at the 1851 Salon, pushed this objectivity too far, and caused him perplexity. For, although Courbet had responded to Gautier's expectations regarding the making of history paintings that were relevant to the contemporary world, his art had at the same time shaken them up,[9] for this so-called Realism was also capable of bombast, or what the critic called the 'mannerism of ugliness'.

THE 'VINTAGE' PROCESS

Courbet's challenging new art encouraged Gautier to seek to clarify the current task that confronted artists. His first article on the Salon of 1852, held a few months after Louis-Napoléon Bonaparte's coup d'état, was particularly brilliant.[10] In addition to pointing out the confusion that existed within the traditional categories of art, the result of a blurring of the boundaries of individual genres, Gautier linked the idea of modernity to the instability of meaning and the need to revise accepted subject-matter: 'There is a strong feeling in the air that something is to be done – but what? Is it a laundress or a dryad, a toilette scene or a hero, a slum or Mount Olympus?'[11] In this context, it was clear that the portrait had a role to play in cleansing the 'grand genre' of all its classical conventions. Writing about Ernest Hébert's portrait of Countess Eugène Pastré (Musée Hébert, Paris) in 1852, Gautier defined the path to follow:

> It is wrong in our view to affect a certain repugnance or at least a certain disdain for purely contemporary subjects. We believe, for our part, that there are new effects, unexpected aspects in the intelligent and faithful representation of what we will call modernity ... More than any other artist, a portrait painter must convey the sense of his time and sign his paintings with their precise 'vintage'.[12]

The effects that could be achieved through consideration of the society portrait were to open Gautier's aesthetic reflection to new developments. The nine articles that he devoted to British painting in 1855, on the occasion of the Exposition Universelle in Paris, praised those proponents of 'modern life' still much in the minority on his side of the Channel: 'the character of British painting is ... modernity. Does this word exist? The feeling it expresses is so new that it could well not be found in dictionaries.'[13] Neologism or not, the word was there to stay and defined many of Gautier's aesthetic concerns in subsequent years. No sooner had he taken a leading role in late 1856 in *L'Artiste* – an influential periodical since the 1830s – he wrote at length about those artists who depicted new imagery in a meaningful way.[14] Significantly, he returned to consider anew the work of Gavarni and Gustave Doré for their fascination with the modern world and its cult of the outsider.[15] A close associate of Doré, Gautier knew that the Romantic illustrator was a keen observer of urban life. His long study of Doré was followed by a series of articles that clearly illustrated the direction his aesthetic was taking over a two-year period. Some texts are well known, especially his telling essay on fashion as the emulation of art, and his articles on Balzac. The publisher Auguste Poulet-Malassis brought these together in book form in 1858 and 1859, having published Baudelaire's *Les Fleurs du mal* in 1857, a controversial collection of poems dedicated to Gautier. At that time, Baudelaire was trying to publish his long essay about Constantin Guys, 'The Painter of Modern Life'; this did not appear until 1863, importantly rephrasing many of Gautier's aesthetic propositions concerning the nature of the modern and modernity.

STRANGE PAINTING

Against this background, Gautier was ready to praise the first public achievements of Manet in 1861, as I mentioned at the outset. The painter quickly understood how his novel aesthetic could be transmitted through a media network in which Gautier had a prominent place. In fact, this conjunction was confirmed by both figures' commitment to the Société Nationale des Beaux-Arts, founded in 1861, and the Société des Aquafortistes, set up a year later.[16] A certain complicity was thus established, as is illustrated in *Music in the Tuileries Gardens* (cat. 26), painted in the autumn of 1862. It is significant that, in this multi-figure work, Manet represented Gautier within the group of 'friends' whose presence gave the painting strong symbolic value. When Manet returned to the Salon in 1864, Gautier as critic and newly appointed juror accorded him much attention. Of Manet's two pictures, one religious, the other of a bullfight, the latter was possibly meant to please the critic's Hispanism, as had *The Spanish Singer* in 1861. But the *Dead Christ with Angels* (1864; Metropolitan Museum of Art, New York) and its excessive Realism left him lost for words. Could Manet also be an advocate of this 'mannerism of ugliness'? Despite its odd perspective, *The Incident at a Bullfight* seemed more in tune with what Gautier perceived to be Manet's style. Above all Gautier was fascinated by the dead toreador lying in the foreground; he even thought that this gripping and moving figure would be a subject sufficient to fill a complete composition. We know that the painter probably took Gautier's advice: by 1867 he had cut up the earlier composition in order to create, under a new title and fuelled with larger meaning, *The Dead Toreador* (fig. 20). Manet, Gautier concluded, had 'a certain power, a certain influence on contemporary painting, of which he represents the most extravagant tendencies'.[17] Alas, in a way, Manet's entries to the Salon of 1865 were to confirm these words beyond Gautier's wildest expectations. Faithful to the Salon's newfound and relatively more liberal stance, the jurors, including Gautier, had accepted two much more provocative works. *Olympia* (fig. 9) looked as monstrous as it seemed to be badly painted, and even dangerously ironic through its references to the Old Masters. *Christ Mocked by the Soldiers* (1865; Art Institute of Chicago) was even worse. However, Gautier

Fig. 20
The Dead Toreador, probably 1864
Oil on canvas, 75.9 x 153.3 cm
National Gallery of Art, Washington.
Widener Collection, 1942.9.40

was sufficiently impressed to leave the door ajar: 'Would not the biggest surprise be for Manet to turn up next year with two good paintings?' Since the artist was not represented at the Salons of 1866 and 1867, Gautier had to wait three years before Manet returned to the official exhibition with two paintings capable of pleasing him. But it did not work out for either of them in 1868. If Gautier quite liked *Emile Zola* (cat. 28) and its allusions to the 'new painting' aesthetic, with its references ranging from Velázquez to Japan, the ambiguous charms of *Young Lady in 1866* (fig. 10) and its redefined eroticism entirely eluded him.[18]

Fig. 21
James Tissot
La Partie carrée, 1870
Oil on canvas, 119.5 x 144.5 cm
Private collection

JAMES TISSOT VERSUS MANET

Despite his only partial appreciation of Manet's work, Gautier was forced to admit in 1869 that it was impossible to remain indifferent to his 'strange painting'.[19] Compared to the rest of the press, Gautier's conclusion was very positive: 'M. Manet's submitted paintings are relatively wise and will provoke no scandal. If he really wanted to take the trouble, he could become a good painter. He has the right temperament for it.'[20] Those last words say everything. But things turned out very differently in 1870. That year, due to the greater liberalism of the Second Empire, the Salon jury was reformed along more democratic lines. As a result Alexandre Cabanel, Jean-Léon Gérôme and Gautier himself were dismissed, and in the wake of this, the critic's tone became more aggressive towards Manet: 'None of the promises of his early years having been realised … each exhibition seems to prove that M. Manet has resolved to die wholly unrepentant, led astray by a false doctrine and imprudent praise.'[21]

Gautier's death in 1872 was to prevent him from returning to a critique of Manet after the Paris Commune. However, he found in James Tissot the perfect candidate to fulfil his expectations of an art that expressed modernity. As early as 1859, Gautier had not only understood that Tissot was more than just a follower of the Dutch painter Henri Leys (a *pasticheur* of Dürer and Holbein), but the critic was also in a position to appreciate Tissot's sensitivity to contemporary British painters and their modernisation of medieval subjects. In the early 1860s Tissot entered a circle that included Degas, Whistler and Manet, and begun to draw inspiration from more mundane scenes of modern Paris. That said, as Baudelaire would have put it, he tried to seize the present in its own historicity. In that sense, 1864 marked a turning point: as Manet provoked a scandal once again at the Salon, Tissot presented *Portrait of Mademoiselle L. L.* and *The Two Sisters* (both Musée d'Orsay, Paris), in which he blurred the boundaries between the society portrait and genre painting. A year later, as Manet was showing *Olympia*, Tissot continued to provide the public with a more acceptable representation of modernity. Nevertheless, his pictures were sufficiently provocative to trouble conservative art critics, and consequently, Gautier rode to his defence and encouraged this new direction in his art. Most of all, he praised Tissot's combination of a visually pleasing, updated style and his witty insights into modern society. For Gautier, Tissot's *La Partie carrée* (fig. 21), shown at the Salon of 1870, was as seductive as the Japanese prints that the artist had started to collect. To us, Tissot's response to Manet's *Déjeuner sur l'herbe* and to Gautier's positive critique gives us the right measure of a common engagement in modernity, a modernity whose scope and romantic roots it is now time to rediscover.

Manet at the Intersection of Portraits and Personalities

EDOUARD MANET'S CAREER as an artist in Second Empire Paris coincided with a moment when the art of painting was being challenged by the burgeoning of photography. The portrait was foremost among those genres of picture in which this challenge was urgently felt, for this was the category of image whose look and meanings were most radically and substantively changed by the proliferation of photographic studios large and small. When in his famous cartoon dubbed *Nadar Raises Photography to an Art Form* (fig. 22) Honoré Daumier lampooned the caricaturist-turned-photographer Nadar, along with the pretensions of photography and the mushrooming of photographic businesses in the city of Paris, he was no doubt also targeting the rise of the photographic portrait more particularly.[1] For not only was Nadar himself the most famed photographic portraitist of the day, but also the majority of those buildings with photography signs on them beneath Nadar's balloon-elevated camera were probably studios that specialised in portraiture.[2]

This was a situation that undoubtedly made a difference to Manet's portrait practice. Indeed, I would like to propose that what Manet did with the portrait was to make it boldly strange, and that he did so at a complicated three-way crossroads between a battle of mediums young and old, 'mechanical' and 'autographic', reproductive and imaginative; in particular, the co-temporal rise of two competing forms of the portrait photograph, the carte de visite and the signature full-plate likeness; and finally, the bohemian culture of the contentious personality. At this intersection of mediums and personalities, competing notions of the portrait, the photograph and the person rubbed up against one another.

Fig. 22
Honoré Daumier
Nadar élévant la Photographie à la hauteur de l'Art (Nadar Raises Photography to an Art Form), 1862
Lithograph, 27.3 x 21.9 cm
Los Angeles County Museum of Art

Fig. 23
Nadar studio
Portrait of Edouard Manet,
c. 1865
Photograph, dimensions unknown
Private collection

A handsome man, Manet is reputed to have had an abundance of wit and charm and a high degree of that *je ne sais quoi* that we call 'presence': we know this, in part, because although he rarely portrayed himself, he was often portrayed by others who were manifestly drawn to just that set of qualities. Indeed, in the 1860s, one after another portraitist rendered him in different mediums: Edgar Degas and Félix Bracquemond drew and etched his face and figure; Alphonse Legros painted him lounging elegantly in his studio in 1863 (Musée du Petit Palais, Paris) and Henri Fantin-Latour painted him top-hatted and dashing in 1867 (Art Institute of Chicago); and he was photographed at Nadar's studio repeatedly.[3] In the next decade, he was to be depicted, among others, by the portrait-specialist Carolus-Duran, as in the little painting of 1876 (fig. 50) that shows him relaxed with his summer straw hat pushed back on his forehead. There are also many photographs of him by other photographers, taken throughout his life.

Fig. 24
Nadar
Portrait of Charles Baudelaire, 1854–60
Albumen print, 9 x 8.5 cm
Musée d'Orsay, Paris, PHO1991-2-53

But, as usual, Nadar's studio portraits of Manet (fig. 23) set themselves apart.[4] They suggest several things about what Manet may have learned both from the experience of sitting (and standing) for his portrait at the Nadar studio, and from looking at the resulting portraits. A number of accounts of the possible effects of photography upon Manet's painting practice have appeared: in particular, those of Anne McCauley and Alexi Worth.[5] There is occasional evidence of a very direct encounter between photography and Manet's painting, such as the in-role cartes de visite made around 1860 by the premier carte-de-visite portraitist A. A. E. Disdéri of actresses and dancers like Henriette Schlosser and Eugènie Fiocre cross-dressing as matadors; these Manet must have seen before he painted *Mlle V… in the Costume of an Espada* (Metropolitan Museum of Art, New York) in 1862. Then there is the curious conjunction of Charles Aubry's photographed peonies and Manet's painting of a similarly arranged bouquet of the same flowers in 1864,[6] not to mention the instances of the photographic basis of *The Execution of Maximilian* (Kunsthalle Mannheim) and *Eugène Pertuiset, Lion-hunter* (cat. 46). But otherwise the photographic 'influences' on Manet's art remain simultaneously obvious and obscure, and difficult to pin down – while the conflicting possibilities suggested by different kinds of portrait photograph remain unexamined.

Manet was among the second generation of bohemian celebrities to be photographed at the Nadar studio, where Nadar the elder (Félix Tournachon) played the directorial role as *auteur* and signatory, whoever else besides Nadar the younger (Adrien Tournachon) acted as the camera-operator. Manet clearly knew Nadar's portraits of Baudelaire (fig. 24) (not to mention the beautiful portrait of the poet by Nadar's competitor Etienne Carjat), and probably translated – even deliberately exaggerated – the photographic tonality of those full-plate photographs and their carbon-print and Woodburytype reproductions in his own, rare little etching of Baudelaire's features of 1865, with its drastic, dark-light contrast. He was to do the same with an etched version of his 1874 portrait of Berthe Morisot in mourning. That Morisot had had her portrait done at Nadar's studio in 1870 therefore seems germane, as does the fact that Manet often made 'autographic' reproductions of his paintings, including *Mlle V... in the Costume of an Espada*, as etchings and/or aquatints – at a time when photography was beginning to take over the much-contested function of reproduction from engravings and etchings.[7] That Baudelaire was a champion of the autographic qualities of the etching revival – his one direct response to Manet's work was to the latter's Cadart portfolio of etchings and aquatints – and a ferocious critic of photography's invasion of the domain of painting, seems just as relevant.[8]

To quote Baudelaire's famous 'Salon de 1859' on the deleterious effects of the invention of photography on painting: 'From that moment our squalid society rushed, Narcissus to a man, to gaze at its trivial image on a scrap of metal. A madness, an extraordinary fanaticism took possession of all these new sun-worshippers. Strange abominations took form. By bringing together a group of male and female clowns, got up like butchers and laundry-maids in a carnival, and by begging these *heroes* to be so kind as to hold their chance grimaces for the time necessary for the performance, the operator flattered himself that he was reproducing tragic or elegant scenes from ancient history. Some democratic writer ought to have seen here a cheap method of disseminating a loathing for history and for painting among the people, thus committing a double sacrilege and insulting at one and the same time the divine art of painting and the noble art of the actor...'[9] Obviously it was *despite* his severity about what photography embodied – a mechanical copyist's attitude to 'Nature' and art, and a banal form of democratic narcissism – that Baudelaire joined the ranks of Delacroix, Daumier and Courbet, Corot and Millet, Balzac and Hugo, Champfleury and Proudhon, Gautier and Goncourt, and had his portrait made, repeatedly, by Nadar and then Carjat.[10]

But not by Disdéri, it appears. Indeed, insofar as they are directed at photography itself (rather than the transformation of art into something trivially photographic, which was his real target), Baudelaire's remarks seem addressed much more to Disdéri's kind of photograph than to Nadar's or Carjat's: the combination of references to the democratised portrait, and to the desecration of the actor's art by playing theatrical roles in front of the camera, suggests the business of the carte de visite more than anything else. Nadar himself was scathing about the carte de visite: writing retrospectively about his earlier life in photography in *Quand j'étais photographe*, he commented about Disdéri and the carte de visite: 'It spelled disaster. Either you had to succumb – that is to say, follow the trend – or resign.'[11] Nadar had started his own portrait studio the year after Disdéri patented his four-lens, sliding-plate-holder camera for making eight photographs on a single sheet in 1854: so the two were in competition from the beginning. Read in context, Nadar's remark indicates that it was not merely the market in photographic portraiture that was at stake; rather, it was the kind of portrait you could make with a camera, the kind of person who would have their portrait made that way, and the ideology of personhood that that portrait would embrace.

Fig. 25
André-Adolphe-Eugène Disdéri
***Portrait of Napoléon III*, 1858–59**
Carte de visite, 10.5 x 6.2 cm
The Library of Nineteenth-century Photography

Baudelaire and Manet both had cartes de visite made of themselves; and Nadar's studio made cartes de visite aplenty. As his own words testify, Nadar felt compelled to capitulate to the trend. But whether he had capitulated or not, the kind of portrait for which Nadar became known by the end of the 1850s marked itself apart from the carte-de-visite image. Full-plate, half-length, close-up, with the subject often gazing directly and piercingly at the camera, and with little or no props or backdrop folderol, Nadar's style of portrait was both compellingly individualised and perfect for compelling individuals. In his portraits, Nadar took the tradition of the painted portrait with the blank background and combined it with his own erstwhile craft of the caricaturist's *portrait-charge*, in order to represent members of the bohemian intelligentsia of Paris not as exchangeable bourgeois likenesses but as one-of-a-kind, non-conformist *differences*, each presence before the camera different from the other. In some of Nadar's portraits, the intransigence of that degree of difference was more marked than in others – as, for example, in his portraits of Baudelaire, in which the poet of scandals met the camera's glass eye with his own fierce, rebarbative gaze.[12] In others it was less so – it depended on the character of the personality before the camera. By the time Manet came before it, the method had become more standardised, Nadar himself was not even there most of the time, others were responsible for his signature look of up-close difference, and other portrait-photographers, such as Carjat, had managed successfully to vie with that signature look. But the fact remains that it was a look – and an ideology of the person, the portrait and the photograph – that was as distinct as it possibly could be from the look of the carte de visite.

The look of Nadar's portraits was precisely autographic, and full of the effect of presence. The look of the carte de visite was exactly not that. Indeed, it is possible to apply Clement Greenberg's famous opposition between 'avant-garde' and 'kitsch' to the disparity between the Nadar-style portrait and the carte-de-visite look that Disdéri made famous overnight when he took Napoléon III's portrait (fig. 25), casting his subject in the diminutive image of the everyday businessman, while at the same time suggesting to the businessman that if the little emperor looked like that, he too could look like a little emperor, and have his image disseminated everywhere.[13] There was no significant difference: or rather, it was the classic case of difference without distinction. By contrast, Nadar strove for distinction – not the class distinction of 'good family' and people 'of quality', but that of avant-garde intransigence setting itself *against* bourgeois conformity and therefore against the bourgeois likeness. This was the same distinction that Courbet had made in his *The Studio: A Real Allegory of Seven Years of My Life as a Painter* (1855; Musée d'Orsay, Paris): between the bourgeois emperor (in disguise) and his ilk on the left-hand side and all those bohemian individualities on the right.[14] Nadar translated that distinction very effectively into photography, at the same time suggesting that not all photography was alike, not all of it was kitsch or banal, and that this was what autographic photography looked like. *That* was what Manet sought – and got – when he went to Nadar's studio and looked straight into the camera's lens with his own personal measure of sharp-eyed acerbity, and *that* was what he attempted to produce, repeatedly, in his own hand-made portraits.

* * *

Manet painted many portraits, in many styles, in the little over two decades of his career. He first began making the portrait strange when he depicted 'Mlle V.', Victorine Meurent, in and out of costume and clothes, in and out of this role and that, between 1862 and 1867. In *Mlle V... in the Costume of an Espada* his move from carte de visite to painted 'portrait' was typically perverse: not only did he use the photographic convention of the actor's in-role portrait pose, in which the posing so derided by Baudelaire was meant to define the person's profession, in order to destabilise the painting's genre-categorisation (it is not very obviously a portrait), but he also took the small size of the visiting-card image and blew it up, making its derivation from the carte de visite difficult to recognise, but also – and this is the really perverse move – utterly subverting its effect and its meaning. Blown up to almost life-size, the pose of 'Mlle V.' looks like nothing more than a nonsense. Moreover, she is simultaneously strangely photographic in her heavily contrasted, front-lit tonality, and exaggeratedly anti-photographic in her painterliness: nowhere is this more evident than in the attribute of the matador's cloak that she holds up as if to point at its caricatured paintedness. If in Disdéri's little portraits of Henriette Schlosser and Eugènie Fiocre (fig. 26) that cloak is a signifier of the role being played before the camera, in Manet's hands it

Fig. 26
André-Adolphe-Eugène Disdéri
Eugènie Fiocre as a Matador in the Ballet Grazioza, 1859–61
Carte de visite, 10.5 x 6.1 cm
The Library of Nineteenth-century Photography

becomes a sign of the transformation of the photographic into the painterly, as if blowing up a small photograph into a large painting revealed what should have been photographic grain to be a big dollop of thickly handled paint. In the meantime, the everybody-is-exchangeable-with-everybody-else commodification of the small carte de visite is turned into its opposite: this is boldly, largely, intransigently, autographically, *Manet*.

'Mlle V.' herself may remain a mystery, but her outward-looking translation into paint has much more of the effect of the masculine gazes of Nadar's gallery of bohemian contemporaries than of Disdéri's little visiting cards. (Even such women as Georges Sand and Sarah Bernhardt tended to lower or avert their gazes before the camera, or at least to make those gazes milder than the men's.) In his later portraits of women, more recognisable as portraits (see Leah Lehmbeck, pp. 50–57), Manet tended to eschew the boldness of facture, lighting, presence and gaze that had characterised his pictures of Victorine Meurent playing different roles, but he continued to stress the fact that they were made by hand in different mediums: not just oil paint, but delicate little watercolours and rococo-looking pastels. This was the case with his portraits of Berthe Morisot (cats 16–19), Isabelle Lemonnier (cats 61, 62) and particularly Méry Laurent (cat. 55), the famous demi-mondaine who served as the real-life model for Marcel Proust's character Odette, and who, as a celebrated beauty, was photographed repeatedly, most often in the carte-de-visite form (figs 64–67). (She went to Disdéri for some of her cartes de visite.) When Manet came to portray her, he made his evanescent handling of pastel and paint into a sign of her femininity, and of his ability to handle paint in different ways: here the virile dash of the 1860s, there the light-handed touch of his charmingly voguish later work. But there was no remaining sign of the photographic in his treatment of her or other women – even when, as in Méry Laurent's case, he may very well have looked at photographs as *aides-mémoire*.[15]

As for Manet's portraits of men, he adopted a wide range of manners over time, and in order to portray different individualities: Théodore Duret, Zacharie Astruc, Emile Zola, Stéphane Mallarmé, George Moore, Georges Clemenceau. Of these, only the Duret portrait (cat. 29) has anything resembling a carte-de-visite pose or look about it. The others are bold, large-scale portraits with some of the effects of the photograph-writ-large to be found in the 'Mlle. V' series, which is the case with the exceptional portrait of Zola (cat. 28). Or they are deliberately casual in presentation and/or facture, as in the case of the portrait of Mallarmé (cat. 30), which ignores standards of photographic finish and self-presentation. But the portrait that stands out from other male portraits in Manet's career in its peculiar, large-scale blend of the photographic and the anti-photographic, is the painting of the Republican arts minister and statesman Antonin Proust of 1880 (cat. 45). Although one finds a few examples of close-up three-quarter-length carte-de-visite photographs, such as one of Disdéri's eight images of the Duke of Coimbra, brother of the King of Portugal (fig. 27), the effect of presence that the artist has achieved in this painted portrait does not resemble the work of Disdéri so much as that of Nadar, as in the Nadar-studio photographs of Manet himself, standing forward and looking straight at the camera (fig. 23) or sitting thighs-akimbo astride a

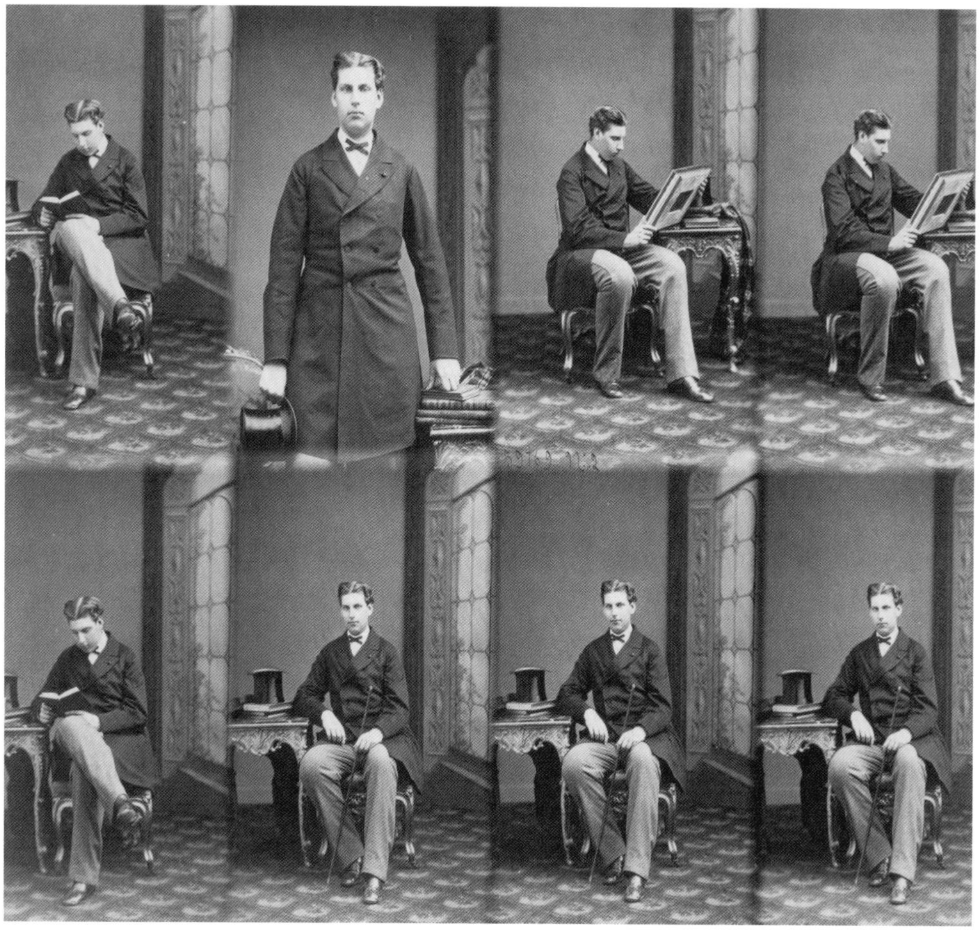

Fig. 27
André-Adolphe-Eugène Disdéri
The Duke of Coimbra, c. 1860
Carte de visite, Albumen print, 20.1 x 23.7 cm
George Eastman House, Rochester, New York

backwards-turned chair (fig. 74). Manet had first possibly portrayed Proust back in the 1850s, in the days when they were both in Thomas Couture's studio: young and bareheaded, and in a style derived from Couture. What a difference two and a half decades had made: the aggressively confident, starkly lit Proust is a Velázquez-style portrait transformed by the modern medium of photography, with the garb and accoutrements of modern urban masculinity. And Proust's hat is brashly on, an in-your-face sign of the defiance of photo-studio decorum. (The Duke of Coimbra had taken off his hat, as had every other gentleman who had his portrait photographed, or for that matter, painted – except for Manet himself, once, in Fantin-Latour's earlier portrait [Art Institute of Chicago].)[16] And for all its photographic style of presentation, Proust's portrait is nonetheless as painterly as can be: Disdéri's bourgeois prince meets Nadar's rule-breaking bohemian, and is transformed into a confrontational painting by Manet. There can be no better example than this of the unsettling, strange-making way that photography inflected portraiture in Manet's career.[17]

LEAH LEHMBECK

'L'Esprit de l'atelier': Manet's Late Portraits of Women, 1878–1883

IN JULY 1878 MANET was forced to leave his beloved studio at 4 Rue de Saint-Pétersbourg, and set up his easel temporarily at 70 Rue d'Amsterdam, just around the corner. His stay there was only to be brief, 'three quarters' of a year as his lease recorded, before he moved into his final studio a few doors down at number 77. And although it was in these few years that Manet began to experience the symptoms that led to his early death at the age of 51, during this time he nevertheless created some of his most brilliant portraits of women.

A gadabout, a wit and a charmer, Manet spent the last five years of his life as gregariously as ever. A parade of *parisiennes* from the monde and the demi-monde walked through his doors, and stood, or sat, for him to capture their smiles, their gazes and their sumptuous costumes. These women, among them his wife, provide a glittering record of his Paris. His late portraits of women also reveal the crucial importance of portraiture to Manet's artistic programme, through his clever engagement with the traditional expectations of the genre: the standardised poses, the idealised identities and the staged compositions. It is in portraiture that Manet's interest in depicting the real world coincides with his deliberately self-conscious approach to picture-making, ultimately revealing the dual nature of his Realism.

By the autumn of 1878 Manet was at work on a group of portraits in his temporary studio.[1] Three portraits of different women, from different social classes and with varying degrees of intimacy with the painter, were created in the same luxuriant setting: a studied double portrait of M. and Mme Jules Guillemet; a lively pastel of the courtesan Jeanne Demarsy; and a genial portrait of his wife, Suzanne Leenhoff. In these three pictures Manet presents us with a brilliant sample of his expansive approach to portraiture, encompassing a range of style, of composition, of finish and of the type of women who sat for him.

Fig. 28
***On the Bench*, 1879**
Pastel on canvas, 61 x 50 cm
Suzuki Collection, Tokyo

The first, and grandest, of the three is *In the Conservatory* (cat. 39), the matrimonial portrait of the Guillemets, completed for the Salon of 1879. The French couple may have owned a fashionable clothing store, and thus Mme Guillemet's sophisticated costume became a focal point for Manet in his highly finished picture. This technical approach was unusual in his *oeuvre*, but was perfectly aligned with the mood of the sitters. Mme Guillemet sits rigidly upright within the lattice of lines created by the bench's slats and posts. The careful fan of her pleats and the neat punctuation of her buttons continue the calculated geometry. The march of the back slats of the bench off the edge of the canvas suggests an infinite divide between husband and wife, and reinforces the female sitter as the primary focus of the composition. Manet underlines this with his palette: a co-ordinated triad of yellow umbrella, gloves and hat, contrasting with the black and beige attire of M. Guillemet. A halo of blue, violet and salmon-coloured petals hovers around Mme Guillemet's head, an obvious reference to her fresh, natural beauty.

The pairing of women and flowers appears in several of Manet's portraits of women, and it is exemplified in his images of Jeanne Demarsy, a young actress and courtesan who was to find success in the theatres of Paris in the 1880s and 1890s. Executed in the same leafy surroundings, her pastel *On the Bench* (fig. 28; see also cat. 57) is a relatively conventional depiction reminiscent of the rigidity of a high-renaissance profile. But the lively execution of chalk perfectly pairs a pink and red rose to like colours in Demarsy's cheeks and lips and beautifully equates petals and flesh. Demarsy's symbolic portrait, *Spring* (fig. 29; see cat. 57), made just a few years after this pastel, takes the relationship between femininity and nature even further. A pendant to Méry Laurent's *Autumn* (cat. 55),[2] the portrait of Demarsy presents the young woman as the bountiful embodiment of the season. Her dress and hat, selected by Manet, are covered in leaves and flowers; she seems herself to blossom from the background verdure. As Maurice Du Seigneur noted upon the work's exhibition in the Salon of 1882, 'Since we are speaking of living flowers, let me introduce you to *Jeanne* by Edouard Manet. She is not a woman, she is a bouquet, truly a visual perfume.'[3]

The relationship between flowers and women in Manet's work goes beyond the relatively facile comparison between feminine beauty and the passivity of the delicate subject; it reveals a more important aspect of his picture-making. In his figural work, Manet was often accused of taking an anti-narrative stance. That is, the people in his pictures seem not to relate to one another, but instead appear simply to have been arranged. Even one of his greatest supporters, Emile Zola, noted that Manet 'treats figure paintings in the same way as in art schools one may treat still-life; I mean that he groups figures before him, somewhat by chance, and that his only concern is then to fix them upon the canvas as he sees them'.[4] Manet's tendency to arrange his compositions is inherent to his studio work, and lies at the core of his artistic approach. This self-conscious method of picture-making also suggests why Manet, whose 'guardian angel protected him'[5] from the commissions of portrait painting and who was so dedicated to capturing life as he saw it, returned again and again to a genre that seemed so limited in format. Portrait painting epitomised the constructs of the studio. The genre not only encouraged Manet's preference for arrangement, it openly acknowledged it.

Fig. 29
Spring (Jeanne de Marsy), 1881
Oil on canvas, 73 x 51 cm
Private collection

The third portrait completed in the same garden setting was a quick but eloquent study of Manet's wife Suzanne (cat. 6). Known for her warmth and grace, Mme Manet cut a distinct figure among the petite Parisians (Demarsy and Guillemet among them) with whom her husband surrounded himself. Born in the Netherlands, she was plump and fair, and although she often stayed out of his studio while he was working, she was the artist's most consistently used female model. Manet's portraits of her number around sixteen (not including early drawings),[6] and these works span his entire career, from the late 1850s to her final portrait, completed around 1882 (cats 3–7, 12). Manet's images of his wife reflect his great comfort with her and, as a result, present some of his most radical experiments within the genre of portraiture.

The freedom with which Manet approached his portraits of Suzanne is unmatched; none were intended for public exhibition. *Mme Manet in the Conservatory* (cat. 6), for example, is strikingly different from the Salon-ready image of the Guillemets. Although both women are posed similarly, the image of Suzanne is much more freely executed. Brushwork is confident and loose rather than tight and pernickety, reflecting the ease of both artist and sitter. Her hat is placed at her side, and the foliage that envelops her appears more natural, less botanically precise, although it is still identifiable. Like Mme Guillemet's, Mme Manet's marital status is revealed by a wedding ring. But instead of including himself in the portrait, Manet hints at his presence with a loosely defined artist's smock hanging over the bench to the right.

Manet's final portrait of Suzanne, the delightful and striking *Woman with a Cat (Portrait of Mme Manet)* (cat. 5), is even more evocative in its demonstration of Manet's relationship with portraiture, a result of both execution and subject. The Dutchwoman is depicted in their apartment, which is defined by a squall of pink and white and red brushwork. Her blush-coloured *peignoir* is as plump as her lustrously black cat Zizi, together a reflection of the embonpoint of the bourgeoisie. Although sexually loaded pairings of women and their cats had been prevalent from the eighteenth century through to the artist's own *Olympia* (fig. 9) and beyond, Manet does not seem to refer to this tradition here. Instead, the cross-hatchings that define Suzanne's person and pet embed her within the fabric of the red couch and the space beyond, an emblem of domesticity rather than of sexuality. Manet encourages her dissolution into the very fabric of the canvas through his application of paint. This female figure – the solidly tangible, real-life wife of Manet – becomes a physical part of the painting, and of the real space that they share together.

By April 1879, the artist had moved into his final, newly renovated studio at 77 Rue d'Amsterdam. The high-vaulted space with its wall of windows served more than anything as a repository for his greatest paintings (*Olympia*, *The Balcony* and *The Execution of Maximilian*, among other works, hung tightly across the walls). Yet here Manet created an extraordinary number of portraits, capturing the steady stream of visitors who came to keep him company, particularly after he could no longer walk to the cafés that he had once frequented. Of the pleasant atmosphere, one such sitter, his cousin René Maizeroy, recalled, 'Once one has come to Manet's studio, even for a casual visit, one cannot make up one's mind to leave.'[7]

Fig. 30
Portrait of Mlle Isabelle Lemonnier (Young Woman in a Ballgown), 1879
Oil on canvas, 101 x 81 cm
Private collection

Many of these friends and acquaintances were captivated by Manet's bold use of pastel. Throughout his career, Manet had utilised the medium occasionally, but as his strength began to wane, he took up chalk much more frequently. With rare exceptions, the dozens of pastels he created after his move into his final studio are markedly similar: conventional bust-height profiles or views *en face* of female sitters. All the women are depicted in the latest fashion and accessories, their hats, gloves, muffs and dresses reflecting contemporary Parisian femininity (and Manet's continued interest in it) (cats 40, 58). Boldly executed and only flirting with finish, they impressed the critics who had often had trouble with these same qualities in his paintings. Indeed, after complaining of Manet's failings in his paintings, Paul Sebillot remarked on the pastels, 'but the same faults, because of the greater freedom of the medium, appear less shocking. They are among the most admired works in the present exhibition and they deserve to be.'[8]

While turning out these delightful fashion plates, during these later years Manet also continued to paint large oils of his sitters. The elegant, wealthy and beautiful Isabelle Lemonnier appeared on his canvases most often. The daughter of a famous jeweller, she was the sister-in-law of Georges Charpentier, a champion of modern art and founder of the review *La Vie moderne* and the eponymous gallery. Isabelle's sister, Marguérite-Louise, was captured beautifully with her children by Renoir for the Salon of 1879 (Metropolitan Museum of Art, New York); she also hosted one of the most important salons of the Third Republic, at which Manet and Lemonnier probably met.[9] The artist's relationship with Lemonnier is preserved through his five oil portraits of her, created around 1879 and 1880, and in a series of flirtatious letters that he wrote to the twenty-three-year old in 1880. Beyond the light-hearted text and drawings, Manet's letters also convey an unexpected vulnerability, no doubt exacerbated by his failing health.[10]

Manet's paintings of Isabelle Lemonnier are an example of how this master of Realism, who embraced modernity on a fundamental level, also deliberately engaged with portraiture's traditional characteristics. All five of his portraits of Lemonnier are three-quarter length, a composition highly unusual in his portraits of women. This was the format that dominated the annual Salon, however, and from the sixteenth century onwards, it had been reserved for cardinals and nobles, making it in turn an appropriately august fit for the society ladies of contemporary Paris.

As did his more academically oriented contemporaries Charles Chaplin, Carolus-Duran or Léon Bonnat, Manet insisted on presenting details of dress, accented with the fashionable accoutrements of the day. The three-quarter-length portraits of Lemonnier allowed him additional room to include such appurtenances. In *Isabelle Lemonnier with a Muff* (cat. 61) the sitter wears a rich fur coat and a bejewelled hair bow while clutching a muff. In *Isabelle Lemonnier with a White Collar* (cat. 62) the sitter's white lace collar with its gold button puffs out of the top of her double-breasted coat. In *Portrait of*

Mlle Isabelle Lemonnier (fig. 30) the sitter is dressed in a gauzy white dress that is nearly indistinguishable from her pallid skin, giving extra vibrancy to her espresso-coloured hair and eyes and her crimson lips.[11] The most vivid colour in the portrait comes from her elbow-length yellow gloves, which appear in several of Manet's portraits, including a three-quarter-length watercolour sketch of Lemonnier dating from the summer of 1880 (fig. 31).

Manet's portraits of Lemonnier are some of his most traditional visions of womanhood. Although they contain Manet's characteristic confidence in his application of paint, as well as his disregard for the notion of completion, Lemonnier is nevertheless presented *comme il faut* – 'as is expected'. She is depicted in a way befitting a woman of her type, age and class. Her beauty is heightened with makeup, her social status demonstrated by her clothes, and her confidence projected by her elegant pose. Given the artifice inherent in these modes of self-presentation, the portraits of Lemonnier not only reflect how she *should* be presented, but how she actually *was*. At once these paintings highlight both that which is created for a painting and that which is real, openly complicating the notion of Realism for this painter of modern life.

Fig. 31
***Portrait of Isabelle Lemonnier*, 1880**
Watercolour on paper, 20 x 10.4 cm
Musée du Louvre, Paris (Musée d'Orsay Collection), RF 11173

Manet's most direct engagement with these two polarities is revealed in his portraits of actors. Throughout his career, in works such as *Lola de Valence* (1862; Musée d'Orsay, Paris), *The Tragic Actor* (cat. 33) or *Faure as Hamlet* (1877; Folkwang Museum, Essen), Manet presented actors and dancers in costume and at work performing. In all of these portraits the artist engaged with notions of identity, performance and the relationship between actor and audience and studio and stage. Because portraiture openly acknowledges the viewer, the medium is particularly fertile territory for playing with ideas of how identity is conveyed.[12] In *Portrait of Emilie Ambre as Carmen* (cat. 35) Manet investigates identity and performance, and cleverly proposes some of the complex issues that underlie his rich engagement with the genre.

In September and October 1880 Manet underwent a course of hydrotherapy in Bellevue, southwest of Paris, to alleviate the pain in his leg. During this time, the singer and actress Emilie Ambre, one of his neighbours in the town, sat for her portrait in the role of Carmen. It is unclear whether she asked for the sitting or if Manet was returning a favour (Ambre had arranged for his extraordinary *Execution of Maximilian* [1868–69; Kunsthalle Mannheim] to be exhibited in New York and Boston the previous winter).[13] Manet, however, did comment on the creation of Ambre's portrait in a letter to Eva Gonzalès in 1880: 'At the moment I am working on a portrait of Mlle Emilie Ambre, a landowning prima-donna neighbour. I go every day to work, as she leaves for America the 8th of October.'[14]

Fig. 32
Unknown photographer
Célestine Galli-Marié as Carmen, undated
Clipping of a photograph
Bibliothèque des Arts décoratifs, Paris

The role was Ambre's favourite, and she even asked Antonin Proust to use his influence in the government to revive Bizet's famous opera for the national stage.[15] Though Proust failed, Ambre nevertheless appears in this important picture in her Carmen costume.[16] A red bolero jacket trimmed in golden pom-poms covers her sky-blue dress. Her hair is topped with a red flower and pinned by a comb that also secures a white lace mantilla. Her right hand clutches a fan. Manet is believed to have completed the portrait at Ambre's residence. Yet her indirect gaze, her position against a table and the uncommon half-length pose may also suggest the use of a photograph, of Ambre or perhaps one of several other actresses identified with the role at that time (fig. 32).

In electing to have herself portrayed as Carmen, Ambre deliberately suppressed her real identity in favour of a fictional character, one that directly recalls her role on stage. She is not enhancing her identity for social reasons, as Lemonnier did in her portraits. Instead, Ambre's inhabiting of another character is more direct. She poses as Carmen: as her *performing* self. And although Manet is undoubtedly indulging in the tradition of making portraits 'in character', by muddling the identity of the sitter in this way his portrait inevitably poses the question: is portraiture a reflection of reality or can it be seen instead as a recognisable, admitted construction?

Manet's late portraits of women show that for the artist these poles are not entirely at odds. He plays with the genre's expectations by varying his stylistic approach and altering the attributes inherent to certain sitters, thereby presenting his contemporary world at the same time as highlighting the artifice of painting. Deeply personal, Manet's Realism was tied to the two parts of his life that were most meaningful to him: his companions and his craft. Portraiture allowed him to connect and to illuminate both simultaneously. So important was the genre to the artist that it seems fitting that as he was slipping towards death, by now away from his studio and at home, his final work was a portrait. The image, a quick pastel of Elisa,[17] the young maid of his friend Méry Laurent, is an exclamation mark at the end of a long career that had repeatedly emphasised the importance of portraiture.

COLIN B. BAILEY

For John House, *in memoriam*

Manet and Renoir: An Unexamined Dialogue

When you admire a master, there is nothing that displeases you in his work.
Pierre-Auguste Renoir

IN THE SUMMER OF 1895, Julie Manet recorded a heated conversation between Renoir and an unnamed 'boring bad painter': her words – those of a well-brought-up, but partisan, seventeen-year-old. The discussion had turned to the work of Julie's uncle, Edouard Manet – who had died twelve years earlier – and Renoir was incensed by his colleague's criticism of certain aspects of Manet's work. 'Well then, Renoir replied, this person simply didn't like Manet at all. For when you admire a master, there is nothing that displeases you in his work.'[1]

Renoir admired all periods of Manet's work.[2] He compared Manet's whites and blacks to Titian's,[3] and had no difficulty in identifying the art-historical quotations in *Déjeuner sur l'herbe* (see cat. 52).[4] For Renoir, even Manet's 'copies' after Velázquez and Goya marked him as 'the standard-bearer of our group', because it was he 'who best captured in his canvases that simple formula towards which we were all striving'.[5] A 'precursor' who ushered in a 'new era in painting', Manet was 'as important to us as Cimabue or Giotto were to the Italians of the Quattrocento'.[6]

Although Renoir owned only two minor watercolours by Manet, acquired in October 1894 for modest sums,[7] it was to his home in the Butte Montmartre that the twenty-eight-year-old Ambroise Vollard was directed that autumn to seek information about the sitter of one of Manet's portraits ('Renoir will know who it is').[8] Renoir identified the top-hatted gentleman shown standing in the Bois de Boulogne as Monsieur Brun (cat. 38) and Vollard was able to sell the portrait to Degas.[9]

Manet, whose collection at the time of his death boasted seven canvases by Monet but nothing by Renoir, had been the first owner of Renoir's *Frédéric Bazille* (fig. 33), which he persuaded Renoir to include in the Second Impressionist Exhibition of April 1876.[10] Renoir later recalled how Manet used to tease him by repeating in front of each of his paintings: 'No, it's not as good as *The Portrait of Bazille*', which led him to believe that 'for once I had done something that was not too bad'.[11] In the 1870s Manet recommended

Fig. 33
Pierre-Auguste Renoir
Frédéric Bazille, 1867
Oil on canvas, 105 x 73.5 cm
Musée d'Orsay, Paris, RF 2448

Renoir's works – and those of his fellow Impressionists – to friends and clients, in March 1875 urging *Le Figaro*'s ferocious art critic Albert Wolff to attend their auction at the Hôtel Drouot.[12] 'My friends Mssrs. Monet, Sisley, Renoir, and Madame Berthe Morisot are holding an exhibition and sale at the Salle Drouot. One of these gentlemen will bring you a catalogue and invitation. You do not yet like their painting, but one day you will.'[13]

In the single exchange of letters between Manet and Renoir that has survived, the tone, on both sides, is bantering, affectionate and a little formal. Both letters are published in full for the first time in the Appendix on p. 207.[14] From Capri in late December 1881, Renoir wrote to express his delight in reading about the French State's acquisition of four masterpieces by Courbet – at the behest of Manet's childhood friend Antonin Proust (see cat. 45), head of the newly created Ministry of Arts in Gambetta's short-lived cabinet.[15] Although it had not yet been confirmed in the press, Renoir also looked forward to being able to congratulate Manet on his decoration (Manet was to be made Chevalier de la Légion d'honneur in the New Year's honours list): 'You are the joyful combatant, without hatred for anyone, like an old Gaul, whom I love for remaining cheerful even in the face of injustice.'[16] Renoir invited Manet to see his latest work as soon as he returned to Paris: 'You will do me the kindness of coming to see what I have brought back with me, but we are not quite there yet… A thousand good wishes and enduring good health.'[17] Manet responded immediately: 'My dear Renoir… No doubt you will bring home a mass of studies that are quite individual and interesting … a thousand good wishes, dear Renoir; come back with many canvases.'[18]

Renoir and Manet shared a sympathy for the aesthetics of 'Irregularity,' as codified by Ruskin in *The Stones of Venice* (1851–53).[19] Renoir's hatred for the architecture of Viollet-le-Duc and Haussmann's remodelling of Paris expressed itself in various articles published in the short-lived journal *L'Impressioniste* and, more trenchantly, in his 'Grammar' and manifesto calling for a Société des Irrégularistes, drawn up in 1883–84.[20] Manet's adherence to Ruskin's principles seems to have been spurred on by his frustrations as a portraitist and the temerity of certain sitters in requesting improvements. Antonin Proust recalled his friend's tirade against contemporary culture's obsession with symmetry – 'the wound of our time' – and his conviction that 'there is no symmetry in Nature. One eye is never exactly the same as the other, it is slightly different. We all have a nose that is more or less crooked, a mouth that is always irregular. Try and make the surveyors understand that!'[21] Manet's outburst is in much the same vein as Renoir's pronouncements on the 'Variety of nature' in his unpublished 'Grammar': 'Look at yourself in a mirror… You'll quickly be convinced that your nose is not in the middle of your face, that your two eyes are neither the same shape or the same size, nor located at the same level.'[22]

Although Renoir was not among the pallbearers at Manet's funeral – Monet and Stevens were the two painters so honoured – he attended the Memorial Banquet in January 1885.[23] Five years later, he was only able to contribute 50 francs towards the subscription for the State's purchase of *Olympia* (Monet, who launched the appeal, gave 1,000 francs).[24] Renoir's most heartfelt homage to Manet was the drawing of *The Fifer* (fig. 34) that appeared as a full-page illustration in *La Vie moderne* on 12 January 1884 (fig. 35), where it accompanied Victor Jannet's churlish review of Manet's posthumous retrospective at the Ecole des Beaux-Arts.[25] Alphonse Tabarant, who mistakenly dated Renoir's drawing to 1866, the time of Manet's painting, praised it as 'very faithful, very lively'.[26]

As the primary figure painter among the Impressionists, who was committed to large formats – above all to the full-length format – and to portraits, Renoir could not help but be attentive to Manet's example. Indeed, in some ways, he might be said to have modelled his career on Manet's, although a fundamental difference between the two artists as portraitists was their speed of execution and relationship with their sitters. Renoir, who established a thriving practice as a 'portraitiste mondaine' in the second half of the 1870s, was renowned for his expeditiousness. 'He worked with such a prodigious virtuosity that a portrait required just one sitting,' his brother Edmond told John Rewald in 1943.[27] Manet, by contrast, demanded innumerable sessions and constantly revisited and revised his portraits, as is confirmed by the litany of complaints from his long-suffering and remarkably patient sitters.[28] Recent assessments of Manet's modernism have tended to stress the differences between his practice and that of the

Fig. 34
Pierre-Auguste Renoir, after Edouard Manet
***The Fifer*, 1883**
Crayon on paper, 44.5 x 27 cm
Collection of Dr and Mrs Michael Schlossberg

Fig. 35
Pierre-Auguste Renoir, after Edouard Manet
The Fifer, published in *La Vie moderne*, 12 January 1884
Lithograph, dimensions unknown
Bibliothèque nationale de France, Paris

Impressionists. But Renoir, no less than Manet, was 'a figure painter fascinated by subjects from modern urban life ... who worked consciously within a grand tradition that simultaneously challenged and sought the admiration of the establishment.'[29] Even Renoir's commitment to 'pleinairisme' was more nuanced and mediated than is generally thought. Like Manet, Renoir, in his treatment of 'quintessentially modern subjects adopted a plein-air illumination that could be elaborated and perfected in the studio'.[30]

Above all, despite having been among the founders of the Société Anonyme des Artistes, Peintres, Sculpteurs, Graveurs in 1873–74, Renoir shared Manet's allegiance to the official Salon. Although Manet in the 1860s had been eager to present his paintings in dealers' galleries and independent exhibitions, he steadfastly refused to participate in the group exhibitions now known as Impressionist.[31] (He did agree, however, to lend paintings by Morisot and Renoir to the First and Second Impressionist Exhibitions.)[32] Between 1859 and 1882 Manet submitted to almost every Salon, was refused outright four times (in 1859, 1863, 1866 and 1876), and partially in 1874 and 1877. Between 1863 and 1883, Renoir sent works to the Salon every year but three, and only in 1874, 1876 and 1877 did he exhibit with his fellow Impressionists of his own accord.[33] He showed at the Salon fourteen times, petitioned in 1867 and 1872 for a reprise of the Salon des Refusés – with Manet a co-signatory on both occasions – and was accepted in all the Salons of the Third Republic to which he submitted.

The calendar of the Salon – the spring deadline for the jury's review, the preparation of forthcoming submissions in the autumn and winter – may be said to have determined the schedule and rhythm of Manet's and Renoir's production for two decades. Both artists were committed to exhibiting large figure paintings in the crowded rooms of the Palais de l'Industrie; with the exception of commissioned portraits, such paintings were made for no obvious destination beyond the Salon.[34] Renoir emulated Manet in his attachment to the single full-length figure of 'insistent frontality', posed against an undefined, indeterminate background in the mode of Velázquez.[35] Large-scale figural compositions also dominated Renoir's presentations at the Impressionist exhibitions.

Despite differences in their age, education, social class and economic standing, the two artists, both of whom considered themselves primarily as figure painters, share unexpected affinities. Manet's first biographer revealed that he nurtured a longstanding interest in ceramics, had decorated a porcelain service early in his career and, at the end of his life 'painted some dozens of plates with exquisite taste'.[36] Renoir, as a native son of Limoges, expected to become a painter at Sèvres before mechanisation led him to seek alternative opportunities in the fine arts. As a twenty-year-old student, in February 1852 Manet copied Boucher's *Diana at the Bath* (1742) almost as soon as it had entered the Louvre's collection.[37] Renoir, at the end of his life, informed Vollard that Boucher's masterpiece was 'the first painting that really had an effect on me, and is one that I have continued to love'.[38] Similarly, both Manet and Renoir copied Rubens's *Portrait of Helena Fourment and Her Children* in the Louvre – Manet in 1857, Renoir in the early 1860s – and both artists made copies after Delacroix.[39]

Although we would expect to find resonances of Manet's formal and compositional innovations in Renoir's figure paintings of the late 1860s and early 1870s – the period in

Fig. 36
Henri Fantin-Latour
Sketch for 'Atelier in Les Batignolles', 1869
Charcoal and graphite on paper, 12.5 x 16.3 cm
Musée du Louvre, Paris (Musée d'Orsay Collection), RF 12551

Fig. 37
Henri Fantin-Latour
Manet's Studio in Les Batignolles, 1869–70
Conté crayon with touches of red, 29.2 x 39.4 cm
The Metropolitan Museum of Art, New York. Gift of Mrs Helena M. Loewel in memory of her brother Charles W. Kraushaar, 19.86

which Manet was acknowledged as leader of the Parisian avant-garde – by the mid-1870s the situation had become more complex, as Michael Fried has noted: 'Manet responded in turn to aspects in Renoir and Monet's practice, above all to their emphasis on painting out of doors, en plein air, in natural light.'[40] Despite Manet's admiration and affection for Monet – whom he also assisted financially in the mid-1870s – he was naturally more attentive to developments in the work of the Impressionist movement's primary figure painter. George Moore (see cat. 32; fig. 5), who enjoyed the company of both artists in the 1870s, found this to be self-evident: 'Manet's last pictures were certainly influenced by Renoir; Manet's last years were spent in thinking about Renoir.'[41] Although there are undeniable differences between Manet as master of the 'tache colorante' and Renoir as the foremost exponent of 'tricotage'[42] – visual distinctions that are social as well as formal[43] – Moore's insight brings into focus a relationship that was both complex and reciprocal, and has generally been overlooked.[44]

One point of departure for assessing this dialogue is a pair of pictorial 'hommages' painted between 1869 and 1871. In Fantin-Latour's *Atelier in Les Batignolles* (fig. 1), Renoir is shown in a pose of solemn veneration, gazing upon the unusually small canvas on Manet's easel.[45] As one of the painters in the 'Batignolles guild', Renoir – with Monet and Bazille – had always been programmed to appear in this group portrait, but at the outset he had occupied a much less prominent position.[46] In Fantin's drawings from October and November 1869 (fig. 36), Renoir is shown wearing a soft hat and cape, carrying a portfolio and standing next to an imposing, more formally attired figure in a top hat.[47] This top-hatted figure was Fantin's London dealer, Edwin Edwards, who appears in most of the preparatory drawings and sketches and for whom Fantin was reserving a place in the final composition. The most elaborate of the preparatory drawings, a large sheet in crayon (fig. 37), shows Edwards entering at left, but with a heavy-set and hatless figure standing behind Manet, who bears little resemblance to Renoir.[48] As late as 1 March 1870, Fantin was still counting upon Edwards's making the journey to Paris: 'I have kept a modest place for you... You represent an artist who has just entered the studio, having come from abroad... I intend to paint you wearing a silk hat and a macfarlane, or traveller's outfit. This will convey the idea of an artist who has just entered the studio.'[49] Since Edwards failed to cross the Channel in time, Renoir was moved to the centre of the composition, ending up as the single artist to be shown in a hat – bowler style, with an upturned brim – which, with his black jacket and cape, conformed to Fantin's desire to include an artist 'who has just entered the studio'. Rather than coming from abroad, however, Renoir has merely entered from outdoors – the site, still contested, of the *actualiste*'s practice. (Fantin was to prove far less sympathetic towards members of the younger generation in the years to come.[50]) Tabarant also claimed that in giving Renoir this 'place of honour', Fantin was following Manet's wishes.[51] Whereas Monet, almost hidden by the tall and elegant Bazille, struggles to keep his footing at the right-hand edge of the composition, Renoir, stationed centre right, is portrayed as Manet's reverential disciple, the artist most eager to learn.[52]

Just over a year later Renoir returned the compliment in a floral tribute to Manet (fig. 38), which may have been painted to welcome him back to Paris in the late spring of 1871.

(However, there is no evidence that Manet ever owned this picture.)[53] *Still-life with Bouquet*, signed and dated 1871, is confidently painted, high-keyed in tonality and dense with allusion. The print hanging by a red ribbon that features prominently is a copy after Manet's *Little Cavaliers*, an etching after a painting in the Louvre then thought to be by Velázquez that Manet had exhibited three times in the previous decade.[54] The Japanese export vase as well as the pampas grass and books in Renoir's painting recall similar accoutrements in Manet's *Emile Zola* (cat. 28), which had been exhibited at the Salon of 1868. The leather-bound volumes in Renoir's picture stand in contrast to the colourful covers of the paperback books and pamphlets in Manet's portrait and suggest his more conservative tastes. The wrapped bouquet resembles the one presented to the reclining courtesan of Manet's *Olympia* (fig. 9), a painting that Philippe Burty claimed had made a strong impression on the young Renoir.[55] (Renoir would have seen the picture at the Salon of 1865, the Pont de l'Alma show of 1867, and on visits to Manet's studio on the Rue Guyot thereafter.) By way of these various homages, Renoir confirms his status as an acolyte.[56] The *uchiwa* fan in Renoir's still-life appears again in his *Portrait of Rapha Maître* (1871; Private collection), probably painted at the same time.[57] This sort of fan was to figure prominently in the background of Manet's *Woman with Fans (Portrait of Nina de Callias)* (Musée d'Orsay, Paris), made in 1873–74, and in Monet's *Camille Monet in Japanese Costume* (1876; Museum of Fine Arts, Boston).[58]

Fig. 38
Pierre-Auguste Renoir
***Still-life with Bouquet*, 1871**
Oil on canvas, 73.2 x 59 cm
The Museum of Fine Arts, Houston. The Robert Lee Blaffer Memorial Collection, Gift of Sarah Campbell Blaffer

On the single occasion in the summer of 1874 when Manet and Renoir painted together en plein air – a fraught experience for the older artist, who had doggedly resisted invitations to participate in the first Impressionist exhibition earlier that year – the acolyte appears to have bested the master. Manet, whose family owned a summer house at neighbouring Gennevilliers, was making his first visit to Monet's rented villa at Argenteuil on 23 July 1874. He set about painting a study of Monet's wife, Camille, reclining under a tree with their seven-year-old son Jean, while Manet's host tended the flowerbeds behind them (cat. 25). Renoir arrived while work was in progress, and, delighted to find a pair of models posed on the grass, borrowed canvas, palette and paint brushes from Monet and executed a vivid close-up of Camille and Jean, joined by a stray rooster at the right (fig. 39). (He excised Monet and his watering can from the composition.) Apparently irritated by Renoir's intrusion, Manet supposedly cast an eye in his direction and confided to Monet: 'He's a nice lad, but since he's your friend, you should encourage him to give up painting straight away; what he does is simply awful.'[59] This, at least, was Monet's recollection of the encounter, many years after the fact.[60]

Renoir's audacity and dynamism in *Camille Monet and Her Son Jean in the Garden at Argenteuil* are striking. His frenetic brushwork and irreverent composition make Manet's portrait of the Monet family appear weighty, formally posed and even a little ponderous – despite its freedom of handling and heightened palette. In its opaque, largely unblended strokes of colour, applied wet on wet, *Camille Monet and Her Son Jean in the Garden at Argenteuil* is Renoir's most Manet-like Argenteuil landscape to date: another reason, perhaps, why Manet was so irritated by his unexpected rival's performance. Indeed, in both Manet's and Renoir's plein-air paintings a certain amount of 'editing' takes place. Monet painted a portrait of Manet, dressed in a straw hat and protective smock, seated by his easel in the garden while at work on the portrait of Camille and Jean (current whereabouts unknown).[61] This throws into question Monet's role as the gardener in Manet's picture, as he could not have been in two places at the same time. Similarly, Renoir incorporated one of Monet's favourite props into his composition. Instead of the crescent of pure red that we see in Manet's picture, Camille holds the tricolour fan that will reappear in *Camille Monet in Japanese Costume* (1876; Museum of Fine Arts, Boston), painted by her husband two years later.[62] For all its spontaneity and the apparent speed with which it was executed, Renoir's exercise in 'painting quickly' was a mediated affair. He later told Vollard that he had painted *Camille Monet and Her Son Jean in the Garden at Argenteuil* in his Paris studio in the Rue Saint-Georges.[63] The possibility of multiple sessions and revisions in the crafting of such a spontaneous scene is consistent with Manet's notoriously deliberative working process.

'He's a nice lad, but since he's your friend, you should encourage him to give up painting straight away; what he does is simply awful.' Alphonse Tabarant was so incensed at the anecdote of Manet trying to persuade Renoir to abandon painting that he devoted an entire chapter of *Manet et ses oeuvres* to disproving this '*monstrous* calumny'.[64] The story, which may or may not be true but has become part of the folklore of Impressionism, has long clouded art-historical accounts of Manet's and Renoir's relationship, and has occluded the commonalities and shared preoccupations that linked the two artists throughout their careers. This is a topic ripe for reappraisal.

Fig. 39
Pierre-Auguste Renoir
Camille Monet and Her Son Jean in the Garden at Argenteuil, 1874
Oil on canvas, 50.4 x 68 cm
National Gallery of Art, Washington, 1970.17.60

LAWRENCE W. NICHOLS

Manet and Hals: Two Geniuses, One Vision

Museums have always driven me to despair. I'm deeply depressed when I go in and see how wretched the pictures look. There are visitors and attendants all milling around. The portraits just don't come alive. And yet some of them (clacking his tongue)... those by Velázquez, Goya, Hals... you have to admit, they really knew what they were doing, those fellows. A bit too contrived, but they never lost sight of reality. Edouard Manet[1]

AVERSION TO CONTRIVANCE. Admiration for reality. These principles in large measure may be said to define Manet's aesthetic creed. That he possessed this artistic vision to no small degree can be traced to the high regard in which he held the works of '*Maître* Velázquez' as he referred to the seventeenth-century Spanish painter. 'I've really come to know Velázquez, and I tell you he's the greatest artist there has ever been,' he wrote to his friend Baudelaire on 14 September 1865, a day after returning from a week in Madrid.[2] His reasoning is explained in a letter he had written to Fantin-Latour a week and a half before, while still in the Spanish capital. Speaking of Velázquez's *The Jester Pablo de Valladolid* (fig. 40), Manet noted, 'He is the supreme master... The most extraordinary piece in this splendid *oeuvre* and possibly the most extraordinary piece of painting that has ever been done is the picture described in the catalogue as a portrait of a famous actor at the time of Philip IV; the background disappears, there's nothing but air surrounding the fellow, who is all in black and appears alive.'[3] Manet's respect for Velázquez, Goya and other Spanish artists, however, had received its initial impetus from works he had seen in the Musée du Louvre. Speaking of *The Spanish Singer* (fig. 18), his Salon submission of 1861, Manet observed: 'When I was painting this figure, I was thinking about the Madrid masters and about Hals as well. You know, I can't believe that Hals wasn't in fact a Spaniard. Which wouldn't be so surprising, since he came from Malines' (he means the former Spanish Netherlands).[4] This rather comical remark about Hals's nationality nonetheless speaks to the high regard in which Manet held him, associating the Dutch master as it does with his Spanish contemporaries that Manet so revered. The importance of Hals for Manet, noted already by critics in the early 1870s, has recently come into sharper focus in the writings of Jowell and Atkins.[5] My aim in this text is twofold: first, to outline Manet's travels to Holland and to note which Hals paintings Manet would have seen, when and where;

Fig. 40
Diego Velázquez
The Jester Pablo de Valladolid, *c.* 1635
Oil on canvas, 209 x 123 cm
Museo del Prado, Madrid, P01198

and second, to explore what captured Manet's eye in the portraiture of Hals and how it resonated with his own aspirations as a portraitist.[6]

At the time the eighteen-year-old Manet entered the studio of Couture in 1850 the critical fortune of Hals was commencing an upswing that was to culminate in a Paris sale in 1865 in which the staggering price of 51,000 francs was paid for his *Portrait of a Gentleman* by the 4th Marquess of Hertford; the work was subsequently rechristened *The Laughing Cavalier* in London, where it now hangs in the Wallace Collection.[7] This and other transactions, including the auction in 1872 of Hals's *Portrait of a Woman* (Kunsthistorisches Museum, Vienna) from the Péreire Collection in Paris,[8] were strongly

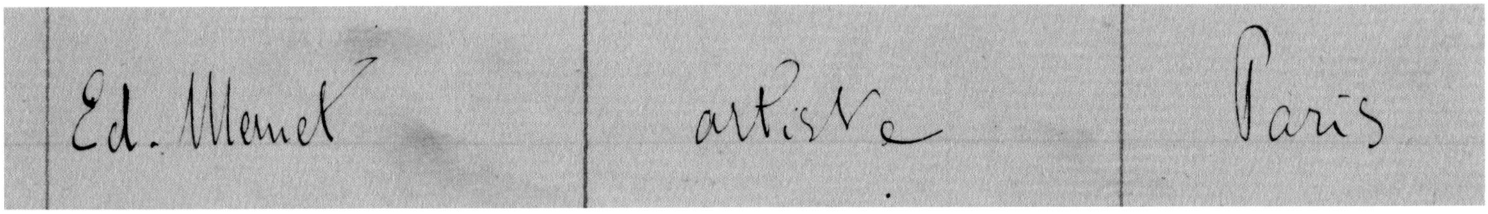

Fig. 41
Manet's inscription in the visitors' book at the Rijksmuseum, Amsterdam, 19 July 1852
Noord-Hollands Archief, Haarlem

spurred on by the influential critic and author Thoré-Bürger, whose major study on the artist appeared in 1868.[9] Two Hals paintings, *Gypsy Girl* and *Portrait of a Woman*, were bequeathed to the Louvre in 1869,[10] and may well have been seen by Manet as early as a decade previously when they were still in the collection of Dr Louis La Caze; it is known that in about 1858 he made a copy of another painting owned by this renowned collector.[11]

In addition to travel in Spain, Germany, Austria and Italy during the course of his professional career, Manet made at least three documented trips to the Netherlands – in 1852, 1863 and 1872 – two of which afforded him the chance to experience Hals's works.[12] On Monday 19 July 1852 the twenty-year-old artist wrote 'Ed. Manet / artiste / Paris' (fig. 41) in the visitors' book at the Rijksmuseum in Amsterdam.[13] There he would have had the opportunity to study a work that was then considered to be a self-portrait of Hals with his second wife Lysbeth Reyniersdr; the painting, now known as the *Wedding Portrait of Isaac Massa and Beatrix van der Laen*, had been auctioned in Amsterdam the previous November and acquired by the Rijksmuseum shortly thereafter.[14] He certainly examined *The Merry Drinker*.[15] Manet conceivably also saw *The Corporalship of Captain Reynier Reael and Lieutenant Cornelis Michielsz Blaeuw, called 'The Meagre Company'*, started by Hals and completed by Pieter Codde in 1637, then on display in the Royal Palace (Town Hall).[16] Visitors' books for the Mauritshuis in The Hague exist only from 1866, so it is not possible to ascertain when precisely Manet ventured there, but he must have done so, for he produced a sketch after Rembrandt's *The Anatomy Lesson of Dr Nicolaes Tulp*.[17] Works by Hals, however, had not yet entered that collection.

On the evening of 6 October 1863 Manet left Paris for Holland.[18] His purpose was to marry Suzanne Leenhoff, who had been Manet's younger brothers' piano teacher, as well as his mistress, since about 1850. The ceremony took place on 28 October 1863 in Zaltbommel, a small town on the south banks of the Rhine north of 's-Hertogenbosch. The couple spent a month in Holland after the wedding. Suzanne's son Léon-Edouard Koëlla, called Leenhoff, had been born eleven years previously, on 29 January 1852, and his paternity remains uncertain, with speculation that the boy was either Manet's half-brother or his son. He was raised in Manet's parents' household in Paris as the younger brother of Suzanne. By the summer of 1860 Manet, Suzanne and Léon were living together on the Rue de l'Hôtel-de-Ville.[19] It seems possible that the reason for Manet's initial visit to Holland in July 1852, less than half a year after Léon's birth, was to visit Suzanne, his future wife, and the infant.

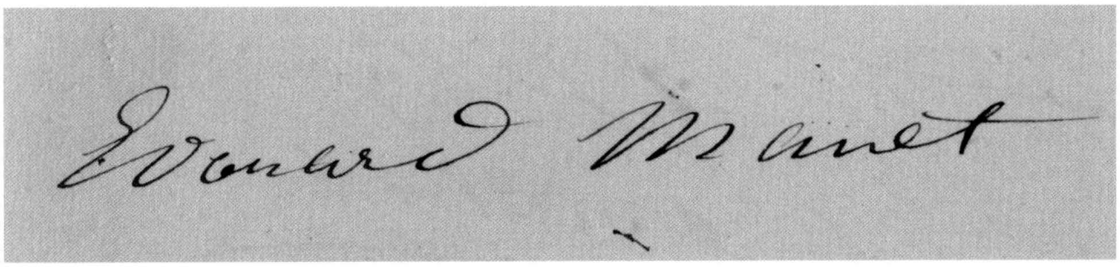

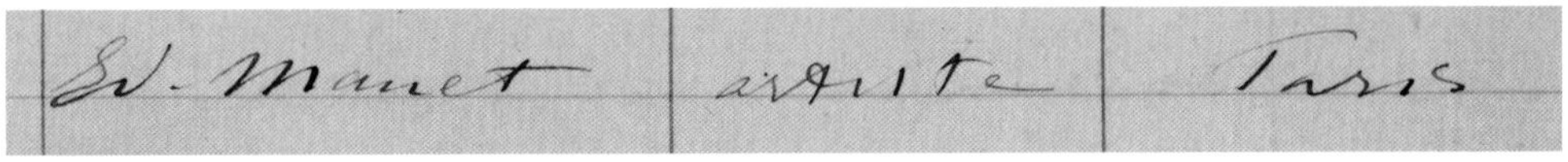

Fig. 42
Manet's inscription in the visitors' book at the Haarlem Municipal Museum, 26 June 1872
Noord-Hollands Archief, Haarlem

Fig. 43
Manet's inscription in the visitors' book at the Rijksmuseum, Amsterdam, 27 June 1872
Noord-Hollands Archief, Haarlem

Manet's third recorded trip north began in May 1872, by which time Hals's reputation had been solidly reaffirmed. Contributing to this was the fact that the Haarlem Municipal Museum had opened its doors for the first time in 1862 in the Town Hall.[20] Manet visited on Wednesday 26 June with his brother-in-law the sculptor Ferdinand Leenhoff, inscribing the visitors' book 'Edouard Manet' (fig. 42).[21] He must have been immensely impressed by the works by Hals that he encountered: five, enormous civic-guard pictures and three large canvases of regents.[22] The following day, just weeks shy of two decades after his first visit, Manet returned to the Rijksmuseum (in the Trippenhuis), still in the company of Ferdinand Leenhoff, and signed the visitors' register 'Ed. Manet / artiste / Paris' (fig. 43).[23] A single picture, *View of Holland* (Philadelphia Museum of Art), a seascape with sailing boats and windmills dotting the shore, is known from this journey to his wife's native country.[24] Tantalisingly, there is only a verbal reference to a copy said to be by Manet after Hals's *Regentesses of the Old Men's Alms House*.[25]

The impact of Manet's admiration for Hals is summed up, as so often in the literature on the artist, in a statement written in 1901 by his lifelong friend Antonin Proust (cat. 45): '[T]he boldness of Franz [*sic*] Hals also made a deep impression. Thus, when he returned to Paris, fortified by all these memories, Manet plunged hardily into the study of the divers aspects of life in the great city.'[26] It should be noted, however, that this sentence begins 'The conscientious sincerity of the primitive Italians moved him, too,' and that the previous paragraph refers to his travel to Holland, Italy and Spain, citing Velázquez by name. For Proust, Manet's *The Absinthe Drinker* (fig. 4), *The Spanish Singer* (fig. 18) and the *Portrait of M. and Mme Auguste Manet* (fig. 2) are all infused with Velázquez, Goya and Hals, and therefore to isolate Hals as an influence in this regard, suggesting that this is how Proust presents Manet, is an oversimplification.[27]

That acknowledged, Manet's most blatant 'Halsian' endeavour, from the vantage point of subject-matter and perhaps also technique, is undeniably his *Le Bon Bock* (1873; Philadelphia Museum of Art), which was exhibited and in the main well received at the Salon that year.[28] The inspiration Manet derived from Hals, his *Merry Drinker* in particular, was readily apparent to contemporary critics, Albert Wolff famously and derogatorily observing that Manet had put 'water in his beer'. Manet's achievement in his depiction of his model, the engraver Emile Belot, was trenchantly articulated by another of the painter's friends and likewise a sitter for a portrait, Théodore Duret (cat. 29). Writing about *Le Bon Bock* in 1923 on its reappearance after a duration in a private collection in Berlin, Duret observed: 'Indeed it gives you the portrait of a certain man. Manet was a realist, but a realist endowed with such superiority that when he rendered the salient aspects of a subject he accentuated and idealised them. He elevated the individual trait to the standard of a general type.'[29]

In the autumn of 1878, five years after painting *Le Bon Bock*, Manet wrote to Duret: 'I've been working hard this summer and hope to have some good things in the next exhibition, and today Proust asked me to do his portrait for the next Salon.'[30] The painting signed 'à mon ami Antonin Proust / 1880 / Manet' was the result (cat. 45). Proust is shown in three-quarter length against an indeterminate space not unlike that often encountered in portraits by Hals and Velázquez, such as the latter's *The Jester Pablo de Valladolid*, which so impressed Manet. The journalist, art critic and politician was briefly to become Minister of Fine Arts a year later, and he is dashingly depicted by his close acquaintance wearing a frock coat with a flower in its lapel and a top hat ever so slightly tilted to his right. The portrait is a compelling image of self-assurance. With one arm akimbo, the other extended to clutch his walking stick, with one hand gloved, the other clutching a glove, Proust jauntily engages directly with the viewer. Manet's vibrant portrait is the antithesis of Proust's report of Manet's response to seeing a portrait by a painter *en vogue*: '"I see clearly", he cried, "that he had painted a frock coat. It even has an irreproachable cut, this frock coat. But where are the model's lungs? He's not breathing under his clothing. He doesn't have a body. This is a portrait for a tailor."'[31] Here and elsewhere within his portraiture, Manet's ambition was to convey a living, breathing likeness, one that 'comes alive' or 'appears alive' to cite the master's words quoted earlier.

And this was Hals's ambition too. Doubtless the sense of immediacy and spontaneity with which Hals endowed his compositions attracted the nineteenth-century French painter to his seventeenth-century Dutch predecessor. More than just an appreciation for Hals's bravura brushwork, Manet surely shared his precursor's vision that a portrait should engage and convince without pretence. 'How do you put on your hat when you do it without thinking and feel completely at your ease? Well then, do it the same way when you're posing, without any affectation.'[32] These are Manet's words but they could just as readily have been spoken by the painter from Haarlem to Isaac Massa or to Gijsbert Claesz van Campen. Hals's *Van Campen Family Portrait* (fig. 44), although unknown to Manet as it was in an English private collection in his day, nonetheless offers telling comparisons of technique that bespeak a common intent.[33]

Fig. 44
Frans Hals
Van Campen Family Portrait, early 1620s
Oil on canvas, 151 x 163.5 cm
Toledo Museum of Art, inv. no. 2011.80

In May 1880 Manet wrote to Proust:

> It's been three weeks, my dear friend, since your portrait has been up at the Salon, badly hung in a narrow section near a door, and received even worse than it's hung. But it's my lot to be vilified and I am philosophical about it. Nevertheless, my dear friend, you cannot believe how discomforting it is to plant a figure alone in a canvas and to invest in this lone and unique figure all one's interest, without its losing its life and presence. To make two figures who draw their attraction from the duality of their personae is child's play in comparison... Your portrait is the sincerest work there can be. I remember as if it were yesterday the rapid and summary way in which I handled the glove of the ungloved hand. And when you said to me at that moment: 'I beg you, not another touch,' I felt we were so perfectly in accord that I could not resist the desire to embrace you. Ah! I trust that later they don't get the idea to stick this portrait in a public collection! I've always had a horror of that mania for piling up art works without letting the light of day between the frames, just as one puts the latest novelties on the shelves of fashionable stores. Anyway, whichever of us lives will see. I leave it to the hands of destiny.
>
> To you,
>
> Edouard Manet[34]

Twenty-one years later, writing at the very outset of the twentieth century, Proust seemed confident that destiny would look kindly on his friend as he wrote: 'A day will come when the truth of Manet's doctrine will be admitted. "Do nothing," said he, "without consulting Nature."'[35]

The Artist and His Family

Manet often drafted in members of his family to serve both as sitters for portraits and as models in his genre paintings, especially during the 1860s, although his wife Suzanne was a constant presence throughout his *oeuvre*.

Manet was born in 1832 into a comfortable, property-owning middle-class family. His father Auguste (1797–1862) was a senior civil servant in the Ministry of Justice, and his mother, Eugénie-Désirée (1811–1895), the daughter of a diplomat and goddaughter of the King of Sweden. Manet had two younger brothers, Eugène (1833–1892), who married Berthe Morisot in 1874, and Gustave (1835–1884), a lawyer and politician. Suzanne Leenhoff (1829–1906), born in Delft in the Netherlands, moved to Paris, where she lived with her grandmother and her four siblings, including Ferdinand, a sculptor, and Rudolphe, a painter. She entered the Manet family circle as piano teacher to the two younger sons in *c.* 1849. In 1852 she gave birth to Léon-Edouard Koëlla Leenhoff (d. 1927), whose paternity remains uncertain, and in 1863 married Edouard Manet (see Locke 2001). Living with the now-widowed Eugénie-Désirée, the Manets held soirées on Tuesdays and Thursdays that were frequented by artists, literary figures, musicians, composers and politicians, many of whom sat for Manet and supported his work.

Although Suzanne had modelled for Manet in *c.* 1860 and again in *Fishing* (cat. 3), after their marriage she became the most frequently painted of his subjects. She sat for straight portraits (cats 4, 5, 7), and served as actor in scenes in which her dress, location or activity subtly proclaimed her husband's commitment to a new aesthetic of modernity. In these scenes of contemporary life she was given either a solo role (cat. 6) or one in partnership with another family member such as Léon (cat. 12) or Mme Manet *mère* (cat. 8), who also sat

Detail of cat. 6
Mme Manet in the Conservatory, 1879

for her son in single portraits and a double portrait with her husband (fig. 2).

Léon Leenhoff made an appearance in Manet's *oeuvre* in three periods between 1859 and 1872: in four paintings produced between 1859 and 1862 (see cat. 3), eight between 1867 and 1869 (see cats 9, 10), and five from 1871 to 1872 (see cats 11, 12). Sometimes seeming to have stepped out of an Old Master painting (cats 3, 9), occasionally playing a fashionable young man, Léon figured alone (cat. 11) and with others, contributing to such potent declarations of Manet's new aesthetic as *The Balcony* (fig. 11; see cat. 34) and *The Luncheon* (cat. 10).

Gustave and Eugène also modelled for Manet, donning Spanish attire in *Young Man in the Costume of a Majo* (1863; Metropolitan Museum of Art, New York), and featuring as part of their brother's social circle in *Music in the Tuileries Gardens* (cat. 26) and as a young student – a composite of both men – in *Déjeuner sur l'herbe* (cat. 52). Even Manet's brothers-in-law Ferdinand and Rudolphe Leenhoff were called upon, the former as the other student in *Déjeuner sur l'herbe* and the latter twice during the summer of 1874 as the stylish yachtsman in *Argenteuil* (Musée des Beaux-Arts, Tournai) and *Boating* (Metropolitan Museum of Art, New York).

Fig. 45 (left)
Photographer unknown
***Edouard Manet, three-quarter-length*, date unknown**
Carte de visite
Bibliothèque nationale de France, Paris
(Cat. 63)

Fig. 46 (right)
Etienne Carjat & Cie
***Léon Koëlla Leenhoff*, date unknown**
Carte de visite, Albumen print on laminated board, 9.4 x 6.3 cm
'Exposition Universelle 1867' inscribed on verso
The Morgan Library and Museum, New York.
Purchased as the gift of Mrs Charles W. Engelhard and children in memory of Charles W. Engelhard, 1974. MA 3950
(Cat. 64)

Fig. 47
Dallemagne
***Edouard Manet, half-length portrait with trompe-l'oeil frame and curtain*, date unknown**
Carte de visite
Bibliothèque nationale de France, Paris
(Cat. 65)

Fig. 48 (below)
David Wilkie Wynfield
***Edouard Manet*, *c*. 1868**
Albumen print on mount with printed surround, 21.4 x 16.3 cm
Royal Academy of Arts, London
(Cat. 66)

1 SELF-PORTRAIT WITH PALETTE, 1878–79
Oil on canvas, 83 × 67 cm
Private collection

2 SELF-PORTRAIT, 1878–79
Oil on canvas, 95.4 × 63.4 cm
Bridgestone Museum of Art, Ishibashi Foundation, Tokyo

3 FISHING, *c.* 1862–63
Oil on canvas, 76.8 × 123.2 cm
Lent by the Metropolitan Museum of Art, New York.
Purchase, Mr and Mrs Richard J. Bernhard Gift, 1957 (57.10)

4 Mme EDOUARD MANET, 1873
Pastel on paper, mounted on canvas, 53.7 × 38.7 cm
Lent by the Toledo Museum of Art.
Gift of Mrs C. Lockhart McKelvy

5 WOMAN WITH A CAT (PORTRAIT OF Mme MANET), *c.* 1880
Oil on canvas, 92.1 × 73 cm
Tate. Purchased 1918

6 Mme MANET IN THE CONSERVATORY, 1879
Oil on canvas, 81 × 100 cm
The National Museum of Art, Architecture and Design, Oslo

7 Mme MANET AT THE PIANO, 1868
Oil on canvas, 38 × 46.5 cm
Musée d'Orsay, Paris. Legs du comte Isaac de Camondo, 1911

8 THE SWALLOWS, 1873
Oil on canvas, 65 × 81 cm
Foundation E. G. Bührle Collection, Zurich

9 BOY BLOWING BUBBLES, 1867
Oil on canvas, 100.5 × 81.4 cm
Calouste Gulbenkian Foundation, Lisbon

10 THE LUNCHEON, 1868
Oil on canvas, 118.3 × 154 cm
Bayerische Staatsgemäldesammlungen, Munich: Neue Pinakothek

11 THE VELOCIPEDE, 1871
Oil on canvas, 53 × 20 cm
Private collection, Paris

12 INTERIOR AT ARCACHON, 1871
Oil on canvas, 39.4 × 53.7 cm
Sterling and Francine Clark Art Institute, Williamstown, Massachusetts

Artists

Manet had a wide circle of artist-friends. They would gather in his various studios, meet at the Cafés Guerbois and Nouvelle Athènes, and attend the Manets' Tuesday and Thursday soirées. As with his representations of literary and theatrical figures (see pages 108–23), Manet's paintings of artists oscillate between convention and innovation, and even when working in an apparently orthodox manner, he explores ways in which traditions can be undermined. Manet took three approaches to this category of sitter: the commonly accepted presentation of the artist in his or her studio; the artist as a private individual; and as an exemplar of a social type or condition.

Eva Gonzalès (cat. 15) is one of only a few representations of artists in which Manet supplied the traditional attributes – brushes, palette, mahlstick, easel – as he also did when recording Claude Monet at work on his floating studio at Argenteuil (1874; Neue Pinakothek, Munich). Yet the picture of Gonzalès also contains certain anomalous details that disturb expectations and suggest irony: her dress seems inappropriate for the potentially messy work in hand, and she is applying paint to a finished, framed work. Manet's admiration for Eva Gonzalès and Berthe Morisot (who became his sister-in-law in 1874) (see cats 14, 16, 17) also led him to depict them as private individuals, without any reference to their vocation, thus making no distinction between them and the many other beautiful women whom he painted.

Manet also cast his artist-friends as exemplars of social types and conditions. Divested of all reference to his profession, Joseph Gall poses as a reader and a smoker (cat. 13); Marcellin Desboutin is the modern urban dweller, having

Detail of cat. 15
Eva Gonzalès, 1870

walked in from the street with his dog and a furled umbrella under his arm (cat. 20); Carolus-Duran stands in a bosky landscape, the landed country gentleman rather than the lionised society portrait-painter (cat. 21); and Berthe Morisot, an artist whose work had already been accepted at the Salon, reclines on a burgundy sofa in a flourish of white muslin to communicate the physical and psychological condition of *The Repose* (cat. 18). Manet took this role-playing even further in his images of his friends Claude Monet (cat. 25) and Giuseppe De Nittis (cat. 24). Each shown with his family in a well-tended garden, the two painters are presented as members of the bourgeoisie enjoying leisure at their semi-rural retreats.

The degree to which it was pertinent that the sitters in the majority of Manet's representations of artists were known practitioners is open to debate. Had his portrait been finished and exhibited, would the critics have been unsettled by the fact that Manet presented Carolus-Duran neither as an elegant, engaging individual – as in John Singer Sargent's portrait (1883; Sterling and Francine Clark Art Institute, Williamstown) – nor demonstrating his skills in his studio? If Manet's portraits of artists recorded friendship and admiration, they also worked towards a wider agenda, like his portraits of family members: the reflection of the contemporary world and its social conditions.

Fig. 49
Photographer unknown
***Portrait of Carolus-Duran*, date unknown**
Carte de visite
Bibliothèque nationale de France, Paris
(Cat. 67)

Fig. 50
Carolus-Duran
***Portrait of Edouard Manet*, 1876**
Oil on canvas, 64.7 x 54.6 cm
Museum of Art, Rhode Island School of Design, Providence
(Cat. 21B)

Fig. 51
Photographer unknown
***Claude Monet in His Garden*, 1880**
Carte de visite
Musée Marmottan Monet, Paris

Fig. 52
Photographer unknown
***Berthe Morisot*, date unknown**
Carte de visite
Musée Marmottan Monet, Paris

13 THE SMOKER, 1866
Oil on canvas, 100.3 × 81.3 cm
Lent by the Minneapolis Institute of Arts. Gift of Bruce B. Dayton

14 PORTRAIT OF EVA GONZALÈS, *c.* 1879
Pastel on paper, 43 × 34.5 cm
Private collection

15 EVA GONZALÈS, 1870
Oil on canvas, 191.1 × 133.4 cm
The National Gallery, London. Sir Hugh Lane Bequest, 1917

16 BERTHE MORISOT WITH A BOUQUET OF VIOLETS, 1872
Oil on canvas, 55.5 × 40.5 cm
Musée d'Orsay, Paris. Acquis avec la participation du Fonds du Patrimoine, de la Fondation Meyer, de Chine Times Group et d'un mécénat coordonné par le quotidien Nikkei, 1998

17 BERTHE MORISOT IN MOURNING, 1874
Oil on canvas, 60 × 48 cm
Private collection

18 THE REPOSE (PORTRAIT OF BERTHE MORISOT), 1870
Oil on canvas, 150.2 × 114 cm
Museum of Art, Rhode Island School of Design, Providence. Bequest of Mrs Edith Stuyvesant Vanderbilt Gerry

19 BERTHE MORISOT, 1868–69, 1870–71
Oil on fabric, 74 × 60 cm
Cleveland Museum of Art. Bequest of Leonard C. Hanna Jr, 1958.34

20 THE ARTIST: PORTRAIT OF MARCELLIN DESBOUTIN, 1875
Oil on canvas, 192 × 128 cm
Museu de São Paulo Assis Chateaubriand, São Paulo

21 PORTRAIT OF CAROLUS-DURAN, 1876
Oil on canvas, 191.8 × 172.7 cm
The Trustees of the Barber Institute of Fine Arts, University of Birmingham

22 PORTRAIT OF ALPHONSE MAUREAU, *c.* 1880
Pastel with gouache on canvas prepared with a gouache ground, 54.7 × 45.2 cm
Art Institute of Chicago. Gift of Edward L. Brewster, 1950.123

23 PORTRAIT OF THE ANIMAL PAINTER LA ROCHENOIRE, 1882
Pastel on canvas, 55.3 × 35.6 cm
Private collection

24 IN THE GARDEN, 1870
Oil on canvas, 44.5 × 54 cm
Collections of Shelburne Museum, Shelburne, Vermont. Gift of Mr Dunbar W. and Mrs Electra Webb Bostwick

25 THE MONET FAMILY IN THEIR GARDEN AT ARGENTEUIL, 1874
Oil on canvas, 61 × 99.7 cm
Lent by the Metropolitan Museum of Art, New York. Bequest of Joan Whitney Payson, 1975 (1976.201.14)

Men of Letters and Figures of the Stage

Novelists, poets, critics, essayists and leading personalities of the theatre traverse Manet's canvases – not least the multi-figure *Music in the Tuileries Gardens* (cat. 26) – conjuring up the literary world of mid- and late nineteenth-century France. They include writers who championed the new artistic programmes, from the Realism of Courbet, supported by Jules-Antoine Castagnary, Champfleury and, with some reservations, Théophile Gautier, to the work of Manet and the Impressionists, advocated by Zacharie Astruc, Théodore Duret, Edmond Duranty, Emile Zola, Stéphane Mallarmé and George Moore. Many frequented the Manets' Tuesday and Thursday soirées and the informal gatherings at the Cafés Guerbois and Nouvelle Athènes, and some – Zola, Mallarmé, Moore (for a time) and, when not travelling, Duret – were regular visitors to Manet's studio.

Manet was well informed about contemporary literature: he followed closely Zola's unfolding epic saga *Les Rougon-Macquart*, was conversant with Charles Baudelaire's poetry and prose, provided illustrations for works by Mallarmé, and maintained a warm correspondence with, among others, Baudelaire, Zola, Duret and Mallarmé. Indeed, Manet's friendship with Baudelaire from the late 1850s was critical to his pictorial articulation of modernity (see cat. 31), and Mallarmé, Duret, Duranty and Zola (the latter with qualifications, eventually) supported his work consistently against unremitting, and often abusive, negative reception, both in the Salon and at his independent exhibitions.

Manet made portraits of his writer-friends. However, as with those of artists (see pages 90–107), they range from the apparently conventional to the highly enigmatic. Astruc (cat. 27) and Zola (cat. 28) are apparently depicted with the traditional attributes of the writer, yet to the side of Astruc can be seen a scene from contemporary life being played out in the background, and the items that

Fig. 53
Photographer unknown
***Portrait of Zacharie Astruc*, date unknown**
Carte de visite
Bibliothèque nationale de France, Paris
(Cat. 68)

Detail of cat. 27
Portrait of Zacharie Astruc, 1866

surround Zola dislodge him as the subject in favour of Manet himself. Equally, Duret (cat. 29) and Moore (cat. 32), both stripped of conventional attributes, are more dandies than literary figures, the former posed within a neutral interior space and the latter in the artist's sun-dappled urban garden. The oblique reference to literature in the portrait of Mallarmé (cat. 30) might summarise the enigmatic, allusive nature of his innovative writing style, just as the dominant white tonality of the painting of Baudelaire's mistress Jeanne Duval (cat. 31) refers to the poet's aesthetic programme and thus transforms it into his own surrogate portrait.

Manet was also familiar with the stage. He shared with Baudelaire an admiration for the tragedian Philibert Rouvière, whose portrait he painted in 1865, the year of the actor's death (cat. 33). Fanny Clauss (cat. 34), model for the first iteration of *The Balcony* (fig. 11), was a talented violonist and friend of Mme Manet, while the not exceptionally talented opera singer Emilie Ambre (cat. 35) was briefly a neighbour as well as a model. Manet made portraits of both in their professional roles, and, in the early 1880s produced more intimate, personal records of the singer Jean-Baptiste Faure. Performers also supported Manet. Faure, who frequented the Manets' Tuesday soirées, was a significant collector of his work. Ambre, a neighbour when Manet was following hydropathic treatment at Bellevue in 1879 and 1880, arranged, possibly with Faure's encouragement, for Manet's controversial modern-history painting *The Execution of Maximilian* (1868–69; Kunsthalle Mannheim) to tour to New York and Boston in the winter of 1879–80.

Fig. 54
Photographer unknown
***Jean-Baptiste Faure*, date unknown**
Carte de visite
Bibliothèque nationale de France, Paris

Fig. 55
Photographer unknown
***Jean-Baptiste Faure in the Role of Hamlet*, date unknown**
Carte de visite
Bibliothèque nationale de France, Paris

Fig. 56
Photographer unknown
***Philibert Rouvière in the Role of Hamlet*, date unknown**
Carte de visite
Bibliothèque nationale de France, Paris
(Cat. 69)

Fig. 57
Dornac
***Stéphane Mallarmé*, date unknown**
Photograph
Bibliothèque nationale de France, Paris
(Cat. 70)

Fig. 58
Dornac
***Portrait of Emile Zola in His Study*, date unknown**
Photograph
Bibliothèque nationale de France, Paris
(Cat. 71)

26 MUSIC IN THE TUILERIES GARDENS, 1862
Oil on canvas, 76.2 × 118.1 cm
The National Gallery, London. Sir Hugh Lane Bequest, 1917

27 PORTRAIT OF ZACHARIE ASTRUC, 1866
Oil on canvas, 90.5 × 116 cm
Kunsthalle Bremen – Der Kunstverein in Bremen, inv. no. 88-1909/1

28 EMILE ZOLA, 1868
Oil on canvas, 146.5 × 114 cm
Musée d'Orsay, Paris. Donation de Mme Emile Zola, 1918

29 PORTRAIT OF THÉODORE DURET, 1868
Oil on canvas, 46.5 × 35.5 cm
Petit Palais, Musée des Beaux-Arts de la Ville de Paris

30 STÉPHANE MALLARMÉ, 1876
Oil on canvas, 27.5 × 36 cm
Musée d'Orsay, Paris

31 LADY WITH A FAN (JEANNE DUVAL), 1862
Oil on canvas, 80 × 113 cm
Szépművészeti Múzeum, Budapest

32 GEORGE MOORE IN THE ARTIST'S GARDEN, *c.* 1879
Oil on canvas, 54.6 × 45.1 cm
National Gallery of Art, Washington. Collection of Mr and Mrs Paul Mellon, 2006.128.24

33 THE TRAGIC ACTOR (ROUVIÈRE AS HAMLET), 1865
Oil on canvas, 187.2 × 108.1 cm
National Gallery of Art, Washington. Gift of Edith Stuyvesant Gerry, 1959.3.1

34 PORTRAIT OF FANNY CLAUSS (STUDY FOR THE BALCONY), 1868–69
Oil on canvas, 71 × 43 cm
Private collection, c/o Robert Holden Ltd, London

35 PORTRAIT OF EMILIE AMBRE AS CARMEN, 1880
Oil on canvas, 92.4 × 73.5 cm
Philadelphia Museum of Art. Gift of Edgar Scott, 1964

The Status Portrait

Status portraits require an artist to communicate the social and economic circumstances of the sitter – power, wealth, position and breeding – in ways immediately recognisable to the viewer. All the portraits in this section, finished and unfinished, appear to aspire to this goal. M. Armand Brun, hands in his pockets, standing on a well-raked gravel path in his manicured garden, surveys his domain (cat. 38). Georges Clemenceau clearly proclaims his political vocation, a speech to hand and his arms folded in a gesture in defence of the Third Republic (cat. 44). If Mme Brunet (cat. 36), Mme Gamby (cat. 37) and M. and Mme Guillemet (cat. 39) inform us through their fashionable dress and their poses that they are members of the wealthy Parisian bourgeoisie, so do the subjects of Manet's unfinished equestrian portraits (cats 41, 42) and the stylishly attired children Henry Bernstein (cat. 49) and Lise Campinéanu (cat. 48).

Manet's financial circumstances ensured that like Degas, but unlike, for example, Renoir, he neither had to seek commissions nor conform to his sitters' expectations. Indeed, Manet received relatively few commissions for status portraits, and those that were executed were not necessarily claimed by the client. His portrait of Mme Brunet, possibly commissioned by the sitter's husband, his friend the sculptor Eugène-Cyrille Brunet, was rejected and remained in Manet's studio, and that of Antonin Proust (cat. 45) did not become the property of Manet's close friend, supporter and biographer, but was offered by the artist to the collector Charles Ephrussi. However, Manet's *Eugène Pertuiset, Lion-hunter*

Fig. 59
Photographer unknown
***Portrait of Georges Clemenceau*, date unknown**
Carte de visite
Bibliothèque nationale de France, Paris
(Cat. 72)

Detail of cat. 44
Portrait of Georges Clemenceau, 1879–80

(cat. 46), possibly the result of a commission, did go to the sitter, where it joined an already significant collection of works by Manet. Equally unusual were Manet's few portraits of children: *Portrait of a Child (The Little Lange)* (fig. 8) and *Portrait of Henry Bernstein*, for example, were commissions, but both appear to be relatively unresolved.

The majority of Manet's status portraits, therefore, were made on his own impulse, motivated by an interest in a specific individual, such as Henri Rochefort (cat. 47) and his 'heroic' exploits, by friendship and shared values, as was the case with Proust and Clemenceau, or by an individual's physical appeal, as in the large number of portraits of women (see Leah Lehmbeck's essay on pages 50–57), including that of Mme Guillemet (cat. 40).

Fig. 60
Studio Benque et Cie
Georges Clemenceau, *c.* 1876
Photograph, 13 x 21 cm
Collection Musée Clemenceau, Paris
(Cat. 73)

Fig. 61
André-Adolphe-Eugène Disdéri
Cabinet Print of Eugène Pertuiset, *c.* 1877/78
Photograph
Bibliothèque nationale de France, Paris
(Cat. 74)

Fig. 62
Franck
***Antonin Proust*, c. 1877**
Carte de visite
Bibliothèque nationale de France, Paris
(Cat. 75)

Fig. 63
Photographer unknown
***Portrait of Henri Rochefort*,**
date unknown
Carte de visite
Bibliothèque nationale de France, Paris
(Cat. 76)

36 PORTRAIT OF Mme BRUNET, 1860–63
Oil on canvas, 132.4 × 100 cm
J. Paul Getty Museum, Los Angeles

37 THE PROMENADE (Mme GAMBY), *c.* 1880
Oil on canvas, 92.3 × 70.5 cm
Tokyo Fuji Art Museum

38 PORTRAIT OF M. BRUN, 1879
Oil on canvas, 194.3 × 126 cm
National Museum of Western Art, Tokyo. Donated by the heirs of Mr Kojiro Matsukata

39 IN THE CONSERVATORY, 1877–79
Oil on canvas, 115 × 150 cm
Staatliche Museen zu Berlin, Alte Nationalgalerie, Berlin

40 Mme GUILLEMET, 1880
Pastel on canvas, mounted on Masonite, 54.8 × 35.2 cm
Saint Louis Art Museum. Funds given by John Merrill Olin

41 PORTRAIT OF M. ARNAUD (THE RIDER), *c.* 1873–75
Oil on canvas, 218 × 136 cm
Galleria Nazionale d'Arte Moderna, Milan

42 THE AMAZON, *c.* 1875
Oil on canvas, 88 × 116 cm
Museu de São Paulo Assis Chateaubriand, São Paulo

43 THE AMAZON, *c.* 1882
Oil on canvas, 73 × 52 cm
Museo Thyssen-Bornemisza, Madrid

44 PORTRAIT OF GEORGES CLEMENCEAU, 1879–80
Oil on canvas, 115.9 × 88.2 cm
Kimbell Art Museum, Fort Worth, Texas

45 PORTRAIT OF M. ANTONIN PROUST, 1880
Oil on canvas, 129.5 × 95.9 cm
Lent by the Toledo Museum of Art. Gift of Edward Drummond Libbey

46 EUGÈNE PERTUISET, LION-HUNTER, 1881
Oil on canvas, 150 × 170 cm
Museu de São Paulo Assis Chateaubriand, São Paulo

47 PORTRAIT OF HENRI ROCHEFORT, 1881
Oil on canvas, 81.5 × 66.5 cm
Hamburger Kunsthalle

48 PORTRAIT OF LISE CAMPINÉANU, 1878
Oil on canvas, 55.6 × 46.5 cm
The Nelson-Atkins Museum of Art, Kansas City, Missouri
(Purchase: William Rockhill Nelson Trust, 36-5)

49 PORTRAIT OF HENRY BERNSTEIN AS A CHILD, 1881
Oil on canvas, 135 × 97 cm
Private collection, c/o Robert Holden Ltd, London

Models

The academic primacy of history painting, which required artists to master drawing from life models for large-scale, morally uplifting compositions, created work for male and female models. They were employed in the official classes of the Ecole des Beaux-Arts and the studios of established artists, as well as in the less formal training institutions, such as the Académie Suisse and the Académie Julien. Outside academic circles, the need to work directly from the human figure also created demand for models in private studios.

Positioned on the margins of society, models tended to come from relatively humble backgrounds and their livelihoods were often precarious. Some went on to have careers on the stage, such as Jeanne Demarsy (cat. 57) and Ellen Andrée, who posed for Manet (cat. 60) and Degas. Some became involved with the artists for whom they sat – Alice Legouvé, who posed for Manet in *A Game of Croquet* (cat. 54) and *The Laundry* (1875; Am Römerholz, Winterthur), was Alfred Stevens's mistress – or even married them, as in the cases of Monet and Renoir, and, it might be argued, Manet.

Manet made only limited use of professional male models, increasingly confining himself to female models, such as Victorine Meurent (cat. 50), and using friends and relations to stand in as their male companions. Although most of Manet's female models have been identified, some remain anonymous, such as the woman who posed beside Manet's brother-in-law Rudolphe Leenhoff in

Detail of cat. 53
The Railway, 1873

Argenteuil (1874; Musée des Beaux-Arts, Tournai). Other identifications are disputed: Ellen Andrée, for example, sat for *At the Café* (1878; Am Römerholz, Winterthur) and, initially, for *Chez le Père Lathuille – en plein air* (cat. 60), but may not have been the model for *La Parisienne* (1875; Nationalmuseum, Stockholm).

Although Manet employed professional female models throughout his career, he also used non-professionals, such as the daughter of a bookseller on the Rue de Moscou, who sat for three surviving versions of *The Amazon* (see cat. 43). As a parallel strategy, he relied on female friends whose beauty and personalities he admired and wished to capture in oil and pastel, for example Méry Laurent, a minor actress and a brilliant salon hostess (cat. 55), Nina de Callias and Isabelle Lemonnier (cats 61, 62), daughter of a society jeweller and sister-in-law of Georges Charpentier, publisher of the journal *La Vie moderne*. Manet's images hover ambiguously between portraiture and genre scene when he uses recognisable personalities such as these in, for example, an allegory of the seasons (cats 55, 56) or the representation of a social type, as in the fashionable Parisienne *Isabelle Lemonnier with a Muff* (cat. 61).

Fig. 64
Photographer unknown
***Portrait of Méry Laurent*, date unknown**
Carte de visite
Bibliothèque nationale de France, Paris
(Cat. 77)

Fig. 65
Photographer unknown
***Portrait of Jeanne Demarsy*, date unknown**
Carte de visite
Bibliothèque nationale de France, Paris
(Cat. 78)

Fig. 66
Photographer unknown
***Portrait of Jeanne Demarsy*, date unknown**
Carte de visite
Bibliothèque nationale de France, Paris
(Cat. 79)

Fig, 67
Photographer unknown
***Portrait of Ellen Andrée*, date unknown**
Carte de visite
Bibliothèque nationale de France, Paris
(Cat. 80)

50 VICTORINE MEURENT, *c.* 1862
Oil on canvas, 42.9 × 43.8 cm
Museum of Fine Arts, Boston. Gift of Richard C. Paine in memory of his father, Robert Treat Paine 2nd

51 STREET SINGER, *c.* 1862
Oil on canvas, 171.1 × 105.8 cm
Museum of Fine Arts, Boston. Bequest of Sarah Choate Sears in memory of her husband, Joshua Montgomery Sears

52 DÉJEUNER SUR L'HERBE, *c.* 1863–68
Oil on canvas, 89.5 × 116.5 cm
The Samuel Courtauld Trust. The Courtauld Gallery, London

53 THE RAILWAY, 1873
Oil on canvas, 93.3 × 111.5 cm
National Gallery of Art, Washington.
Gift of Horace Havemeyer in memory of his mother, Louisine W. Havemeyer, 1956.10.1

54 A GAME OF CROQUET, 1873
Oil on canvas, 72.5 × 106 cm
Städel Museum, Frankfurt am Main.
Property of the Städelscher Museums-Verein e.V.

55 AUTUMN (PORTRAIT OF MÉRY LAURENT), 1881
Oil on canvas, 72 × 51.5 cm
Musée des beaux-arts, Nancy

56 JEANNE (SPRING), 1882; printed 1890
Etching with aquatint
Bibliothèque nationale de France, Paris

57 GIRL IN A SUMMER BONNET (JEANNE DEMARSY), *c.* 1879
Pastel on canvas, 56 × 35 cm
Collection of Diane B. Wilsey

58 Mlle SUZETTE LEMAIRE, FULL FACE, *c.* 1880/81
Pastel on canvas, 53 × 33 cm
Private collection. On long-term loan to the Ashmolean Museum, Oxford

59 PORTRAIT OF M. GAUTHIER-LATHUILLE FILS, *c.* 1879
Pastel on canvas, 56 × 46 cm
Private collection

60 CHEZ LE PÈRE LATHUILLE – EN PLEIN AIR, 1879
Oil on canvas, 92 × 112 cm
Musée des Beaux-Arts, Tournai

61 ISABELLE LEMONNIER WITH A MUFF, *c.* 1879
Oil on canvas, 91.4 × 73 cm
Dallas Museum of Art. Gift of Mr and Mrs Algur H. Meadows and the Meadows Foundation Incorporated

62 ISABELLE LEMONNIER WITH A WHITE COLLAR, *c.* 1879–82
Oil on canvas, 86.5 × 63.5 cm
Ny Carlsberg Glyptotek, Copenhagen

Chronology

SARAH LEA

1832 23 January: Edouard Manet is born at 5 Rue des Petits Augustins (now 5 Rue Bonaparte), the eldest son of Auguste and Eugénie-Désirée (see fig. 2). He has two younger brothers, Eugène and Gustave.

1838–40 Manet studies at the Institut Poiloup.

1839 Louis Daguerre exhibits the first 'daguerreotypes'. In England, Henry Fox-Talbot reports his 'art of photogenic drawing' to the Royal Society.

1841 Fox-Talbot patents his calotype positive–negative photographic process, allowing multiple prints of a single image.

1844–48 While studying at the Collège Rollin, Manet begins a lifelong friendship with Antonin Proust. Manet's maternal uncle Captain Edouard Fournier encourages his nephew's artistic talent, funding his attendance at a drawing class and accompanying Manet and Proust on regular trips to the Louvre.

1848 The government of King Louis-Philippe, known as the July Monarchy, collapses following the February Revolution and the Second Republic is declared. 9 December: having failed the entrance exam for the Ecole Navale in July, Manet sails for Rio de Janeiro as a trainee on the ship *Havre et Guadeloupe*, arriving on 4 February 1849. During the voyage he draws caricatures of shipmates. 10 December: Louis-Napoléon Bonaparte is elected President.

1849 After his return to Le Havre on 13 June, Manet again fails the entrance exam for the Ecole Navale. His family agrees that he may pursue an artistic career. Suzanne Leenhoff becomes his brothers' piano teacher.

1850 Manet and Proust enrol at the studio of Thomas Couture on the Rue Laval; Manet is to study there for six years. Although attracted by Couture's independent stance and his keenness to challenge traditional academic practice, on a number of occasions Manet takes exception to his teaching.

1851 2 December: Louis-Napoléon Bonaparte stages a military coup d'état. The National Assembly is dissolved and the Second Empire established. Louis-Napoléon declares himself Emperor Napoleon III the following year.

1852 29 January: birth of Suzanne Leenhoff's illegitimate son Léon-Edouard Koëlla. His paternity remains uncertain. July: Manet travels to the Netherlands, where he visits the Rijksmuseum in Amsterdam (see fig. 41).

1853 Summer: Manet visits Normandy with Couture's students. September: he travels to Italy, including Venice, Florence and possibly Rome, returning via Germany and Austria, possibly visiting Kassel, Dresden, Munich, Prague and Vienna. Nadar

Fig. 68
Photographer unknown, Manet aged fourteen, 1846
Private collection

Fig. 69
Photographer unknown, Suzanne Manet
Carte de visite
The Pierpont Morgan Library, New York, MA 3950

So you've had more excitement in Paris; try and keep a decent republic against our return, for I fear L[ouis] Napoleon is not a good republican …

Manet to his father, 22 March 1849

We've been perverted by all the artistic tricks of the trade … Who's going to give us back a clear, direct kind of painting and do away with the frills?

Manet, *c.* 1858–60, reported later by Proust

Fig. 70
Album of photographs belonging to Manet
On the left page, three photographs of Manet (by Franck), and, on the right page, Suzanne Leenhoff (by Chardin), Edgar Degas (by Carjat), Eva Gonzalès (by Lebas) and an unidentified woman
Bibliothèque nationale de France, Paris

(Gaspard Félix Tournachon) (see figs 22–24, 73–74) opens a studio pioneering a new type of bust- or half-length photographic portrait emphasising the sitter's personality.

1854 André-Adolphe-Eugène Disdéri (see figs 25–27) patents the printing of multiple photographs on a single sheet, initiating a popular and commercially successful craze for cartes de visite.

1855 15 May – 15 November: the Exposition Universelle is held in Paris. Gustave Courbet erects his own independent Pavillon du Réalisme nearby to show his works. Accompanied by Proust, Manet visits Eugène Delacroix at his studio and requests permission to copy *The Barque of Dante* (1822; Musée du Louvre, Paris).

1856 February: Manet leaves Couture and moves into a studio with the animal painter Albert de Balleroy on the Rue Lavoisier, where he will stay until 1859.

1857 Manet's father falls ill, possibly from a stroke or tertiary syphilis. Manet meets the painter Henri Fantin-Latour at the Louvre. November: he visits Italy with the sculptor Eugène-Cyrille Brunet (see cat. 36).

Fig. 71
After A. Provost, *The Salon, Palais de l'Industrie*, 1857
Engraving, dimensions unknown
Musée de la Ville de Paris, Musée Carnavalet, Paris

Fig. 72
Honoré Daumier, *The Exhibition of 1859* (series, plate 4), 1859
Lithograph, 26.2 x 21.7 cm
Published in *Le Charivari*, 20 April 1859
Private collection

'Just look where they squeezed in my painting!' – 'I say, my friend ... you are not happy? ... you should be more than satisfied since they are hanging higher than those by Meissonier!'

His painting is a kind of challenge

Thoré-Bürger, *L'Indépendance belge*, 15 June 1864

Never has anyone distorted lines so appallingly and made tones howl

Paul de Saint-Victor, *La Presse*, 1863

Manet has a gift for displeasing the jury

Edouard Lockroy, *Courrier artistique*, 15 May 1863

A pronounced taste for reality, for modern reality

Charles Baudelaire, *Boulevard*, 14 September 1862

Fig. 73
Nadar, *Charles Baudelaire in a Louis XIII Armchair*, before March 1855
Albumen print, 28 x 16 cm
Musée d'Orsay, Paris, PHO1991-2-1

Fig. 74
Nadar, *Edouard Manet*, 1865
Private collection

1858 Manet meets the poet Charles Baudelaire.

1859 Despite Delacroix's support, Manet's first submission to the Salon, *The Absinthe Drinker* (fig. 4), is rejected; Couture does not vote in its favour. Manet moves to a studio on the Rue de la Victoire. He meets Edgar Degas at the Louvre.

1860 From the summer until the following year Manet uses a studio on the Rue de Douai. He rents an apartment for himself, Suzanne and Léon on the Rue de l'Hôtel-de-Ville in the Batignolles *quartier*, their home until 1864. From *c.* 1860 to 1866 Manet frequents the Café Tortoni and Café de Bade.

1861 Together with Louis Martinet, Théophile Gautier, Fantin-Latour and Alphonse Legros, Manet is a founding member of the Société Nationale des Beaux-Arts, established to promote artists and challenge the dominance of the Salon. May: *Portrait of M. and Mme Auguste Manet* (fig. 2) and *The Spanish Singer* (fig. 18) are accepted by the Salon; the latter earns an 'honourable mention'. Artists and writers such as Fantin-Latour, Carolus-Duran and Baudelaire visit Manet's studio to express their admiration for *The Spanish Singer*. Manet establishes a studio at 81 Rue Guyot, where he will stay until 1870. The painter Joseph Gall (see cat. 13) is one of his neighbours. August: Manet places work for sale at the Galerie Martinet, 26 Boulevard des Italiens. September: he exhibits *The Surprised Nymph* (Museo Nacional de Bellas Artes, Buenos Aires) at the Imperial Academy of Arts, St Petersburg.

1862 Manet is a founding member of the Société des Aquafortistes, created to promote the revival of etching. April: prints by Manet are exhibited at the print dealer and publisher Alfred Cadart's premises at 66 Rue de Richelieu. 25 September: death of Manet's father. Manet meets the professional model Victorine Meurent (see cat. 50), who poses for *Street Singer* (cat. 51).

1863 February: exhibits with the Société Nationale des Beaux-Arts. From 1 March, he exhibits fourteen paintings at the Galerie Martinet, his first solo exhibition. May: he exhibits three paintings rejected by the Salon at the first Salon des Refusés, sanctioned by the government in response to public complaints over the large number of works refused by the Salon jury. 17 August: he attends Delacroix's funeral with Baudelaire. 28 October: he marries Suzanne Leenhoff at Zaltbommel in the Netherlands. He meets Frédéric Bazille and Nadar. He paints *Olympia* (fig. 9).

1864 *Episode from a Bullfight* (Frick Collection, New York, and National Gallery of Art, Washington) and the *Dead Christ with Angels* (Metropolitan Museum of Art, New York) are accepted by the Salon. Both are criticised and their reliance on the Spanish

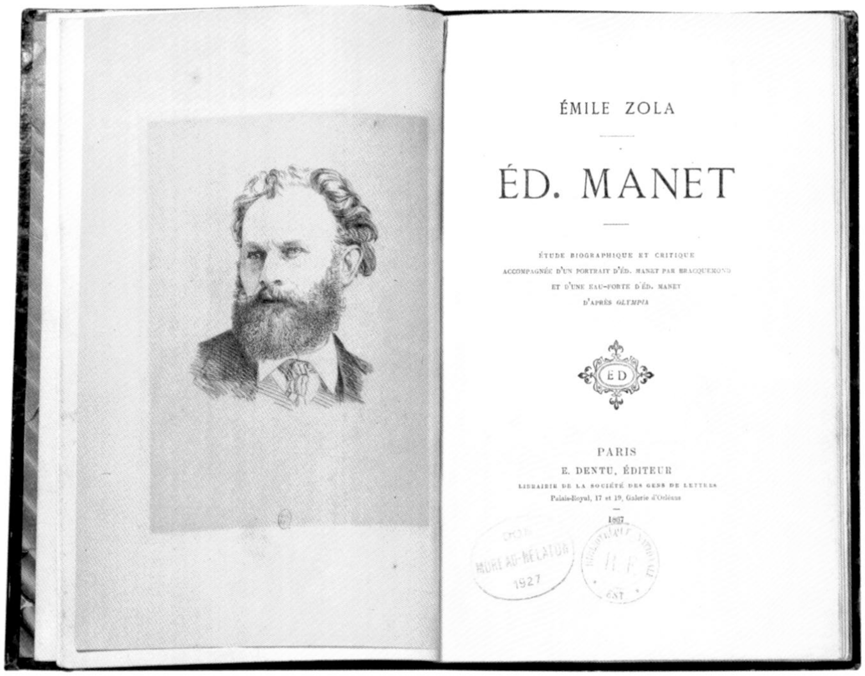

Fig. 75
Emile Zola, *Edouard Manet*, Paris, 1867
Frontispiece with etching of Manet by Félix Bracquemond
Bibliothèque nationale de France, Paris

school of painting is noted. November: Manet moves to an apartment at 34 Boulevard des Batignolles, where he will stay until 1866.

1865 February: an exhibition of the Société Nationale des Beaux-Arts is held at the Galerie Martinet. Manet had initially planned to exhibit nine works, but only two are shown and he resigns. *Christ Mocked by the Soldiers* (Art Institute of Chicago) and *Olympia* (fig. 9) are accepted by the Salon. The Annual Exhibition of the Royal Academy of Arts, London, rejects Manet's paintings. End August – 11 September: Manet visits Burgos, Valladolid, Toledo and Madrid, where he visits the Prado and meets the collector and critic Théodore Duret (see cat. 29). October: Manet falls ill during a cholera epidemic.

1866 *The Fifer* (Musée d'Orsay, Paris) and *The Tragic Actor* (cat. 33) are rejected by the Salon jury. 7 May: Emile Zola defends Manet in his review 'Salon de 1866' (*L'Evénement*). The public confuse Monet's work with Manet's. Zacharie Astruc (see cat. 27) introduces them. The Café Guerbois (see fig. 77), 11 Grande Rue des Batignolles (present-day Avenue de Clichy), becomes a regular meeting place for Manet and his circle, including Marcellin Desboutin (see cat. 20), Zola, Bazille, Renoir and Cézanne. Autumn: Manet, Suzanne and Léon go to live with Manet's mother at 49 Rue de Saint-Pétersbourg, their home until 1878.

1867 1 January: Zola publishes a study of Manet's life and work, 'A New Style in Painting: M. Edouard Manet', in *L'Artiste: Revue du XIXe siècle*. 1 April – 31 October: the Exposition Universelle is held in Paris. May: Manet opens an independent one-man exhibition of 50 paintings in a pavilion on the Avenue de l'Alma, which he advertises in the catalogue of the Exposition Universelle but which receives little critical or public attention, except Randon's cartoons (fig. 76). In Mexico the Emperor Maximilian (installed by Napoleon III) and two of his generals are executed by firing squad. Manet makes a series of works on the subject. 2 September: Manet attends Baudelaire's funeral.

We are not accustomed to seeing such simple and direct translations of reality. Then, as I said, there is such a surprisingly elegant awkwardness … it is a truly charming experience to contemplate this luminous and serious painting which interprets nature with a gentle brutality

Emile Zola, 'Une nouvelle manière en peinture: M. Edouard Manet' / 'A new style in painting: M. Edouard Manet', *Revue du XIXe siècle*, 1 January 1867

Fig. 76
G. Randon, Caricatures of Manet's paintings in his own exhibition, *Le Journal amusant*, 29 June 1867, no. 600, pp. 6–8

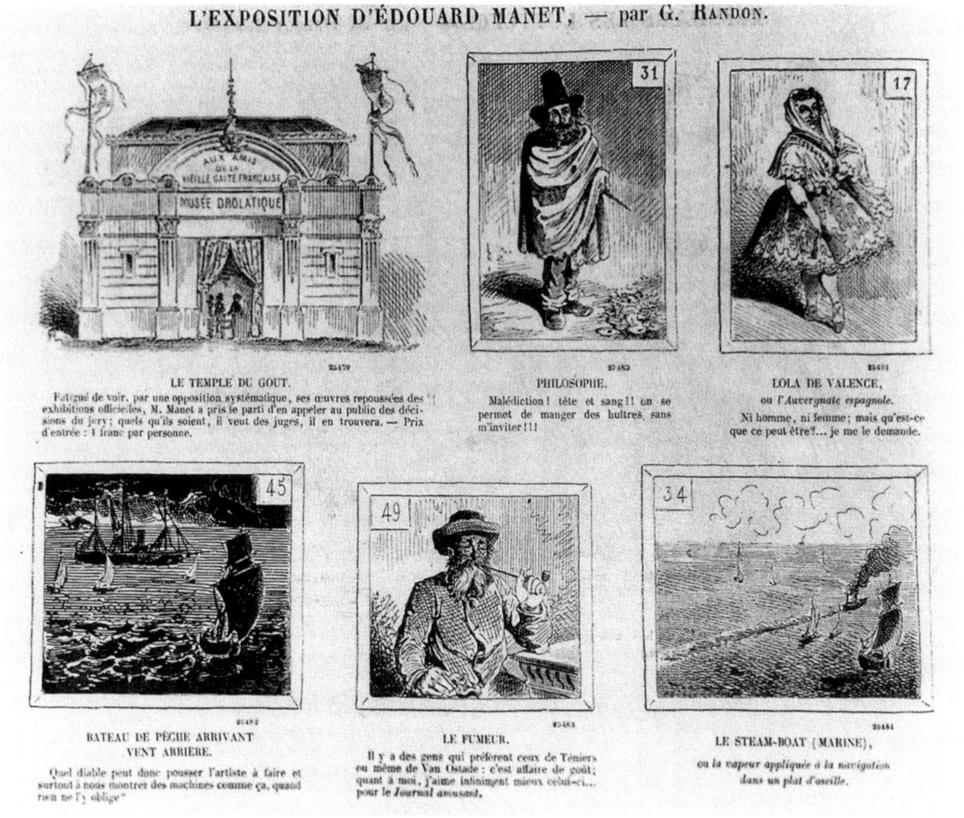

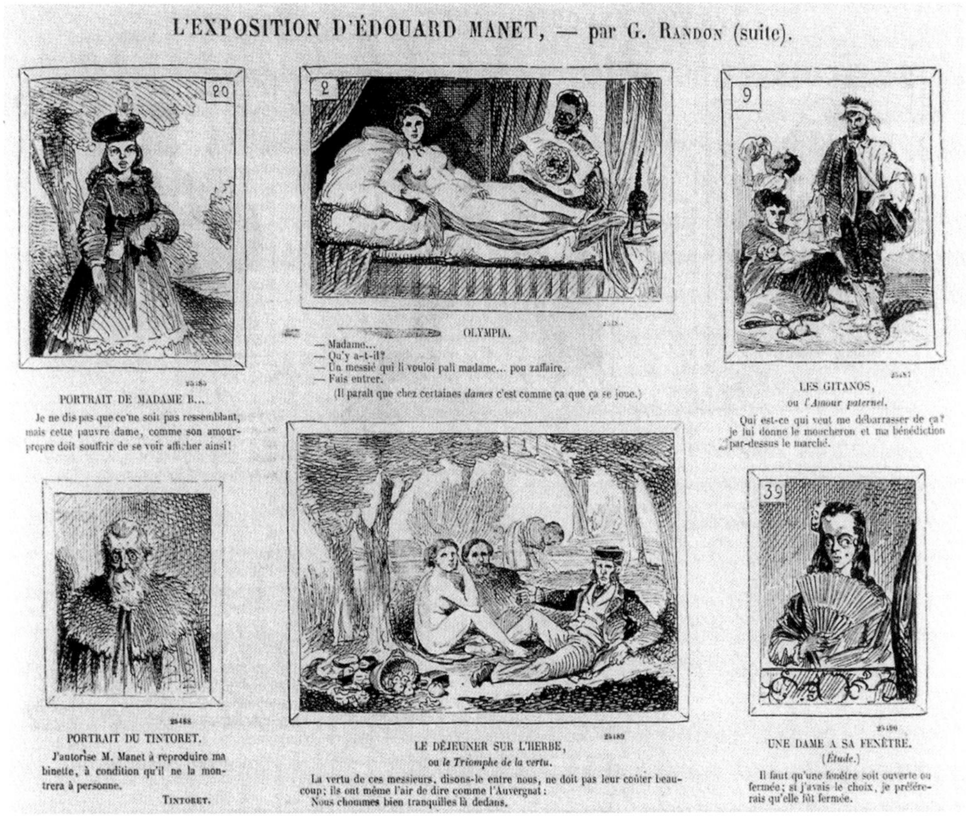

It is a vital matter, a sine qua non, for an artist to be able to exhibit his work … To exhibit is to find friends and allies for the fight

'Reasons for a Private Exhibition,' May 1867, preface to the catalogue of Manet's independent exhibition

Fig. 77
***At the Café (Café Guerbois)*, 1869**
Lithograph, 26.3 x 33.4 cm
National Gallery of Art, Washington, Rosenwald Collection, 1953.6.82

Fig. 78
Pierre Petit, *Berthe Morisot*, 20 February 1869
Photograph, dimensions unknown
Private collection

Fig. 79
Photographer unknown, Eva Gonzalès, *c.* 1874
Photograph, dimensions unknown
Private collection

1868 May: *Emile Zola* (cat. 28) and *Young Lady in 1866* (fig. 10) are accepted by the Salon. Summer: Manet and his family holiday at Boulogne-sur-Mer. Late July – early August: Manet visits London, travelling by steamboat, and is welcomed by the painter Alphonse Legros, whom he had known in Paris. Legros probably introduced Manet to the artist and photographer David Wilkie Wynfield (see fig. 48). Manet possibly visited an exhibition of British portraits at the South Kensington Museum. Back in Paris he is introduced to Berthe Morisot and her sister Edma, both painters, by Fantin-Latour. Berthe poses for *The Balcony* (fig. 11). Manet meets the prominent French statesman Léon Gambetta.

1869 January–February: Manet is informed that *The Execution of Maximilian* (Kunsthalle Mannheim) will be refused by the Salon; the publication of the related lithograph is banned. February: Alfred Stevens introduces Manet to Eva Gonzalès, who becomes his pupil and model (see cat. 15). May: *The Balcony* and *The Luncheon* (cat. 10) are accepted by the Salon. July–September: the Manets holiday at Boulogne-sur-Mer.

1870 23 February: Manet fights a duel with the critic Edmond Duranty over an article; Duranty is wounded, but friendly relations are soon re-established. March: Manet joins a committee aiming to reform the method of selecting the Salon jury. *The Music Lesson* (Museum of Fine Arts, Boston) and *Eva Gonzalès* (cat. 15) are accepted by the Salon. Fantin-Latour exhibits his tribute to Manet, *Atelier in Les Batignolles* (fig. 1). Summer: Manet stays with the painter Giuseppe de Nittis at Saint-Germain-en-Laye (see cat. 24). 19 July: France declares war on Prussia. 4 September: following the defeats suffered by the French army and the fall of Napoleon III, the Third Republic is proclaimed. Manet sends his family to Oloron-Sainte-Marie in the Pyrenees and closes his Rue Guyot studio, placing thirteen paintings in store at Duret's apartment (see fig. 80). He takes a studio at 51 Rue de Saint-Pétersbourg. By 23 September

We've reached the decisive moment ... There's fighting everywhere, all round Paris

Manet to Suzanne, 20 September 1870

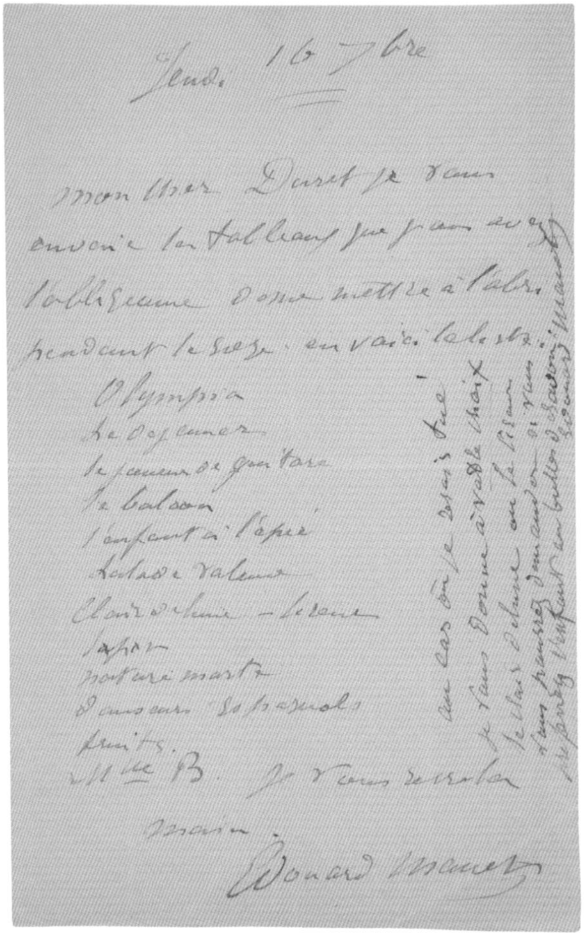

Jeudi 16 7bre

mon cher Duret je vous envoie les tableaux que vous avez l'obligeance de me mettre à l'abri pendant le siège. en voici la liste:

Olympia
le Déjeuner
le joueur de guitare
le balcon
l'enfant à l'épée
[illegible]
[illegible]
[illegible]
nature morte
danseurs espagnols
fruits
Mlle B. je vous serre la main.

Edouard Manet

[illegible]

Fig. 80
Autograph letter from Manet to Théodore Duret, 16 September 1870
Pierpont Morgan Library, New York

'My dear Duret I am sending you the pictures you have kindly offered to shelter during the Siege – here is the list'

Degas and I are in the artillery, as volunteer gunners ... My paintbox and portable easel are stuffed into my military kitbag, so there's no excuse for wasting my time

Manet to Eva Gonzalès, 19 November 1870

Prussian forces surround Paris. Manet remains in the city until the end of the Siege of Paris (28 January 1871) and in November enlists in the National Guard.

1871 End of January: Paris surrenders to Prussian forces. A treaty is prepared, leading to the payment of compensation by France and the loss of Alsace and Lorraine. February: Manet joins his family in the Pyrenees; they stay for a week in Bordeaux. March: the Paris Commune is declared and the city is cut off from the rest of France. Manet stays at Arcachon for the month (see cat. 12). Unable to return to Paris, he travels up the west coast. Late May–June: he returns to Paris after the 'semaine sanglante' or 'bloody week' (21–28 May), during which thousands of Communards are killed in the streets of Paris and the political journalist Henri Rochefort (see cat. 47) is arrested and sentenced to life imprisonment. July: Manet frequently visits Versailles, following the election of Léon Gambetta to the National Assembly. He asks Gambetta to sit for his portrait but the politician cannot spare the time. August: psychologically drained, Manet follows medical advice to rest and stays with his family at Boulogne-sur-Mer. The collector and art dealer Paul Durand-Ruel acquires two of his paintings.

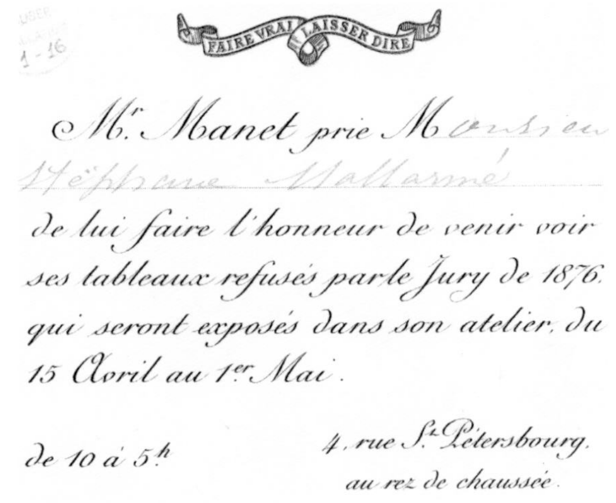
FAIRE VRAI LAISSER DIRE

Mr. Manet prie Monsieur
Stéphane Mallarmé
de lui faire l'honneur de venir voir
ses tableaux refusés par le Jury de 1876.
qui seront exposés dans son atelier, du
15 Avril au 1er. Mai.

de 10 à 5h

4, rue St. Pétersbourg,
au rez de chaussée.

Fig. 81
Photographer unknown, *Portrait of Stéphane Mallarmé*, c. 1873
Bibliothèque Litteraire Jacques Doucet, Paris

Fig. 82
Manet's invitation to Mallarmé to see an exhibition of his pictures rejected by the Salon, 12 April 1876
Musée départemental Stéphane Mallarmé, Vulaines-sur-Seine, DAPMD/CG7

1872 January: Durand-Ruel purchases 24 of Manet's paintings for 35,000 francs, many of which he shows at exhibitions of the Société des Artistes Français in London during 1872. The Café Nouvelle Athènes at 9 Place Pigalle becomes the new meeting place for Manet and his artistic and literary friends. He visits Haarlem and Amsterdam with Suzanne and her brother Ferdinand (see figs 42, 43). 1 July: Manet moves his studio to the second floor of 4 Rue de Saint-Pétersbourg, near the Gare Saint-Lazare, where he will stay until 1878.

1873 *Le Bon Bock* (Philadelphia Museum of Art) and *The Repose* (cat. 18) are accepted by the Salon. July: the Manets visit Etaples, near Berck-sur-Mer, where Manet paints and draws *en plein air* (see cat. 8). In Paris, he meets the poet Stéphane Mallarmé (see cat. 30) through Nina de Callias; the two men become firm friends. November: he sells five paintings to the well-known baritone Jean-Baptiste Faure (see figs 54, 55).

1874 March: Henri Rochefort (see cat. 47) escapes from a penal colony on the Pacific island of New Caledonia. April: *The Railway* (cat. 53) and the watercolour *Polichinelle* (RWII, no. 563) are accepted by the Salon, but *The Swallows* (cat. 8) and *Masked Ball at the Opera* (1873; National Gallery of Art, Washington) are rejected. May: Mallarmé publishes 'The Painting Jury of 1874 and M. Manet' in *La Renaissance littéraire et artistique* in response. An exhibition is organised by the Société Anonyme des Artistes, Peintres, Sculpteurs, Graveurs at Nadar's studio on Boulevard des Capucines; subsequently known as the First Impressionist Exhibition, this comprised 165 works by 30 artists, including Degas, Monet, Morisot and Renoir. Determined to exhibit at the Salon, Manet declines to participate in this or any other of the Impressionist exhibitions held between 1879 and 1886 but lends works by Morisot and Renoir. August: Manet holidays at Gennevilliers, near Argenteuil, where Monet is living (see cat. 25). Renoir also visits. October: Manet visits Venice with Suzanne and the painter James Tissot. 22 December: Eugène Manet and Berthe Morisot marry.

1875 May: *Argenteuil* (1874; Musée des Beaux-Arts, Tournai) is accepted by the Salon. Around this time the press begin to describe Manet as the leader of the Impressionists.

1876 15 April – 1 May: in the weeks before the official opening of the Salon, Manet opens his studio to the public to show works, including two paintings rejected that year: *The Laundry* (1875; Am Römerholz, Winterthur) and *The Artist* (cat. 20). The actress Méry Laurent (see cat. 55) is among the visitors. April/May: Mallarmé's article

Each time he begins a picture, says he, he plunges headlong into it … the eye should forget all else it has seen, and learn anew from the lesson before it

Stéphane Mallarmé, 'The Impressionists and Edouard Manet', *Art Monthly Review*, [probably April or May] 1876

Fig. 83
At the Paintings Exhibition,
***c.* 1876**
Blacklead, wash and watercolour on paper, 14 x 9 cm
Musée du Louvre, Paris (Musée d'Orsay collection), RF 30528

And Manet! One could say that criticism has gathered up all the insults which it has poured on his precursors for half a century, to throw them at his head all at one time. And yet criticism has since then made amends, the public is full of admiration

Théodore Duret, *Les Peintures Impressionistes*, May 1879

Fig. 84
***Café at the Place du Théâtre Français*, 1877–81**
China ink, wash, pencil and graphite on graph paper, 14.1 x 18.7 cm
Musée du Louvre, Paris (Musée d'Orsay Collection), RF 30527

'The Impressionists and Edouard Manet' is published (*Art Monthly Review*). Summer: Manet spends four weeks at Fécamp, Channel coast; July: he stays with the businessman and collector Ernest Hoschedé at Montgeron (see cat. 21).

1877 March: Manet supports the third Impressionist exhibition by lending works from his own collection, two by Monet and one by Sisley. April: *Faure as Hamlet* (Folkwang Museum, Essen) is accepted by the Salon, but *Nana* (Hamburger Kunsthalle) is rejected. Manet shows *Nana* in the window of a luxury goods shop on the Boulevard des Capucines.

1878 Unwilling to submit work to the jury for the Exposition Universelle or the Salon, as in 1867, Manet considers another independent show of 100 paintings but cannot secure funding for the venture. Duret's *Les Peintres Impressionistes* is published. Summer: the Manet family moves from 49 to 39 Rue de Saint-Pétersbourg. July: Manet is forced to leave the studio at 4 Rue de Saint-Pétersbourg, he temporarily rents a space at 70 Rue d'Amsterdam until 1879.

1879 April: he moves to his final studio at 77 Rue d'Amsterdam. May: *Boating* (1874; Metropolitan Museum of Art, New York) and *In the Conservatory* (cat. 39) are accepted by the Salon. Spring: Manet meets the Irish writer George Moore (see cat. 32; fig. 5). September–October: he stays at Bellevue and undergoes hydrotherapy for Locomotor ataxia, caused by syphilis. He meets the opera singer Emile Ambre (see cat. 35), who organises the exhibition of *The Execution of Emperor Maximilian* (Kunsthalle Mannheim) in New York and Boston that winter.

1880 January: Manet's health deteriorates; his left leg causes him pain and he becomes less mobile. 8–30 April: a solo exhibition of ten oil paintings and fifteen pastels is held at the gallery of the journal *La Vie moderne* (see fig. 86). May: *Portrait of M. Antonin Proust* (cat. 45) and *Chez le Père Lathuille – en plein air* (cat. 60) are accepted by the Salon; although the former is hung 'on the line', both receive a mixed reception.

Fig. 85
Photographer unknown, Isabelle Lemmonier wearing fancy dress, *c.* 1876
Private collection

Fig. 86
***Catalogue of Recent Works by Edouard Manet Exhibited at 'La Vie moderne'*, April 1880**

Fig. 87
'Vive l'amnistie!': Illustrated letter from Manet to Isabelle Lemonnier, 14 July 1880
Watercolour, 18 x 11.2 cm. Musée du Louvre, Paris (Musée d'Orsay Collection), RF 11183

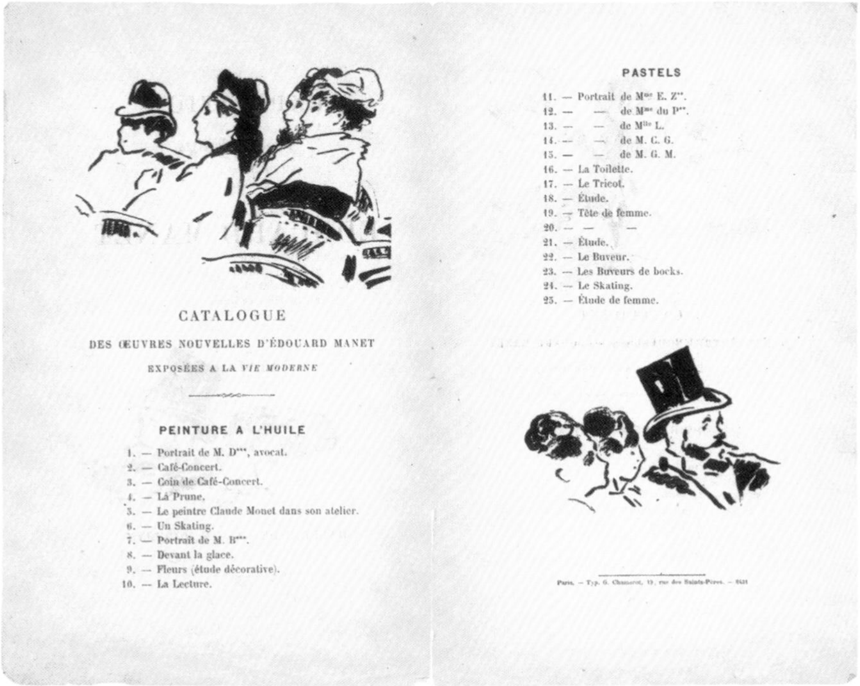

CATALOGUE

DES ŒUVRES NOUVELLES D'ÉDOUARD MANET

EXPOSÉES A LA *VIE MODERNE*

PEINTURE A L'HUILE

1. — Portrait de M. D***, avocat.
2. — Café-Concert.
3. — Coin de Café-Concert.
4. — La Prune.
5. — Le peintre Claude Monet dans son atelier.
6. — Un Skating.
7. — Portrait de M. B***.
8. — Devant la glace.
9. — Fleurs (étude décorative).
10. — La Lecture.

PASTELS

11. — Portrait de Mme E. Z**.
12. — — de Mme du P**.
13. — — de Mlle L.
14. — — de M. C. G.
15. — — de M. G. M.
16. — La Toilette.
17. — Le Tricot.
18. — Étude.
19. — Tête de femme.
20. — — —
21. — Étude.
22. — Le Buveur.
23. — Les Buveurs de bocks.
24. — Le Skating.
25. — Étude de femme.

Paris. — Typ. G. Chamerot, 19, rue des Saints-Pères.

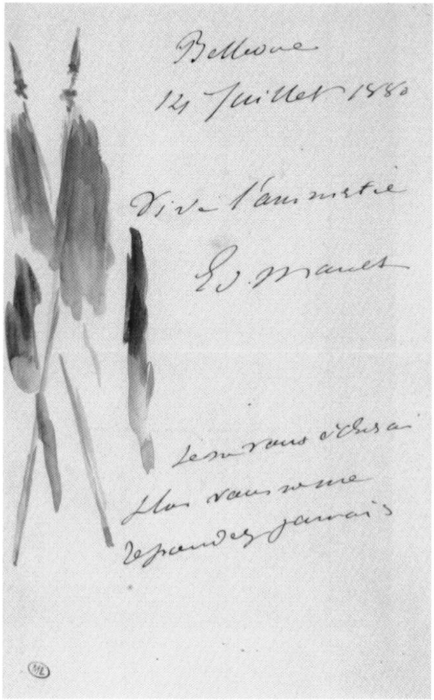

Fig. 88
Alfred Le Petit, 'Edouard Manet, King of the Impressionists', illustration on the cover of *Les Contemporains*, 16 June 1881
Private collection

July–November: prescribed rest in the country, Manet rents a house at 4 Route des Gardes, Bellevue, and continues treatment. He sends illustrated letters to Eva Gonzalès, Isabelle Lemonnier and Zacharie Astruc. December: Manet meets Henri Rochefort and persuades him to sit for a modern-history painting recording his 1874 escape.

1881 *Eugène Pertuiset, Lion-hunter* (cat. 46) and *Portrait of Henri Rochefort* (cat. 47) are accepted by the Salon. Manet receives a second-class medal for the latter, affording him the privilege of exhibiting at subsequent Salons without having to submit work to the jury. June: he stays for the summer at 20 Avenue de Villeneuve l'Etang, Versailles, to receive further medical treatment. Marcel Bernstein has a house in the area and Manet makes a portrait of his son Henry (cat. 49). 14 November: following Gambetta's appointment as Prime Minister, Proust is made Minister of Fine Arts. 30 December: Manet is made a Chevalier de la Légion d'honneur, the highest decoration in France.

1882 January: Manet's health deteriorates further. May: *A Bar at the Folies-Bergère* (Courtauld Institute of Art, London) and *Spring* (fig. 29; see cat. 56) are exhibited at the Salon. July–October: Manet takes a villa at Reuil. September: he writes a will naming Suzanne as his heir, Léon Leenhoff as residuary legatee, and Duret as executor with responsibility for the sale or destruction of his works.

1883 20 April: Manet's left leg is amputated, but he fails to recover. He dies on 30 April, aged 51, and is buried on 3 May at Passy Cemetery. Proust, Zola, Duret, Fantin-Latour, Philippe Burty, Alfred Stevens and Monet are his pallbearers.

1884 January: a retrospective exhibition of 179 of Manet's works is held at the Ecole des Beaux-Arts. 4–5 February: a studio sale is held at the Hôtel Drouot, Paris.

Manet understands the human countenance … A portrait by Manet is the physical and moral counterpart of an individual

Charles Flor (signed 'Flor O'Squarr'), *Le National*, 11 May 1880

One of M. Manet's most constant preoccupations has been to envelop his characters with the atmosphere of the world to which they belong

Joris-Karl Huysmans, *L'Art moderne*, 1883

Catalogue Entries

MARYANNE STEVENS | LEAH LEHMBECK

1
SELF-PORTRAIT WITH PALETTE, 1878–79
Oil on canvas, 83 × 67 cm
Private collection

SELECTED EXHIBITIONS:
Paris 1983A, no. 164;
New York 2003, no. 160
SELECTED REFERENCES:
RWI, no. 276

NOT EXHIBITED

2
SELF-PORTRAIT, 1878–79
Oil on canvas, 95.4 × 63.4 cm
Signed bottom right: E. M.
Bridgestone Museum of Art, Ishibashi Foundation, Tokyo

SELECTED REFERENCES:
RWI, no. 277

LONDON ONLY

'One October evening in 1878, I was walking down the Rue Pigalle when I saw coming towards me a man of seemingly youthful appearance, with a distinguished presence combined with an elegant simplicity. A fair-haired man with a well-kept beard … grey eyes, straight nose, mobile nostrils; hands gloved, feet alert and nervous. It was Manet' (Jeanniot 1907, p. 847).

Although Manet had included representations of himself in two genre paintings of the 1860s, *Fishing* (cat. 3) and *Music in the Tuileries Gardens* (cat. 26), and possibly in one of the 1870s (*The Masked Ball*, 1873–74; National Gallery of Art, Washington) (see Paris 1983A, p. 151), he executed only two independent self-portraits. Both address his complex relationship with the Old Masters and his crafting of a visual language of modernity, his view of the connections between portraiture and paintings of modern life, and his understanding of the duality of his professional and personal personae within contemporary society.

On the one hand, *Self-portrait with Palette* (which he painted over an effaced portrait of his wife) presents the artist as a figure of modernity: he proudly sports a soft felt hat and a stylish tan jacket, and he executes the work with the open, free brushwork that reflects his consideration during the early 1870s of the techniques of his younger, more radical contemporaries the Impressionists. His pose, however, echoes the one chosen by Velázquez for his self-representation in *Las Meninas* (Museo Nacional del Prado, Madrid). Furthermore, close examination of the way in which Manet builds up the form of his figure and the mere touch with which, for example, he suggests the hand holding the paint brush, reflects his admiration for the two great Old Masters of the Low Countries, Rubens and Frans Hals (see Lawrence W. Nichols on pp. 66–71 of the present volume; and cat. 3). *Self-portrait with Palette* eloquently and succinctly summarises Manet's artistic programme. It simultaneously acknowledges the profound significance of the great tradition in laying the foundations for his new visual language and unequivocally declares his contemporaneity, his modernity.

Self-portrait announces the same relationship, albeit in a less direct manner. With one hand thrust firmly into a pocket of the same tan jacket, with a seemingly identical tie and pin, his soft felt hat now replaced by a skullcap, worn at a slightly rakish angle, Manet depicts himself as a man of his time. His handling of paint again suggests his consideration of the techniques of the Impressionists, and his relationship with the Old Masters is explored here too, but in a more circumspect manner. Overtly, Manet's pose refers to his own monumental single-figure compositions of the 1860s, such as *The Philosopher* (1865–66; Art Institute of Chicago), or to such portraits as the standing figure of Théodore Duret (cat. 29), yet all three works make potent reference to the art of Velázquez (see cats 26, 33).

Significantly the two self-portraits show the artist in two distinct guises. *Self-portrait with Palette* is an unequivocal proclamation of Manet's professional status: he stands with the tools of his trade in hand, ready to depict himself. *Self-portrait* presents him stepping into another role, that of the man of leisure, caught in a moment of informality: adopting the frontal pose that he chose for his portrait of his fellow artist and friend Marcellin Desboutin (cat. 20), Manet wears headgear associated with informal social activities such as smoking. Taken as 'pendants', the two self-portraits demonstrate the interaction in Manet's artistic programme between the portrait and the scene from contemporary life: his transition from straightforward 'sitter' into an actor who illustrates a facet of modernity and hence underscores the authenticity of that very representation.

The modernity of these two images is further enhanced by Manet's innovative compositional formats. In *Self-portrait with Palette*, both by deliberately allowing his physical form to dominate the canvas and by placing the palette as the entry point into the composition, Manet asserts, as Armstrong (2002, p. 315) has observed, the integration of two previously separate approaches to portraiture: the painter painting, and the painter painted. In *Self-portrait*, deliberately lacking his professional attributes yet patently of his era, Manet appears somewhat anxious, slightly diminished by the surrounding, undefined space, a figure of uncertainty; does he perhaps presage that contemporary urban condition, *anomie*, as defined by Emile Durkheim?

The sequence of these two self-portraits has been much discussed (Paris 1983A, no. 164; New York 2003, no. 160). More important, perhaps, is the rationale for their creation, which is related to the supposed year of their execution. If made in 1878, they might stand as a defiant statement of Manet's own self-esteem in the wake of his 1877 rejection by the selection panel of the 1878 Paris Exposition Universelle (Reff 1982, no. 1). If created in 1879, they might mark the acceptance of *Boating* (1874; Metropolitan Museum of Art, New York) and *In the Conservatory* (cat. 39) by the Salon, or, reflecting Léon Leenhoff's statement to Duret, the onset of Manet's illness from this year (New York 2003, no. 160), which could have provoked a desire to record his two personae: the artist and the man about town.

Both self-portraits remained within the private domain of Manet and his family. Neither was exhibited publicly during Manet's lifetime, and neither was included in the 1884 posthumous exhibition. Both works were later referred to by Mme Suzanne Manet as 'sketches' (Tabarant 1947, p. 357). However, the fact that Tabarant reported (p. 355) that Manet himself 'invited all his friends' to see *Self-portrait with Palette* suggests that he considered that work resolved. Viewing this self-portrait next to the seemingly less resolved *Self-portrait* raises the question of what constitutes 'finish' in Manet's work (for more on this see pages 22–24).

Testimony to the innovative significance of both self-portraits can be found in their impact on subsequent artists. *Self-portrait* entered the collection of Max Linde, the Lübeck patron of Edvard Munch, who appears to have adopted both pose and handling of paint for such portraits as that of Dr Daniel Jacobsen (1909; Munch Museet, Oslo). *Self-portrait with Palette* can be seen to have informed self-portraits by such artists as Cézanne, Van Gogh and Picasso (see Copenhagen 1989, no. 31; Armstrong 2002, p. 316). MAS

3
FISHING, *c.* 1862–63
Oil on canvas, 76.8 × 123.2 cm
Signed and dated lower left (by Mme Manet): Ed Manet
Lent by the Metropolitan Museum of Art, New York. Purchase, Mr and Mrs Richard J. Bernhard Gift, 1957 (57.10)

SELECTED EXHIBITIONS: Paris 1867, no. 50; Paris 1983A, no. 12; Martigny 1996, no. 8; Madrid 2003, no. 28
SELECTED REFERENCES: RWI, no. 36

This painting, initially known as 'Landscape', brings together an amalgam of contemporary and Old Master references in a range of genres: 'family' portrait, costume piece, and a scene making direct reference to contemporary life. Set within a landscape derived from the Ile Saint-Ouen, close to the Manet property at Gennevilliers to the west of Paris, the work presents Manet and Suzanne Leenhoff in the guise of Rubens and his second wife Hélène Fourment. Léon Koëlla Leenhoff, Suzanne's illegitimate son (1852–1927), who here makes his second appearance in Manet's *oeuvre* (see cats 9–12), fishes from the other side of the riverbank, and, like the fishermen in the boat who hold the centre of the composition, wears seemingly more contemporary attire.

Locke (2001, p. 78) has proposed that *Fishing* is a pendant of *Music in the Tuileries Gardens* (cat. 26). Both works contain self-portraits of the artist and both respectively communicate the public (social) and private sides of his life. Furthermore, both summarise Manet's relationship to contemporary academic art practice and his reflections on the possibilities that the Old Masters offered him in crafting a new visual language through which to describe the modern age. While *Music in the Tuileries Gardens* appropriates Velázquez, *Fishing* draws upon Annibale Carracci, Rubens (notably *Château de Steen* [Kunsthistorisches Museum, Vienna] and *Landscape with Rainbow* [Musée du Louvre, Paris], and Watteau for compositional and technical models; the landscape may also be informed by Delacroix's landscapes of the 1850s (see Paris 1983A; Fried 1996; Rubin 2010, p. 36; for John Constable as another putative source, see Madrid 2003). Yet both paintings also present their subjects in contemporary spaces pertinent to mid-century Parisian life: the Tuileries Gardens, where the prosperous bourgeoisie disported itself in the city, and a country property that provided a retreat for rural leisure pursuits (Locke 2001, pp. 78–81).

Whether the painting was intended as an allegory of the impending marriage of Manet and Suzanne Leenhoff remains unproven (Reff 1982; Paris 1983A; Locke 2001, pp. 71–72). However, the work is significant within the context of Manet's portrait practice: it incorporates two people who were to pose fairly consistently over the next two decades as both sitters for straight portraiture and actors in scenes of contemporary life; it presents one of only four firmly identified self-portraits made by the artist; and it demonstrates Realism's contention that the veracity of the sitters/actors in a scene of contemporary life ensures its objective truth. MAS

4
MME EDOUARD MANET, 1873
Pastel on paper, mounted on canvas, 53.7 × 38.7 cm
Lent by the Toledo Museum of Art. Gift of Mrs C. Lockhart McKelvy

SELECTED EXHIBITIONS: Paris 1950, no. 67; Toledo 1964, p. 13
SELECTED REFERENCES: RWII, no. 2; Oshima 1981, no. 36; Adler 1986, no. 208

5
WOMAN WITH A CAT (PORTRAIT OF MME MANET), *c.* 1880
Oil on canvas, 92.1 × 73 cm
Tate. Purchased 1918

SELECTED EXHIBITIONS: Philadelphia 1966, no. 182; Copenhagen 1989, no. 46; Stuttgart 2002, no. 64
SELECTED REFERENCES: RWI, no. 337; Tate 1991, no. 03295

6
MME MANET IN THE CONSERVATORY, 1879
Oil on canvas, 81 × 100 cm
Signed and dated, lower left: Manet / 1876
The National Museum of Art, Architecture and Design, Oslo

SELECTED EXHIBITIONS: Paris 1983A, no. 181; Stuttgart 2002, no. 58
SELECTED REFERENCES: RWI, no. 290; Paris 1983A, no. 181; Wilson-Bareau 1991, p. 268

LONDON ONLY

There are more representations of Manet's wife, Suzanne Leenhoff (1829–1906), than of any other female figure in the artist's *oeuvre*, and indeed she was represented in paint, pastel and ink over the course of nearly his entire career. Born in the Netherlands, Suzanne moved to Paris with four of her siblings and her grandmother, and she was introduced to the Manet family as their music teacher in *c.* 1849. Although little is known about her reasons for moving to Paris, or much of her life before she married Manet in 1863, we do know that she gave birth to a son, Léon-Edouard Koëlla, in 1852, and that he was named as Manet's godson in 1855. Suzanne played the piano beautifully and graced her mother-in-law's Tuesday-evening soirées with her music. While Baudelaire lay paralysed on his deathbed, she played Wagner for the author, who once described her as 'beautiful, very nice, and a very good musician' (Baudelaire 1973, vol. 2, p. 323).

The portraits of Suzanne relate the natural ease between painter and sitter, as well as the resultant blurring of the boundary between portraiture and genre scene. Throughout Manet's *oeuvre*, Suzanne sits, stands, leans and lounges; she is captured *en face*, in profile, in *profil perdu* and from behind. She is depicted in the studio, outside and in the domestic space of the home she and Manet shared with Mme Manet *mère* and Léon. This variety, along with the rapid execution and the seemingly relatively unresolved state of so many of these paintings, suggests both a kind of experimentation permitted by this most intimate relationship and a perception of the degree of 'finish' required for a work that was to remain in the private domain. Suzanne's portrait in the verdant setting of the conservatory, for example, hung in their bedroom even after the artist's death. The portrait of Suzanne with her beloved cat Zizi was sold by her to Manet's friend and fellow artist Edgar Degas. Because these portraits of Suzanne were not intended for public view, they can instead be seen as images in which Manet felt free to subvert convention and explore boldly. LL

7
MME MANET AT THE PIANO, 1868
Oil on canvas, 38 × 46.5 cm
Musée d'Orsay, Paris. Legs du comte Isaac de Camondo, 1911

SELECTED EXHIBITIONS: Paris 1884, no. 47; Paris 1983A, no. 107
SELECTED REFERENCES: RWI, no. 131

This work inhabits the uncertain borderlands between the portrait and the genre scene. It is one of the numerous representations of Suzanne Manet (*née* Leenhoff) that Manet made from early in his career (see cats 4–6). Showing his wife seated at one of her instruments (Manet to Suzanne Manet, 11 September 1870, in Wilson-Bareau 1991, p. 55) in the apartment at 47 Rue de Saint-Pétersbourg, Manet celebrates her talent as a pianist who had entered his life as piano teacher to his younger brothers, and who subsequently entertained guests at the Manets' Tuesday evening gatherings of politicians, artists, writers, musicians and composers, and at musical soirées elsewhere, such as those organised by Paul Meurice, where she would perform duets with Mme Meurice and accompany singers. Suzanne was a champion of contemporary German music, especially that of Robert Schumann and Richard Wagner, then relatively little known in France.

The painting reflects a number of sources, and is symptomatic of Manet's artistic procedures in the 1860s. Suzanne adopts the profile pose of the Dutch seventeenth-century artist Gabriel Metsu's *Dutchwoman at the Harpsichord* (Musée du Petit Palais, Paris), which was published as an engraving in Charles Blanc's *Histoire des peintres de toutes les écoles* (vol. 1, 1861, 'Metsu', p. 3). However, there is also an echo of Degas's representation of Suzanne at the piano on the right of his double portrait of Manet and his wife (*c*. 1865; Municipal Art Museum, Kitakyushu), which Manet cut after receipt. As Dorment has noted (London 1994, p. 72), both Degas and Manet appear to have drawn inspiration from James McNeill Whistler's *At the Piano* (1858–59; Taft Museum, Cincinnati). Whistler's canvas was exhibited twice in Paris during Manet's lifetime: in 1859 at the studio of the artist Bonvin (where it was admired by Gustave Courbet) and secondly at the Salon of 1867 (to which Manet did not submit but held his own solo exhibition on the Avenue de l'Alma). Whistler's rigorous arrangement of piano and performer in profile in a narrow space parallel to the picture plane, and his use of gilded picture frames on the wall behind to indicate a domestic setting, are echoed in *Mme Manet at the Piano*, although Manet replaces the picture frames with the gilded panel delineation and a mirror, whose position and reflection of the chimneypiece across the room recall similar treatment in the work of Ingres.

Whistler's title deliberately avoided the identity of the performer, instead characterising his work as an intimate, private engagement with music itself. Given that Manet referred in 1872 to this representation of Suzanne as 'Jeune dame à son piano' (Paris 1983A, p. 287), it seems reasonable to suggest that he initially intended to emphasise the work's theme – the making of music – rather than to paint a straight portrait of his wife. Indeed, it could be argued that, by painting the act of music-making, Manet infers parity between the two art forms, which parallels Baudelaire's contemporaneous assertion of a parity between poetry and music. In a further parallel, it is telling that, during the period when Manet was making this painting, Suzanne was often to be found playing the works of, among others, Wagner – chief proponent of the *Gesamtkunstwerk* (the complete work of art) – to Baudelaire as he lay dying in a clinic at Chaillot. MAS

8
THE SWALLOWS, 1873
Oil on canvas, 65 × 81 cm
Signed bottom right: Manet
Foundation E. G. Bührle Collection, Zurich

SELECTED EXHIBITIONS: Paris 1884, no. 63; Paris 1983A, no. 135
SELECTED REFERENCES: RWI, no. 190

LONDON ONLY

The Swallows was painted during the summer of 1873, when Manet spent three weeks at Etaples, near Berck-sur-Mer, with his family, including his widowed mother (Wilson-Bareau 1991, p. 166). Two figures sit in a meadow behind the sand dunes characteristic of this part of the Pas-de-Calais coast. The weather is unsettled, as the parasol resting on the ground, the scudding grey clouds and the swallows wheeling above the seated figures indicate. The models are Suzanne Manet, in grey and white, and the artist's widowed mother, Mme Auguste Manet, dressed in black. Manet had already presented both women in straight portraiture (see cat. 4, and *Portrait of Mme Manet mère* [1862; Isabella Stewart Gardiner Museum, Boston]). Thus, his use of two already recorded and yet unidentified figures as models firmly underscores Manet's genre translation from portrait to a scene of contemporary life, the latter's authenticity confirmed by his familiarity with his 'models' – his wife and his mother. As such, the painting complements other scenes of contemporary life beside the sea, including *On the Beach* (1873; Musée d'Orsay, Paris), also made that summer and which uses Suzanne Manet and her brother-in-law Eugène as models; and *Afternoon at Arcachon* (cat. 12), in which, in place of his mother, Manet presses Léon Leenhoff into service as the second of his two actors.

Manet's ambition to present a work seemingly made 'en plein air' and utilising a more vibrant technique and a lighter palette indicates his determination to move away from his earlier dependence upon the Spanish and Dutch Old Masters. However, although *The Swallows* found an immediate purchaser in Albert Hecht, the work was presumably deemed too 'unfinished' to be acceptable to the Salon Jury of 1874. The critic and writer Stéphane Mallarmé disagreed: 'What is an unfinished painting when all of its parts harmonise and it has a charm that one additional touch of paint would mar?' (Mallarmé 1970, p. 698). MAS

9
BOY BLOWING BUBBLES, 1867
Oil on canvas, 100.5 × 81.4 cm
Signed bottom right:
Ed. Manet
Calouste Gulbenkian Foundation, Lisbon

SELECTED EXHIBITIONS:
Paris 1884, no. 45; Paris 1983A, no. 102; Madrid 2003, no. 77; Paris 2011A, no. 82
SELECTED REFERENCES:
RWI, no. 129

Léon-Edouard Koëlla Leenhoff (1852–1927) was the illegitimate child of Suzanne Leenhoff. His paternity remains uncertain: he was referred to in public as either Manet's young brother-in-law or godson, and was only legitimised by Mme Manet in 1900.

This work has been understood as a homage primarily to the Old Masters of the Northern School (Paris 1983A, no. 102; Locke 2001; Rubin 2010). The image of a figure blowing bubbles has a long tradition in Western iconography as a comment on the transience of human life and an intimation of mortality. While Manet's teacher Thomas Couture's work of the same title (*c.* 1859; Metropolitan Museum of Art, New York) gives a meticulous description of the subject, Manet's is an austere composition, with the figure set frontally behind a parapet and against a sober, generalised background. The subdued palette and dense painterly technique reinforce the work's debt to the art of the past. The canvas's dependence on Dutch seventeenth-century models, mediated through the work of Jean-Siméon Chardin, most especially his *Soap Bubbles* (1737; National Gallery of Art, Washington), has been noted. Knowledge of Chardin and the influence upon his work of Dutch seventeenth-century art was widespread in France by the early 1860s. Furthermore, Manet had demonstrated an early interest in eighteenth-century French art, notably that of Watteau and Chardin (Proust 1996, p. 15), and had the opportunity to study Chardin's painting when it appeared in the Laperlier sale in Paris on 11 April 1867.

It has been suggested that Manet purposefully used this treatment of his young 'relation' as a means to look again at Dutch seventeenth-century art as an important alternative source for both his technical and compositional explorations (see Lawrence W. Nichols in the present volume, pp. 66–71; Fried 1996, p. 109). However, Manet's interpretation of the theme, stripped of narrative incident, is much sparer than either Chardin's model or the almost contemporaneous treatment of the subject by Couture. Manet gives no clue to location and invests the scene with as few attributes as possible to convey his theme: the bowl and the bubble on the end of a straw must suffice. The absence of direct interaction between model and viewer draws attention to such formal elements as the richly articulated paint surfaces and the limited palette. Although these elements perhaps suggest a sense of being out of time and thus seemingly contradict Manet's 'modern' programme, the work's use of an identifiable model and its reference to Chardin, whose 'feeling for truth' Manet admired, according to Antonin Proust (Proust 1996, p. 31), suggest that its Realist credentials were guaranteed. This uneasy balance between reference to an Old Master and the contemporary can also be found in other paintings by Manet of the 1860s, such as *The Old Musician* (1862; National Gallery of Art, Washington).

Léon posed for seventeen works made during the 1860s and early 1870s, including *Boy with a Sword* (1861; Metropolitan Museum of Art, New York), *Fishing* (cat. 3), *Young Man Peeling a Pear* (fig. 3), *The Velocipede* (cat. 11), *The Luncheon* (cat. 10) and *Interior at Arcachon* (cat. 12). MAS

10
THE LUNCHEON, 1868
Oil on canvas, 118.3 × 154 cm
Signed at centre: E. Manet
Bayerische Staatsgemäldesammlungen, Munich: Neue Pinakothek

SELECTED EXHIBITIONS: Paris Salon 1869, no. 1617; Brussels 1869, no. 755; Paris 1884, no. 48; Paris 1983A, no. 109; London 2004B, unnumbered
SELECTED REFERENCES: RWI, no. 135; London 2004B

LONDON ONLY

The Luncheon uses as its three models the sixteen-year-old Léon Leenhoff, dramatically forced up against the picture plane and staring disconcertingly beyond the viewer; the artist Auguste Rousselin (a pupil of Gleyre and Couture), who painted portraits, horses and genre pictures and had his debut at the Salon in 1863; and an unidentified woman. Claude Monet initially posed for the seated male figure. In an earlier iteration of the composition, a female figure was included on the extreme left, possibly Suzanne Manet. The location and precise date of execution of the composition are uncertain. An X-ray of the canvas revealed that the scene was originally unambiguously set in an artist's studio lit by large north lights in the background on the right. In the final version, Manet replaced these with a framed painting or mirror and a new window on the left, through which a sailing boat and a steamer can be seen. This has led to the suggestion that the interior is derived from that of the Hôtel Folkestone at Boulogne-sur-Mer, where the Manet family summered in 1868 (London 2004B, pp. 101–05).

Despite the overt modernity of Léon's outfit, the painting retains specific references to Old Master paintings. For his composition, Manet looked to seventeenth-century Dutch prototypes, specifically Vermeer, although the informal arrangement of the figures may also suggest the eighteenth-century conversation piece or group portrait on a modest scale produced by such French artists as Jean-Baptiste Charpentier and Charles Lepeintre and in England by Hogarth and Zoffany. For the still-life, the model appears to be Chardin (Fried 1996, pp. 105, 109; London 2004B, pp. 106–11). Technically and tonally, with the rich blacks and the subtle range of whites and greys arranged rhythmically across the composition, Manet refers again to the art of Velázquez.

The Luncheon is possibly one of the most enigmatic works in Manet's *oeuvre* (see Locke 2001, pp. 128–34; London 2004B, pp. 99–101). Although it portrays a domestic scene, the two principal protagonists are disengaged, denying the scene any apparent narrative. The composition is majestically static, and yet the pose and position of Léon implies his imminent departure from the scene. The work is possibly an affirmation of Manet's interpretation of Realism in two senses. Studio props more appropriate to the Romantic painters of an earlier generation but still to be found in the studios of Manet's fellow Realists perhaps make an ironic allusion to the Realists' confused adherence to the new doctrine. Secondly, Manet revisits the subject of the end of a meal that Courbet had addressed in his large 'manifesto' painting *After Dinner at Ornans* (1849; Palais des Beaux-Arts, Lille). By reducing that work's scale and relocating it to an apparently urban setting, Manet declares his reading of the Realist programme as one that is unequivocally engaged with the representation of contemporary, urban, bourgeois France. MAS

11
THE VELOCIPEDE, 1871
Oil on canvas, 53 × 20 cm
Private collection, Paris

SELECTED EXHIBITIONS: Martigny 1996, no. 35
SELECTED REFERENCES: RWI, no. 171

This painting of a young man jauntily riding what is probably a velocipede, or 'bone-shaker', was identified by Léon Leenhoff as a picture of himself in the inventory of Manet's studio that he made immediately after the artist's death in 1883 (Leenhoff Inventory, vol. 1, no. 79). Léon also records that the work was 'painted in the Rue Guyot around 1871'. However, Manet moved his studio from the Rue Guyot to 51 Rue de Saint-Pétersbourg in September 1870, and the reference to the sea in the background might suggest that the painting was made in March 1871, when Manet and his family were staying at Arcachon on the Atlantic coast (see cat. 12). The composition originally encompassed a small greyhound on the right (RWI, no. 172). Despite its unfinished status, the work was included in the Manet studio sale of 1884, where it was acquired by a private collector.

Léon rides a quintessentially modern device. The velocipede was developed during the 1860s as the first bicycle to be equipped with pedals. These were mounted on the larger, front wheel. Both the frame and the wheels were made of wood and the ride was consequently notoriously uncomfortable. Despite the bicycle craze of 1868, the velocipede was soon overtaken by new advances in materials and design.

On one level *The Velocipede* presents a scene unequivocally taken from contemporary life. The painting shows speed being achieved by modern mechanical means, an idea originally reinforced by the inclusion of the greyhound running competitively at the velocipedist's side, an image in common currency among caricaturists of the later 1860s illustrating the properties of this new mode of transport. However, by using a recognisable sitter as his model, Manet makes the painting into a 'portrait in motion'. Thus it is related to similar representations of movement through the picture space, such as Manet's treatments of Isabelle Lemmonier (cats 61, 62) and Berthe Morisot (cat. 19), which inhabit that ambiguous zone between straight portraiture and genre scene. MAS

12
INTERIOR AT ARCACHON, 1871
Oil on canvas, 39.4 × 53.7 cm
Sterling and Francine Clark Art Institute, Williamstown, Massachusetts

SELECTED EXHIBITIONS: Paris 1983A, no. 127
SELECTED REFERENCES: RWI, no. 170

Interior at Arcachon was made during March 1871, while Manet was staying at the seaside town with his family following the Seige of Paris during the Franco-Prussian War and the subsequent Paris Commune. The work records two people who regularly sat for the artist (see cats 4–6, 9–10) at leisure within the mid-nineteenth-century domestic interior of the Chalet Servanti at 41 Avenue Ste-Marie. Léon Leenhoff pauses in his reading and draws on a cigarette while the artist's wife Suzanne contemplates the view of the wide bay of Arcachon, the subject of several small, rapidly executed works that Manet also made that month (RWI, nos 165–69). A pen-and-ink drawing (Fogg Art Museum, Cambridge, Mass., RWII, no. 345) shows that the relative positions of the sitters within the composition have been modified, with Léon becoming more recessive and engaging more equally with the figure of Suzanne (Paris 1983A, nos 127, 128). The work seems to share the interest that Degas displayed in 1862–72 in making portraits of individuals in typical poses within characteristic environments.

Interior at Arcachon also contributes in two important ways to the artist's programme for a new, modern art informed by a reassessment of Realism. The painting's modest scale and its subject-matter make reference to seventeenth-century Dutch genre scenes and eighteenth-century conversation pieces (see cats 7, 10), thus placing it squarely within the group of works dating from the 1860s in which references to the art of the past provided a starting point for composition, handling of paint and choice of tonalities, liberating Manet from the ruling academic aesthetic and enabling him to forge a new style of painting appropriate to the modern age. Intriguingly, the open window with the sunlit bay beyond and the less closely applied brushwork and more informal composition presage Manet's careful consideration of Impressionism during the early 1870s (see cats 8, 25).

Equally, *Interior at Arcachon* presents a modern subject: leisure. Cultivated by the recently enriched urban bourgeoisie, then benefiting from greater access to sources of unearned income, leisure as a hallmark of modern Parisian life had been recorded by Manet as early as 1862 in *Music in the Tuileries Gardens* (cat. 26), and was to continue to be addressed in such works as *Boating* (1874; Metropolitan Museum of Art, New York) and *Chez le Père Lathuille – en plein air* (cat. 60). *Interior at Arcachon* transposes the modern subject of leisure to the Atlantic coast yet retains overt references to its urban source through the identity of its two Parisian sitters. By using actual identifiable individuals to act out the narrative scene, Manet confirms its contemporaneity. MAS

13
THE SMOKER, 1866
Oil on canvas, 100.3 × 81.3 cm
Signed right: Manet
Lent by the Minneapolis Institute of Arts. Gift of Bruce B. Dayton

SELECTED EXHIBITIONS:
Paris 1867, no. 49;
Paris 1884, no. 26
SELECTED REFERENCES:
RWI, no. 112

Manet had met the landscape painter Joseph Gall, sitter for *The Smoker*, in 1861, when the two artists had studios at 81 Rue Guyot. Gall (b. 1807) exhibited at the Salon from 1842 to 1876. *The Smoker* was probably executed in 1866; Zola records that it was only recently finished in his article on Manet published on 1 January 1867.

The subject of a smoker was common in Dutch seventeenth-century art, and indeed Manet is known to have made a copy in 1858 in the Musée du Louvre of *The Smoker*, then attributed to Adriaen Brouwer (RWI, no. 17; Private collection). However, he apparently shifted the meaning from life's transience to life's simple pleasures. This nineteenth-century meaning also underlies his treatment of smoking in such works as *Interior at Arcachon* (cat. 12), *Stéphane Mallarmé* (cat. 30) and *Le Bon Bock* (1873; Philadelphia Museum of Art). Given his close friendship with Baudelaire, Manet's painting may have been engendered by the poet's use of such imagery as an escape from harsh reality, as in *Les Paradis artificiels* (1860), or as consolation against sorrow and weariness, as in 'La Pipe' (*Les Fleurs du mal*, 1857).

The Smoker can be seen as a 'pendant' to *The Reader* (1861; Saint Louis Art Museum), made five years earlier and using the same model. In both paintings the figure is set against a neutral ground and dominates the composition, like other near-contemporaneous but full-length images of self-absorbed figures such as the two paintings of 'philosophers' (*Beggar with a Duffle Coat* and *Beggar with Oysters*, 1865/67; Art Institute of Chicago). Painted the year after Manet's visit to Madrid, *The Smoker*'s palette and technique reflect the influence of Spanish seventeenth-century art, although the uncompromisingly frontal position adopted by Gall, very close to the front of the picture plane, gives the work a sense of immediacy.

The Smoker was shown in Manet's solo exhibition in 1867 and again in the memorial exhibition of 1884. It was initially purchased by Eugène Pertuiset (see cat. 46), and was subsequently in the collection of the operatic baritone Jean-Baptiste Faure. MAS

14
PORTRAIT OF EVA GONZALÈS, *c.* 1879
Pastel on paper, 43 × 34.5 cm
Signed lower right: Manet
Private collection

SELECTED REFERENCES:
RWII, no. 16

15
EVA GONZALÈS, 1870
Oil on canvas,
191.1 × 133.4 cm
Signed and dated on the rolled canvas: Manet 1870
The National Gallery, London. Sir Hugh Lane Bequest, 1917

SELECTED EXHIBITIONS:
Paris Salon 1870, no. 1852;
Paris 1884, no. 56
SELECTED REFERENCES:
RWI, no. 154

The daughter of the novelist, playwright and journalist Emanuel Gonzalès, Eva (1843–1883) trained with Charles Chaplin. She was introduced to Manet by Alfred Stevens (see cat. 54) in February 1869 and became his only formal pupil. Unlike Berthe Morisot, who regarded her as a rival for Manet's advice, instruction and affection, Gonzalès openly proclaimed herself to be the artist's student (Rouart 1987, p. 44). She was a gifted artist and, despite adopting a somewhat Impressionist style in the early 1870s, she remained a regular exhibitor at the Salon; she had an exhibition at the Galerie Georges Petit in 1883, and a posthumous retrospective at La Vie moderne the following year.

Unlike his representations of Berthe Morisot (cats 16–19), Marcellin Desboutin (cat. 20) and Carolus-Duran (cat. 21), in which the artists have been taken out of their discrete professional contexts to act as members of contemporary bourgeois society, Manet shows Gonzalès at work in front of her easel (Armstrong 2002, pp. 184–89; Rubin 2010, pp. 161–63). The portrait, painted in Manet's studio at 81 Rue Guyot, was probably started in February 1869. After a painful gestation, involving numerous sittings, it was finally finished by 12 March 1870 (Rouart 1987, pp. 44, 45). It was shown at the Salon of that year, where it received the usual mixed critical reception. Duret, however, recognised that it proclaimed Manet as 'an innovator, one of the rare beings who has his own view on nature and who, for that reason, is very much alive' (Hamilton 1969, p. 147). Even Berthe Morisot found words of praise: 'Manet has never done anything as good as his portrait of Mademoiselle Gonzalès' (Rouart 1987, p. 49).

This is not a straightforward work. Gonzalès puts the finishing touches to an already framed flower piece; the peony on the ground, a flower personalised by Manet in still-lifes of the 1860s, and the half-rolled canvas, which bears Manet's signature, indicate the presence of her teacher. Her pose, the colour of her dress and the brilliant fluidity of the brushwork may make reference to the work of Goya, notably *The Marquesa de Villafranca Painting Her Husband* (1804; Museo del Prado, Madrid). The veritable cascade of Gonzalès's white dress, which dominates the composition, echoes Manet's use of a single light tone to communicate an elision between white and light, a device that he had already explored in *Lady with a Fan* (cat. 31), *Reading* (1865–73; Musée d'Orsay, Paris) and *The Balcony* (fig. 11; see cat. 34). Radical within the context of contemporary French art, this appreciation of the dual qualities of the colour white may have been inspired by James McNeill Whistler's controversial *Little White Girl*. Subsequently entitled *Symphony in White No. 1: The White Girl* (fig. 7), this painting was exhibited in the 1863 Salon des Refusés.

Gonzalès married Manet's friend the graphic artist Henri Guérard (1846–1887) in 1879. Manet probably made his ravishing head-and-shoulders pastel portrait of her at the end of the 1870s, as part of a series of pastel portraits of beautiful women (see cats 40, 58 and Leah Lehmbeck in the present volume, pp. 50–57). Pastel's ease of execution appealed to the ailing artist since it produced brilliant results without the physical exertion demanded of painting in oil. These pastels also reflect Manet's admiration for the expert manipulation of the medium in eighteenth-century French art. MAS

16
BERTHE MORISOT WITH A BOUQUET OF VIOLETS, 1872

Oil on canvas, 55.5 × 40.5 cm
Signed and dated upper right: Manet 72
Musée d'Orsay, Paris. Acquis avec la participation du Fonds du Patrimoine, de la Fondation Meyer, de Chine Times Group et d'un mécénat coordonné par le quotidien Nikkei, 1998

SELECTED EXHIBITIONS:
Paris 1983A, no. 130; Martigny 1996, no. 29; Madrid 2003, no. 89; New York 2003, no. 156; Paris 2011A, no. 95
SELECTED REFERENCES:
RWI, no. 179

17
BERTHE MORISOT IN MOURNING, 1874

Oil on canvas, 60 × 48 cm
Private collection

SELECTED EXHIBITIONS:
Paris 1983A, no. 144; Martigny 1996, no. 34
SELECTED REFERENCES:
RWI, no. 228

LONDON ONLY

Berthe Morisot (1841–1895), the daughter of a high-ranking civil servant, was a talented artist. She trained under, among others, Joseph Guichard and Achille Oudinot, and exhibited for the first time at the Salon of 1864 and from 1874 at all but one of the Impressionist exhibitions. Acquainted with Bracquemond and Fantin-Latour, she was introduced to Manet at the Musée du Louvre in either June or July 1868, and subsequently frequented the Manets' Thursday soirées with her artist sister Edma and her mother. An informal student of Manet, her relationship with the artist was close but bound by bourgeois convention, and productive and creative for both parties. She first sat to Manet in September 1868 for *The Balcony* (fig. 11; see cat. 34) and subsequently served as model for ten other oil paintings (see cats 18, 19), two watercolours and three prints created between the late summer of 1868 and the end of 1874, when she married Manet's brother Eugène (Lille 2002, pp. 440–71).

Both *Berthe Morisot with a Bouquet of Violets* and *Berthe Morisot in Mourning* present apparently straight portraits of the sitter, two of seven such treatments. *Berthe Morisot with a Bouquet of Violets* was made in 1872 with apparently no more than two sittings (Paris 1983A, no. 130; Copenhagen 1989, no. 25; Lille 2002, no. 165; Paris 2011A, pp. 185–86). A virtuoso technical feat, this immediate, brilliant and direct image presents Morisot dressed in the height of fashion, adopting a format that Manet was to employ extensively in the series of pastel portraits of beautiful, fashionably dressed women that he made during the final years of his life (cats 14, 40, 58). Embedded within the image and its predominant use of black are more complex messages. The portrait summarises the object of Manet's aesthetic regard and records the physical attributes of a fellow professional artist. Equally, it encapsulates Manet's appreciation of Baudelairean modernity, to which he had already given pictorial form in his portrait of Jeanne Duval (cat. 31). Hence it stands as an example of Manet's move away from dependence upon the Old Masters as he developed a style of painting commensurate with Baudelaire's definition of the modern as proclaimed through the latest fashions (Paul Valéry, in Paris 1932, pp. xiv–xv; Armstrong 2002, pp. 175–78).

Berthe Morisot in Mourning was made in the wake of the sitter's father's death on 24 January 1874 (Lille 2002, no. 170). Morisot rests her face on her right hand in a traditional representation of mourning, and her hollow cheeks, sunken eyes and black mourning gown and hat, complete with a long mourning veil, intensify the viewer's sense of her loss. Like *Berthe Morisot with a Bouquet of Violets*, the painting was executed at immense speed and with great energy, its elements loosely brushed in and barely resolved. With its predominant but appropriate use of black, the work is a straight portrait but also an image of the darker, more fragile side of Morisot's personality, which Manet had also captured in another 'dark' painting, *Portrait of Berthe Morisot with a Veil* (Musée du Petit Palais, Geneva), made between 1872 and 1874. MAS

18
THE REPOSE (PORTRAIT OF BERTHE MORISOT), 1870

Oil on canvas, 150.2 × 114 cm
Signed on the corner of the Japanese print: Manet
Museum of Art, Rhode Island School of Design, Providence. Bequest of Mrs Stuyvesant Vanderbilt Gerry

SELECTED EXHIBITIONS:
Paris Salon 1873, no. 998; Paris 1884, no. 57; Paris 1983A, no. 121
SELECTED REFERENCES:
RWI, no. 158

TOLEDO ONLY

This second full-length representation of Berthe Morisot was started in the early summer of 1870, a year after Manet had undertaken the equally monumental portrait of Eva Gonzalès (cat. 15). Ambitious in its scale, *The Repose* was made in Morisot's studio (the framed work behind Morisot's head is an *ukiyo-e* triptych print by Kuniyoshi), and was the product of lengthy and seemingly tortuous sittings (Paris 1983A, no. 121). The painting was intended for the Salon of 1871, which was annulled. It was accepted two years later with *Le Bon Bock* (1873; Philadelphia Museum of Art) (Lille 2002, no. 161; Paris 2011A, p. 185).

Portrait or genre painting? The work was exhibited in 1873 under the title 'Repose', making no reference to the identity of the sitter. However, certain critics, including Paul Mantz and Théodore de Banville, clearly referred to it as a portrait, the latter declaring it to be 'an engaging portrait which holds our attention and which imposes itself on our imagination by an intense character of modernity' (Hamilton 1969, pp. 169, 172). Indeed, in this work Manet's determination to create a meaningful image of modernity seems to have led him to collapse straight portraiture into genre painting through a series of complex literary and pictorial references. On the one hand, the modernity of the work is articulated by Morisot's fashionable, tight-waisted summer dress. It takes centre stage within the composition, a device that Manet had already explored in his portraits of Jeanne Duval (cat. 31), Eva Gonzalès (cat. 15) and Mme de Nittis (cat. 24) and in the genre painting *Reading* (1867–73; Musée d'Orsay, Paris), in which Suzanne plays the leading role (Armstrong 2002, pp. 194–98). As noted elsewhere (see cats 15, 31), Manet's espousal of high fashion within his female portraits aligns his art with Baudelaire's articulation of the properties of modern beauty (Dolan 1997). On the other hand, Manet's concentration on the expanse of Morisot's white dress also demonstrates his application of Whistler's innovative elision between white and light, as explored in his three *Symphonies in White* (1862, 1863 and 1865; see fig. 7).

Whistler may also be relevant to Manet's choice of subject and its visualisation in the form of the reclining Morisot, for, in a print made in 1863, Whistler associated the image of a half-seated, half-reclining woman (*Weary*, 1863, drypoint and roulette; Singletary 2012) with physical and emotional states.

Insofar as the painting is also a representation of an individual, in this case, a practising artist, the work could also be seen as a dialogue between two artists. With no recourse to the attributes of her profession, unlike Eva Gonzalès, her 'rival' for Manet's attention, Morisot with her air of reverie suggests that Manet appreciated Baudelaire's recognition of art's potential to provide an escape from mundane existence, which in the case of Morisot meant her bourgeois milieu (Singletary 2012, p. 61).

In comparison with the more heavily and closely painted *The Balcony* (fig. 11), *The Repose* has a looser technique akin to that used by Morisot herself. It seems possible that Manet was emulating Morisot's more open brushwork in recognition of her own achievements as a painter. Significantly, Manet must have thought *The Repose* sufficiently finished to enter the public domain at the Salon of 1873, although its apparent lack of resolution did engender negative criticism. MAS

19
BERTHE MORISOT, 1868–69, 1870–71
Oil on fabric, 74 × 60 cm
Cleveland Museum of Art. Bequest of Leonard C. Hanna Jr, 1958.34

SELECTED EXHIBITIONS:
Baltimore 1999, no. 35
SELECTED REFERENCES:
RWI, no. 138

This rapidly executed painting is generally regarded as another straight portrait of Berthe Morisot (see cats 16, 17). The date of its execution is uncertain, with opinion divided between 1868–69, the year during which Morisot sat for *The Balcony* (fig. 11; see cat. 34) or the winter of 1870–71. If the latter is correct, the painting was created at a time when both Manet and Morisot had remained in Paris during the Seige (Lille 2002, no. 163; Paris 2011A, p. 185).

In contrast to her dress and pose in cats 16 and 17, Morisot is shown here in winter outdoor attire against a neutral background. She moves across the picture space, casting a brief glance in the viewer's direction before passing out of the frame. This transient quality places *Berthe Morisot* between the straight portraits of her clutching a bouquet of violets (cat. 16) or in mourning (cat. 17) and her presence as model in a genre scene such as *The Balcony* and *The Repose* (cat. 18). Manet is apparently exploring an innovative form of portraiture, which positions a known sitter between a straight portrait and an actor within a scene of contemporary life. Perhaps deriving inspiration from the *intimiste* portraits of Whistler and Degas, he was to pursue this hybrid portrait/genre approach later in the 1870s in his representations of Isabelle Lemonnier (cats 61, 62).

Berthe Morisot was neither exhibited during Manet's lifetime nor in the 1884 memorial exhibition, suggesting that the work was considered 'unfinished'. However, the technique and application of colour are seemingly carefully considered: Morisot's figure is robustly modelled with long, broad brush strokes; the violet-blue of her hat is echoed in her left sleeve; and the articulation of light on her collar is caught in two deft, thin strokes of white. The work is less resolved than *The Balcony*, and, if made in 1870–71, possibly reflects the influence of the sitter herself, since by this date she was beginning to adopt a looser handling of paint, indicating her eventual engagement with the rapid brushwork and 'plein-air' execution of the Impressionists. MAS

20
THE ARTIST: PORTRAIT OF MARCELLIN DESBOUTIN, 1875
Oil on canvas, 192 × 128 cm
Signed and dated bottom right: Manet 1875
Museu de São Paulo Assis Chateaubriand, São Paulo

SELECTED EXHIBITIONS:
Paris 1876; Paris 1884, no. 78; Paris 1983A, no. 146; Martigny 1996, no. 46; New York 2003, no. 158
SELECTED REFERENCES:
RWI, no. 244

The writer, painter and brilliant engraver Marcellin Desboutin (1823–1902) met Manet on his return to Paris in the early 1870s following financial ruin in Italy. He frequented the Cafés Guerbois and Nouvelle Athènes, and enjoyed close friendships with the Impressionists, especially Degas and Renoir, exhibiting at the Second Impressionist Exhibition in 1876.

This painting was probably made in Manet's studio in the Rue de Saint-Pétersbourg between May and August 1875 (Martigny 1996). As with his *Self-portrait* (cat. 2) and his representations of Berthe Morisot (cats 16–19) and Carolus-Duran (cat. 21), Manet does not present his sitter with the attributes of his profession. Furthermore, rather than the dishevelled bohemian who appears in Degas's *The Absinthe Drinker* (1876; Musée d'Orsay, Paris), Desboutin is presented on a monumental scale, within a neutral setting, modestly dressed and dignified, with a furled umbrella under his arm, filling his pipe and accompanied by his dog. According to Antonin Proust, Manet considered that the portrait represented a type rather than a specific individual: 'I do not presume to have summarised an epoch, but to have painted the most extraordinary character in the *quartier*. I have painted Desboutin with as much passion as Baudelaire' (Proust 1996, p. 51).

Despite the artist Jacques-Emile Blanche's recollection of a garden chair in the composition, suggesting that the setting was initially intended to be out of doors, Desboutin's costume and the now unarticulated background indicate that the sitter has just walked in from an urban stroll. The portrait of Carolus-Duran posed within a landscape was made a year later but on the same monumental scale as the present work, and it is possible that Manet saw the two 'portraits' as pendants: two artist-friends, in interior and external settings, in the city and the countryside. Although the work's scale, neutral background and focus on the single figure refer back to such monumental figure paintings of the 1860s as *The Tragic Actor* (cat. 33) and the two representations of 'philosophers' (1864–67; Art Institute of Chicago), the replacement of heavy black and dense greys with browns and a range of ochres and the use of looser, almost nervous brushwork reflect Manet's engagement with the work of the Impressionists from the early 1870s.

Refused by the Salon of 1876, *The Artist* was shown in Manet's studio with *The Laundry* (1875; Am Römerholz, Winterthur) and other works two weeks before the opening of the official Salon. It received significant and positive critical acclaim, Armand Silvestre seeing the painting as worthy of Velázquez, and Castagnary, the celebrated Realist critic, declaring that had it not been refused it would have been one of the most powerful paintings in the Salon (Hamilton 1969, pp. 198–99). MAS

21
PORTRAIT OF CAROLUS-DURAN, 1876
Oil on canvas, 191.8 × 172.7 cm
The Trustees of the Barber Institute of Fine Arts, University of Birmingham

SELECTED EXHIBITIONS:
Paris 2011A, no. 117
SELECTED REFERENCES:
RWI, no. 245

LONDON ONLY

21B
CAROLUS-DURAN
PORTRAIT OF EDOUARD MANET, 1876
Oil on canvas, 64.7 × 54.6 cm
Museum of Art, Rhode Island School of Design, Providence

TOLEDO ONLY

ILLUSTRATED ON PAGE 92

Carolus-Duran (Charles Auguste Emile Durand, 1837–1917) was one of the most successful portrait painters in Paris in the second half of the nineteenth century and a teacher with his own independent atelier, established in 1872, which attracted students from Europe and America, including John Singer Sargent. Carolus-Duran was a close friend of Manet, and the two shared an interest in Spain and especially the art of Velázquez.

Manet's portrait of Carolus-Duran (cat. 21) was made during a fortnight in July 1876, when Manet was staying with Ernest Hoschedé, the department store magnate and patron of the Impressionists, at his country estate, the Château de Rottembourg at Montgeron, southeast of Paris (Wilson-Bareau 1991, p. 180). Carolus-Duran had a property in the vicinity and during the period of Manet's visit not only sat for this portrait but also made two records of Manet himself (cat. 21B and Musée d'Orsay, Paris). Both are sketches, although cat. 21B is more resolved, and both present Manet out of doors, making no reference to his profession but showing him as the man of fashion, complete with trilby hat and, in cat. 21B, a straw boater casually pushed back from his forehead. Although it is a sketch, the rich painterly technique of cat. 21B reflects the artists' shared enthusiasm for Spanish art as well as Carolus-Duran's appreciation of the licence of an oil sketch, which could not apply to his highly sought-after society portraits.

Carolus-Duran's intimate portrait of Manet stands in sharp contrast to Manet's presentation of him (Paris 2011A, pp. 194, 203). Set in the woodland of Hoschedé's domain, the *Portrait of Carolus-Duran*, like Manet's *Self-portrait* (cat. 2) and his treatment of Marcellin Desboutin (cat. 20), presents the artist without reference to his profession. Rather, through monumentality of scale and the swagger of pose – which is derived from Velázquez's *Portrait of Philip IV* (Museo del Prado, Madrid), an etching of which Manet made in 1862 from a copy of the painting now in the Musée du Louvre, Paris, or possibly from Van Dyck's *Portrait of Charles I at the Hunt*, which entered the French royal collection in 1775 – Carolus-Duran is transformed into a member of the landed gentry in command of the surrounding landscape, just as he was of his profession. Indeed, despite the work's unfinished state, the pose and the integration of figure and landscape suggest the English eighteenth-century portrait type of the sitter within the landscape favoured by Reynolds or Gainsborough. Manet would not only have known of their work through the publications of Gautier and Thoré-Bürger, but may also have studied examples at an exhibition of British portraits at the South Kensington Museum (Exhibition of National Portraits, 13 April – 22 August 1868) during his brief visit to London in late July to early August 1868.

Carolus-Duran's temporary absence from Montgeron, followed by Manet's return to Paris, led to the work's apparently unfinished state, with great sweeps of broad brushwork hastily describing costume and foliage. However, the finish of the sitter's features and the convincing unity between him and the landscape may indicate that Manet chose to take the portrait no further before presenting it to Carolus-Duran. *Portrait of Carolus-Duran* could be seen as a 'pendant' to *The Artist: Portrait of Marcellin Desboutin* (cat. 20), Manet's other full-length representation of an artist, which was made at almost the same time but is decidedly urban in its setting. MAS

22
PORTRAIT OF ALPHONSE MAUREAU, *c.* 1880
Pastel with gouache on canvas prepared with a gouache ground, 54.7 × 45.2 cm
Signed bottom right on curtain: Manet
Art Institute of Chicago. Gift of Edward L. Brewster, 1950.123

SELECTED EXHIBITIONS:
Paris 1884, no. 154
SELECTED REFERENCES:
RWII, no. 6

TOLEDO ONLY

23
PORTRAIT OF THE ANIMAL PAINTER LA ROCHENOIRE, 1882
Pastel on canvas, 55.3 × 35.6 cm
Private collection

SELECTED EXHIBITIONS:
Paris 1884, no. 149
SELECTED REFERENCES:
RWII, no. 66

Both Alphonse Maureau and Emile-Charles-Julien la Rochenoire were landscape and animal painters. Alphonse Maureau, whose work is similar to that of Gustave Caillebotte, was sufficiently associated with the Impressionists to have exhibited four works (nos 86–89) at their Third Exhibition held in 1877. His paintings were favourably received by the critic Roger Ballu: 'the four sketches are excellent, with a light, fine tonality' (Berson 1996, vol. 1, p. 126, and vol. 2, p. 75). Like the sketch in oils of the Irish writer George Moore (see cat. 32, fig. 5), *Portrait of Alphonse Maureau* shows the subject in the Café Nouvelle Athènes, which he frequented. Manet's treatment of la Rochenoire (1825–1899) equally belies his professional status. Trained with Léon Cogniet, Charles Gleyre and, informally, with Constant Troyon, he exhibited at the Salon from 1857 to 1878, associated with Daubigny, organised a committee in 1870, of which Manet was a member, to reform the Salon jury, and appears to have collected eighteenth-century pastels. Both of these pastel portraits were shown in the posthumous exhibition of 1884, the latter designated merely as 'Portrait' and lent by the sitter.

Alongside the Tuesday and Thursday soirées at home, Manet socialised in the cafés of Paris. After frequenting the more fashionable Cafés Tortoni and Bade on the Boulevard des Italiens, Manet switched his allegiance in *c.* 1866 to the Café Guerbois at 11 Grande Rue des Batignolles (now Avenue de Clichy), where key figures of the literary and artistic avant-garde gathered, including Zola (cat. 28), Astruc (cat. 27), Duranty, Fantin-Latour and the young proto-Impressionists, notably Monet (cat. 25) and Degas. However, it was his further move to the Café Nouvelle Athènes at 9 Place Pigalle in *c.* 1872 that marked the moment when café and café-cabaret subjects were to become part of his repertoire.

Of Manet's 89 recorded pastels (others may be lost), 57 were portraits of identified and unidentified women (see cats 40, 57), and only twelve of men. With one exception, these pastels were made in the closing years of his life. Manet's male sitters were primarily friends of his, such as his physician Dr Materne, the artist Constantin Guys, the musicians Chabrier and Cabaner, and the son of the restaurant proprietor Louis Gauthier-Lathuille (cat. 59). The majority present the sitter as the subject of a straight head-and-shoulders portrait, although two of René Maizeroy (Museum of Fine Arts, Boston; Art Institute of Chicago) show the figure in full length. While la Rochenoire shares the neutrality of his pose with his fellow artist Constantin Guys, the boldly patterned background recalls that of *Autumn* (cat. 55). The present representation of Maureau, dressed in contemporary attire, is however different, in that it casts the sitter in the role of a modern Parisian 'type': the café *habitué*. From the 1850s, cafés experienced significant change and expansion as part of the modernisation of Paris, becoming a neutral space for social, intellectual and amorous encounters (Reff 1982, pp. 73–75). Presented in this context, Maureau inhabits the transitional zone between straight portraiture and a scene of contemporary life, in contrast to Manet's earlier, more timeless presentation of another artist, Joseph Gall (cat. 13). MAS

24
IN THE GARDEN, 1870
Oil on canvas, 44.5 × 54 cm
Signed bottom right: Manet
Collections of Shelburne Museum, Shelburne, Vermont.
Gift of Mr Dunbar W. and Mrs Electra Webb Bostwick

SELECTED EXHIBITIONS: Paris 1884, no. 58; Paris 1983A, no. 122; Copenhagen 1989, no. 22
SELECTED REFERENCES: RWI, no. 155

There has been much discussion concerning the identity of the models in this work, its location, the date of its execution, the possible later insertion of the male figure, and the role that the painting plays within Manet's development towards a greater consideration of Impressionist procedures. Furthermore, if *In the Garden* does indeed represent an artist and his family, it is a striking translation of the traditional presentation of a practitioner.

The sitters may have been Berthe Morisot's artist-sister Edma, recently married, their brother Tiburce and Edma's four-month-old daughter, and the location the Morisots' garden at 16 Rue Franklin in Paris. If, as seems more likely, the sitters were instead the Italian artist Giuseppe de Nittis (1846–1884), who had moved to Paris in 1868, his wife Léontine Gruville (whom he married in 1869) and their child, the scene would be located in the garden of the de Nittis villa, between Reuil and Saint-Germain-en-Laye, to the west of Paris. The case for arguing that the sitters were indeed de Nittis and his family rests on the fact that Manet stayed with de Nittis in the summer of 1870 (Proust 1996, p. 36), and that Manet gave the painting to de Nittis, who greatly appreciated the work (Tabarant Archive), giving Manet a painting of his own in return. De Nittis also served on the selection committee for the 1884 memorial exhibition for Manet.

If it is a representation of an artist and his family, this scene presents a radical revision of the projection of the role and status of an artist. No longer working at an easel in a studio, de Nittis is shown surrounded by his family, partaking of the newfound pleasures of the leisured life that had become available to the expanding middle classes during the course of the nineteenth century.

It has been argued that the luminosity, the angle of Manet's viewpoint and the truncated perspective suggest that *In the Garden* may have been an early exercise in creating a composition out of doors directly in front of the motif (Copenhagen 1989, no. 22). However, in contrast to the immediacy of execution and the integration of the figures, garden and surrounding atmosphere in *The Monet Family in Their Garden at Argenteuil* (cat. 25), made four years later, the density of impasto and the handling of paint in the present work are in large measure characteristic of the artist's *oeuvre* of the previous decade. MAS

25
THE MONET FAMILY IN THEIR GARDEN AT ARGENTEUIL, 1874
Oil on canvas, 61 × 99.7 cm
Signed bottom right: Manet
Lent by the Metropolitan Museum of Art, New York.
Bequest of Joan Whitney Payson, 1975 (1976.201.14)

SELECTED EXHIBITIONS: Paris 1983A, no. 141; Baltimore 1999, no. 36
SELECTED REFERENCES: RWI, no. 227

This work, started in late July 1874, shows the painter Claude Monet (1840–1926) with his first wife Camille and their son Jean in the garden of their villa at Argenteuil, the town where Monet had settled after his return from London in 1871 (Madeline 2011). The family is mirrored by a cockerel, a hen and a chick. The relationship between Monet and Manet dates back to 1865, becoming firmly established two years later. Monet frequented the Cafés Guerbois and Nouvelle Athènes and the Manets' Thursday soirées. He rushed to Manet's bedside ten days before he died on 30 April 1883, participated in Manet's funeral cortège, and led the ultimately successful 1889–90 campaign to acquire *Olympia* (fig. 9) for the French State. Manet returned Monet's friendship and admiration: 'there is no member of the School of 1830 who can establish a landscape like he can. And then water. He is the Raphael of water' (Proust 1996, p. 46).

Manet spent much of July and August 1874 at his family's property at Gennevilliers, on the opposite bank of the Seine from Argenteuil, and while there he created two quintessential records of modern bourgeois leisure: *Argenteuil* (Musée des Beaux-Arts, Tournai) and *Boating* (Metropolitan Museum of Art, New York). He also made two paintings (and a sketch) of his friend Monet, one showing him painting on his floating studio (Neue Pinakothek, Munich), and the other, the present work, showing Monet as *pater familias* and horticulturalist, two roles that Monet was to consolidate after he had settled at Giverny in 1883. The Munich painting might stand as a pictorial manifesto for the 'new' painting revealed at the First Impressionist Exhibition the previous April. The present work, in contrast to Renoir's record made the previous year of Monet painting at his easel in the same garden at Argenteuil (Wadsworth Atheneum, Hartford), is an image of bourgeois leisure; it dismisses any overt reference to Monet's profession, mirroring Manet's earlier representation of another artist, Giuseppe de Nittis, and his family (cat. 24), whom he had similarly brought out of the studio into the manicured garden of a villa outside Paris.

A painting by Monet showing Manet at work on this painting in his garden (location unknown), and a 'portrait' by Renoir of Mme Monet and Jean (fig. 39), seen from a viewpoint slightly further to the right, confirm that Manet executed his work en plein air in front of the motif (see Ottawa 1997, pp. 130–31; and Colin B. Bailey in the present volume, pp. 64–65). This gives the present work a freshness of touch, an immediacy of execution and an integration of figures and surroundings, characteristics absent from the image of the de Nittis family.

At this moment Manet was involved in the interrogation of the nature of painting and the painting process, and its relationship to the past and to the contemporary: the figure as posed in the studio or as caught within the context of contemporary urban or rural environments. Manet's commitment to recording his artist-friend painting on his floating studio and tending his flowers while surrounded by the subjects of his art – wife, child and garden – elevates both works from mere portraiture to the representation of the subject and process of painting itself. MAS

26
MUSIC IN THE TUILERIES GARDENS, 1862
Oil on canvas, 76.2 × 118.1 cm
Signed and dated bottom right: Ed Manet 1862
The National Gallery, London. Sir Hugh Lane Bequest, 1917

SELECTED EXHIBITIONS: Paris 1863, no. 135; Paris 1867, no. 24; Paris 1884, no. 9; Paris 1983A, no. 38; Madrid 2003, no. 29
SELECTED REFERENCES: RWI, no. 51

LONDON ONLY

This multi-figured composition is both a group portrait and a painting of modern life. It is also a self-portrait of the artist. Manet included himself, standing partially cropped by the frame, on the extreme left of the picture, observing the viewer not the social gathering. By summarising his social and artistic worlds through his selection of 'actors', he also created a cultural 'self-portrait' that includes: the artists de Balleroy (with whom Manet had shared a studio), Fantin-Latour (who was to introduce him to the Morisot sisters, see cat. 16), Eugène-Cyrille Brunet (the sculptor, see cat. 36) and Charles Monginot (the painter); the critics and writers Astruc (see cat. 27), Champfleury, Gautier, Baudelaire and Baron Taylor (a leading proponent of Spanish art in France); the musician Jacques Offenbach (see cat. 60); and the society figures Mme Loubens and Mme Lejosne (at whose salon Manet met both Bazille and Baudelaire). Members of Manet's own family may also be seen at the centre of the composition (Paris 1983A, no. 38; Armstrong 2002; Dolan 2012).

The sitters/actors are assembled in the Tuileries Gardens, the extension of Napoleon III's palace where 'the music, which was played twice weekly, drew a fashionable and elegant crowd' who relaxed under the trees on recently introduced wrought-iron chairs. At one level the painting respects the tradition of group portraits of people with shared values that evolved in Dutch seventeenth-century art and was explored extensively during the nineteenth century (Bailey 1997, p. 68; Bonnet 2007). However, the painting has many complex layers of meaning, demonstrating perhaps most consistently the shared aesthetic concerns of Manet and Baudelaire, whom the artist had met in 1858 (see cat. 31) and whom he regularly accompanied to the Tuileries Gardens (Proust 1996, p. 29). Since 1846, Baudelaire had been investigating the meaning and implications of 'modernity', which included identifying the appropriate subject-matter and mode of expression of a new art, a redefinition of beauty and a consideration of the relationship between music, literature and the visual arts. These he summarised in poetry, prose poems and essays, notably in 'The Painter of Modern Life', eventually published in 1863. *Music in the Tuileries Gardens* focuses on male and female high fashion, that manifestation, according to Baudelaire, of transient beauty, which intimated the heroism of modern life, and beauty's unchanging eternal counterpart. The person capable of comprehending this dual beauty was the dandy, or *flâneur*, the role that Manet adopts for his self-portrait on the far left. The painting's composition and format also underscore its commitment to presenting a 'scene of contemporary life'. In contrast to Courbet's *The Studio: A Real Allegory of Seven Years of My Life as a Painter* (1855; Musée d'Orsay, Paris), a monumental, carefully crafted allegory of his artistic life in which he is placed centre stage (Armstrong 2002, pp. 22–24), Manet's account is on a relatively small scale, distributing its protagonists seemingly informally across the entire picture plane and relegating the artist to the 'wings'. It has been proposed that the informality of the composition, while aware of Velázquez (Fried 1996), was derived from popular prints and the watercolours of Gavarni and Guys, both artists admired by Baudelaire. Finally, Manet's reference to music in the title, presumably to inform the viewer that the protagonists are listening to one of the twice-weekly open-air band concerts, not only highlights Manet's own interest in music, but also suggests Baudelaire's identification of music's formal, non-mimetic qualities, which, when translated into Manet's art, play off direct representation against abstract compositional components articulated through the repetition of a limited range of colours across the surface of the canvas and the uncompromised presence of brushwork.

The painting was made in Manet's 81 Rue Guyot studio in the summer or early autumn of 1862 (Locke 2001, p. 74). Locke has suggested that Manet employed carte-de-visite photographs for some of the sitters, and also that, given its autobiographical content, the work is a pendant of *Fishing* (cat. 3) (Locke 2001, p. 78). MAS

27
PORTRAIT OF ZACHARIE ASTRUC, 1866
Oil on canvas, 90.5 × 116 cm
Signed and dated left on a book:
Au poète Z. Astruc, son ami: Manet, 1866
Kunsthalle Bremen – Der Kunstverein in Bremen, inv. no. 88-1909/1

SELECTED EXHIBITIONS: Paris 1867, no. 43; Paris 1983A, no. 94
SELECTED REFERENCES: RWI, no. 92

LONDON ONLY

Zacharie Astruc (1833–1907) was a writer, critic, editor, composer, painter and, later, an officially honoured sculptor. He championed Courbet, Manet and the Impressionists. He met Manet between *c.* 1854/55 and 1857.

Portrait of Zacharie Astruc is one of a trilogy of portraits made between 1866 and 1868 of writers who provided Manet with crucial support in the form of friendship and critical reviews (see cats 28, 29; see also cat. 26) (see Armstrong 2002). The work represents an art-historical dialogue between artist and sitter, standing as a powerful testament to a friendship that was to provide Manet not only with the first considered defence of his art (in 1863), but also a critical commentary that contributed to the development of his personal artistic voice from the later 1850s and throughout the 1860s.

This complex painting appears to pay homage to the Old Masters. Although the pose that Astruc adopts is not conventionally that of a man of letters, his books – both ancient and modern – and the quills on the table recall the iconography of the writer extending back to the sixteenth century. Likewise, the somewhat more fluid brushwork, especially the treatment of the left hand, implies lessons learnt from Hals (see the essay by Lawrence W. Nichols in the present volume, pp. 66–71), while the scene glimpsed in the background on the left is derived from Titian. Equally important are the overall richness of the handling of the paint, the sombre, narrow tonal range, especially of the figure and the background on the right, and the relatively fluid brushwork. All point to the influence of Spanish art, notably Velázquez: Manet visited Spain in 1865, and Astruc was responsible for planning his trip meticulously.

However, the portrait also proclaims Astruc's commitment to the creation and support of a contemporary art that embraced modern idioms. His enthusiasm for Japanese art, with its emphasis on naturalism, novelty and modernity, characteristics that he recognised as directly relevant to contemporary French art, is acknowledged in the sewn book and the red lacquer tray. This parallels Manet's recourse to the Old Masters, which was merely the means by which he liberated his art from the technical and compositional constraints of the ruling academic aesthetic.

As with so many of Manet's representations of his family and friends, *Portrait of Zacharie Astruc* hovers between straight portraiture and genre painting. A known sitter is placed off-centre, allowing a domestic scene to be shown on the left. Although derived from Titian's *Venus of Urbino* (Galleria degli Uffizi, Florence), it is clearly being re-enacted by figures in mid-nineteenth-century dress within a space containing a strikingly nineteenth-century rocking chair. It is not clear whether the scene is a reflection in a mirror, a view through to another room or a painting hanging on the wall behind the table, but its inclusion reveals that Manet intended this work to be more than a mere portrait: this is an image of the sitter within his contemporary environment, and hence both a work that subscribed to the criterion of Realist portraiture and a scene of everyday life.

Astruc served as model for Manet's *Music Lesson* (1870; Museum of Fine Arts, Boston) and was one of Manet's literary and artistic friends to appear in *Music in the Tuileries Gardens* (cat. 26). MAS

28
EMILE ZOLA, 1868
Oil on canvas, 146.5 × 114 cm
Signed on the cover of the reprinted article: Manet
Musée d'Orsay, Paris. Donation de Mme Emile Zola, 1918

SELECTED EXHIBITIONS: Paris Salon 1868; Paris 1883, no. 304; Paris 1884, no. 42; Paris 1983A, no. 106; Basel 1999, no. 1; Madrid 2003, no. 82; New York 2003, no. 153; Paris 2011A, no. 83
SELECTED REFERENCES: RWI, no. 128

Emile Zola (1840–1902) was one of the most significant writers of the latter decades of the nineteenth century. Critic, novelist, playwright and political activist, he was the author of twenty novels gathered under the collective title *Les Rougon-Macquart*, which give a vivid, panoramic account of Second Empire France between 1851 and 1871. Zola met Manet after his defence of the artist in 1866, beginning a firm relationship that endured until Manet's death.

Emile Zola was made at Manet's request in January 1868. Intended for the Salon of that year, it was produced at great speed over the following two months, Zola reporting that he was sitting for the artist every afternoon (Paris 1983A, no. 106; Basel 1999, no. 1, and pp. 21–41; New York 2003, no. 153). The work was accepted at the Salon, and received significant critical acclaim. Manet gave the portrait to Zola.

Although purporting to represent the writer in his study, the portrait was in fact executed in Manet's studio at 81 Rue Guyot. As in *Portrait of Zacharie Astruc* (cat. 27), the iconography of the work generally conforms to the traditional representation of a writer. Zola is shown directly engaged with the worlds that he inhabits, literature and art criticism, and these are described through the writing equipment, the old and modern books clustered on the back of his writing table and the reprint of Zola's 1 January 1867 biographical and critical study of Manet. The presence of both author and artist on the reprint's cover indicates that Manet is as powerful a presence within the composition as his more youthful sitter. Indeed, the majority of the attributes displayed reflect Manet's interests and achievements. The print by Goya after Velázquez's *The Triumph of Bacchus* (Museo Nacional del Prado, Madrid) provided a source for Manet's *The Old Musician* (1862; National Gallery of Art, Washington) and summarises Manet's interest in the Old Masters, as does the print after Manet's *Olympia* (fig. 9) with its reference to Titian. The print of a sumo wrestler by Kuniaki II and the screen on the left reflect Manet's interest in Japanese art, which he shared with his contemporaries Astruc, Duret, Fantin-Latour and Whistler. Even the volume lying open in Zola's hand identifies Manet's interests, for it is the first in a series of articles published in the *Gazette des Beaux-Arts* on Goya's prints and deals with his copies after Velázquez (New York 2003, no. 153). As in cats 15 and 27, the accumulation of still-life detail serves as a means of creating what Nochlin has called the 'Realist specificity of the occasion' (Ottawa 1997, p. 71).

Despite its relatively conventional approach, the portrait's capacity to capture the spirit of the Realism demanded by the more advanced critics of the day and its innovative treatment of the figure were commented upon when it was exhibited at the Salon. Castagnary declared it 'one of the best portraits in the Salon' (Hamilton 1969, p. 123), and Ernest Hache praised Manet's truth to nature in announcing: '[he] paints what he sees, and as he sees it, and he sees truly' (Hamilton 1969, p. 125). Thoré-Bürger felt that 'the books ... were astonishingly realistic', and then identified the key characteristics of Manet's style: 'Certainly the technique is broad and generous. But the principal merit of the portrait, as in other works by Manet, is the light which circulates in this interior and which everywhere determines the modelling and the relief' (Hamilton 1969, p. 124). MAS

29
PORTRAIT OF THÉODORE DURET, 1868
Oil on canvas, 46.5 × 35.5 cm
Signed and dated lower left: Manet 68
Petit Palais, Musée des Beaux-Arts de la Ville de Paris

SELECTED EXHIBITIONS: Paris 1884, no. 43; Paris 1983A, no. 108; Madrid 2003, no. 83; New York 2003, no. 154; Paris 2011A, no. 84
SELECTED REFERENCES: RWI, no. 132

Théodore Duret (1838–1927) came from a family of cognac dealers. He was a committed Republican, and his private means permitted him to pursue a career as a journalist, author, art critic and keen traveller. His commitment to the new painting made him one of the first advocates of Manet and the Impressionists and an avid and lifelong collector of their work. He was also a connoisseur of Japanese art and knowledgeable about British contemporary art, including that of Whistler. Manet met Duret by chance in Madrid in the summer of 1865, and despite a negative critical text published in 1867, artist and writer established a close relationship: Duret wrote in defence of Manet, provided safe storage for some of his paintings during the Siege of Paris and the Commune, was executor of his will, and oversaw arrangements for his memorial exhibition at the Ecole des Beaux-Arts in 1884.

Portrait of Théodore Duret is one of three portraits that Manet made between 1866 and 1868 of writers who gave him crucial support in the form of critical reviews (see cats 27, 28). Duret probably commissioned the work in June 1868 (Wilson-Bareau 1991, p. 46) after attending the innumerable sittings that Zola had had to endure earlier that year for his own portrait (cat. 28), and paid for it with a case of cognac (Tabarant Archive). Like the other two portraits, the work reflects the influence of Spanish art, which is especially pertinent here given Manet's and Duret's shared enthusiasm for this school. The full-length standing figure, set against an unarticulated backdrop, painted within a relatively narrow tonal range and with long, fluid brush strokes, refers to Velázquez's treatment of single figures and, on a more modest scale, to works by Goya that Manet could have studied in Madrid and through engravings in Blanc's *Histoire des peintres de toutes les écoles* (Paris 1983A, no. 108; Loyrette 2002; New York 2003, no. 154).

Portrait of Théodore Duret encapsulates the modern, the enigmatic and the contradictory. Christened 'the last of the dandys' by Manet, Duret is presented as an elegantly dressed young man, kid glove in hand and sporting a cane. Just as in Whistler's portrait of him (1883–84; Metropolitan Museum of Art, New York), Duret is cast as the Baudelairean *flâneur* who graces modern Paris, always in transit, observing but unengaged, someone who has either just entered the space or is about to leave it, gloves half on and cane in hand.

Unlike the other two literary portraits in this 1866–68 trilogy, *Portrait of Théodore Duret* contains no conventional writer's attributes. The still-life of table, lacquer tray, carafe, glass, lemon and unidentifiable book has little explicit connection with the profession of the sitter. Instead they may represent Manet's own search, derived from Baudelaire, for an element of the timeless within images of contemporaneity.

The scale of the portrait is disturbing and runs counter to portrait conventions. The concept of the single figure seen slightly from below is generally reserved for life-size portraits that seek to communicate the status of the sitter through monumentalising strategies. Although these strategies have been adopted here, *Portrait of Théodore Duret* is very modest in scale, making it more akin to eighteenth-century English and French cabinet paintings. MAS

30
STÉPHANE MALLARMÉ, 1876
Oil on canvas, 27.5 × 36 cm
Signed bottom left: Manet (date added later)
Musée d'Orsay, Paris

SELECTED EXHIBITIONS: Paris 1884, no. 87; Paris 1983A, no. 149; Madrid 2003, no. 95; Paris 2011A, no. 116
SELECTED REFERENCES: RWI, no. 249

LONDON ONLY

The poet and critic Stéphane Mallarmé (1842–1898) was a leading figure of the Symbolist movement at the end of the nineteenth century; his experimental approach to language and poetic form was to have a major influence on twentieth-century art and literature. Mallarmé returned to Paris from Avignon in 1871, and was introduced two years later to Manet either by Philippe Burty or Nina de Callias. The friendship between the two men lasted until Manet's death, and included daily visits to the studio, with the opportunity to interrogate Manet on his painting practice and to meet such leading literary figures as Zola, and artists, notably the Impressionists. The sympathy that Mallarmé had for Manet's work was reflected in the supportive articles that he published in 1874 and 1876, commissions for illustrations to his poetic works (1875, 1876, 1880–81), and a profound understanding of the artist's modernity ('a complete vision of contemporary life'), his engagement with the challenge of plein-air painting and the significance of the critical issue of finish in his art.

This portrait acknowledges this friendship. It was in progress in the artist's 4 Rue de Saint-Pétersbourg studio by October 1876 and shows the poet reclining on a sofa against a faintly *japoniste* background in a pose similar to that of Berthe Morisot in *The Repose* (cat. 18) (Armstrong 2002, p. 225).

Unlike the relatively conventional treatments of the writers Astruc and Zola made in 1866 and 1868 respectively (cats 27, 28), this small yet exceptionally powerful portrait represents a new typology for the representation of the writer as a cultural figure. Mediated possibly by the neutral *Portrait of Théodore Duret* (cat. 29), Mallarmé is invested with only the subtlest indication of his profession. His right hand rests on some sheets of paper and a notebook with a marbled cover. However, he does not address these but rather gazes into the undefined space beyond the left edge of the canvas, cigar in hand in place of a writing tool, as a reference to modernity and contemporary leisure (see cats 12, 13). The focus of the composition is no longer the accumulation of literary attributes but the sitter's expression of internal reflection. Mallarmé has made the transition from the specificity of a portrait to the personification of creative activity – intellectual reverie. MAS

31
LADY WITH A FAN (JEANNE DUVAL), 1862
Oil on canvas, 80 × 113 cm
Signed bottom left: Manet
Szépművészeti Múzeum, Budapest

SELECTED EXHIBITIONS: Paris 1865, unnumbered; Paris 1983A, no. 27; Copenhagen 1989, no. 5; Madrid 2003, no. 32; Paris 2011A, no. 46
SELECTED REFERENCES: RWI, no. 48

TOLEDO ONLY

The genesis of this portrait is unclear. The Creole sitter, Jeanne Duval (*c.* 1820–1862), was the mistress and muse of the poet and critic Charles Baudelaire (1821–1867). They met in 1842. By the date of this portrait, their stormy and unstable relationship had deteriorated and Duval was in poor health, having suffered a stroke three years before. Created probably at the behest of the poet (Strauber, in Copenhagen 2006), the portrait may have belonged to the poet; it was recorded as being in Manet's studio on the artist's death. It was possibly exhibited for the first time in 1865 (Paris 1983A, no. 27; Copenhagen 1989, no. 5).

Although Baudelaire appears in *Music in the Tuileries Gardens* (cat. 26) and had two portrait heads etched by Manet, he never sat to the artist for a painted portrait despite the fact that he was probably the figure who, more than any other, most immediately informed Manet's understanding of modernity and inspired him to define his own formulation of the 'painter of modern life'.

As a statement about the emergence of Manet's idea of the modern, the portrait underlines the debt he owed to Baudelaire. Just as Baudelaire both provided a physical description of Duval and used her as a vehicle for his aesthetic meditations concerning a new literature appropriate to his age, so Manet encapsulates her physical presence as the sitter of the portrait and uses the image to probe the nature of femininity, the significance of fashion and the idea of modernity within the context of contemporary art, not least the transformation of the portrait to a modern 'tableau' (Strauber, in Copenhagen 2006, p. 99). Confronting a cheval mirror glimpsed on the extreme left, Jeanne reclines within an indeterminate space, adopting a pose that Manet was subsequently to revisit (see cat. 18). The dominance of the great crinoline skirt within the composition makes reference to Constantin Guys, mocks Xavier Winterhalter and illustrates Baudelaire's contention that the modern woman is only beautiful if attired in the highest of fashion. The poet's proposal of a new aesthetic based upon the ephemeral overturns traditional academic norms, and Manet appears to espouse it, by placing so much emphasis upon the extent of Duval's skirt in the painting (Dolan 1997). Given these Baudelairean connections, it could be argued that Manet's portrait of Jeanne Duval serves as a surrogate representation of the poet himself.

That the dress is white, and hence establishes the dominant colour note of the composition, brings another facet of Manet's definition of modernity into the portrait. Possibly echoing Whistler's recent use of white as the dominant colour in his controversial painting *Little White Girl* (subsequently entitled *Symphony in White No. 1*; fig. 7), Manet experiments with the capacity for a single, light tone to communicate an elision between white and light, a process that he was to work through in paintings made over the succeeding decade, such as *Reading* (1865–73; Musée d'Orsay, Paris), *The Balcony* (fig. 11) and *The Repose* (cat. 18).

Lady with a Fan brought to the fore the contemporary debate about Manet's finish. It is remarkably loosely worked, with areas such as the hem of the dress, the position of the paralysed foot and the description of the physical setting left unresolved. Yet Manet signed the painting and considered including it in the 1865 Galerie Martinet exhibition, suggesting that he found its level of 'unfinish' consonant with his own aesthetic of the modern. MAS

32
GEORGE MOORE IN THE ARTIST'S GARDEN, *c.* 1879
Oil on canvas, 54.6 × 45.1 cm
National Gallery of Art, Washington. Collection of Mr and Mrs Paul Mellon, 2006.128.24

SELECTED REFERENCES: RWI, no. 297

The Irish poet, playwright, novelist and critic George Moore (1852–1933) trained initially as an artist at the South Kensington Schools in London and, on his move to Paris in 1873, at the Ecole des Beaux-Arts under Cabanel and the Académie Julien. Having turned to writing, he rejected an early flirtation with the Decadent movement to become a leading exponent of Naturalist literature in such novels as *A Modern Lover* (1883) and *Esther Walters* (1895). He championed Zola's novels and the plays of Ibsen and Strindberg, criticised the malign influence of French academic training in *Impressions and Opinions* (1891) and advocated the new painting, notably of Manet and Degas, in *Modern Painting* (1893). He presented Manet as an exemplar of the 'modern' for British artists at the end of the nineteenth century. Moore was introduced to Manet's work by Mallarmé, but the two actually met in April 1879 at the Café Nouvelle Athènes, possibly through the writer Paul Alexis (Frazier 2000, pp. 55–58).

Apparently intrigued by Moore's conversation, wit and youthful good looks, Manet made three portraits of the nascent writer during the spring and summer of 1879. The most finished is the pastel portrait (Metropolitan Museum of Art, New York), the other two being an outline sketch in oil on canvas (fig. 5) and the present work, which records Moore seated on a folding green garden chair, his hands resting on one of its arms, in the garden of the artist's studio at 77 Rue d'Amsterdam (Paris 1983A, nos 176, 177).

Manet's representations of Moore suggest neither his artistic nor his literary ambitions, but rather capture a young dandy about town: in the café, elegantly attired as in the oil sketch and the pastel portrait, or relaxing en plein air. Indeed, in the oil sketch and the portrait shown here, Manet appears to be using his sitter to create the image of the modern urban type. Despite its external setting, the scale of *George Moore in the Artist's Garden* aligns it more with the cabinet-sized representation of Théodore Duret (cat. 29), made eleven years earlier, than with the ambitious, life-size presentation of another artistic figure out of doors, the painter Carolus-Duran, in Manet's portrait of 1876 (cat. 21).

George Moore in the Artist's Garden remained in Manet's studio. Not included in the 1884 memorial exhibition, it was sold at the posthumous studio sale. Although rapidly painted, and seemingly unfinished, evidence of its physical condition in the studio in 1883 (Lochard Album, vol. 1, no. 64) indicates that it was not subsequently completed by another hand, as was the case with other works (see cats 41, 55). MAS

33
THE TRAGIC ACTOR (ROUVIÈRE AS HAMLET), 1865
Oil on canvas, 187.2 × 108.1 cm
Signed bottom right: Manet
National Gallery of Art, Washington. Gift of Edith Stuyvesant Gerry, 1959.3.1

SELECTED EXHIBITIONS:
Paris 1867, no. 18; Paris 1983A, no. 89; Madrid 2003, no. 67; New York 2003, no. 150
SELECTED REFERENCES:
RWI, no. 106

Philibert Rouvière (1809–1865) was a brilliant tragedian whose career on the Paris stage was uneven. His style of highly expressive acting and mastery of make-up and costume were informed by his initial training as a painter under Baron Antoine Gros; he exhibited at the Salon from 1831 to 1837, and again in 1864. He established his reputation as one of the leading interpreters of the Romantic theatre in the title role of Shakespeare's *Hamlet* in the season of 1846–47, but by the later 1850s, his career went into decline, and, already in failing health, he appeared for the last time on stage in January 1865. Gautier was a loyal supporter, and Baudelaire viewed him as a hypnotic natural actor but a troubled genius.

Manet invited Rouvière to sit for him shortly after the actor's retirement, but progress was so slow that the work remained unfinished on Rouvière's death on 19 October 1865. It is reported that Manet resorted to using Proust and the artist Paul Roudier as models for the actor's hands and legs respectively. Even before the work was presented, unsuccessfully, to the Jury of the Salon of 1866, Velázquez's portrait of the jester Pablo de Valladolid (fig. 40) was noted as a major source; indeed, Manet copied Velázquez's canvas (RWI, no. 3; Private collection) on his visit to the Spanish capital in the summer of 1865 and noted that it was not only 'the most extraordinary example of painting in [Velázquez's] splendid *oeuvre*' but also 'the most extraordinary example of painting that has ever been made'. Manet may also have been aware of the French tradition, which extends back to at least the seventeenth century, of making engravings of actors in their roles against neutral backgrounds and with minimal props (Paris 1983A, no. 89).

The status of this work is enigmatic. In a letter to Baudelaire (27 March 1866) concerning his entries to the Salon, Manet declares: 'There is a portrait of Rouvière in the role of Hamlet. I call it The Tragic Actor to avoid criticism of people who will say it is not enough like him' (Wilson-Bareau 1991, p. 38). Here Manet appears to consider the work a portrait, a genre in which the public expected a likeness of a sitter. But equally, in order to deflect such expectations, he converts Rouvière into a generic and hence less individualised figure, referring to him as a type: the tragic actor.

Manet shared Baudelaire's admiration of Rouvière's prowess. The poet published a study of Rouvière in 1855, and also wrote his obituary. Perhaps Manet's painting can also be seen as a homage to the poet, then failing in health, and a recognition of their friendship. MAS

34
PORTRAIT OF FANNY CLAUSS (STUDY FOR THE BALCONY), 1868–69
Oil on canvas, 71 × 43 cm
Private collection, c/o Robert Holden Ltd, London

SELECTED EXHIBITIONS:
London 1983, no. 11
SELECTED REFERENCES:
Duret 1902, p. 57 (ill.); RWI, no. 133

Fanny Clauss (1845–1877) was a friend of Suzanne Manet. A violinist and viola player, she was the second of four musical daughters of a Belgian conductor based in Besançon. She trained at the Paris Conservatoire with Charles Dacla from *c.* 1860 to 1863, before establishing a career as a soloist and a member of chamber-music groups, including the Quattuor Feminin (1865/66) and the Quattuor Ste-Cécile (founded 1876). After her marriage to Manet's friend the artist Pierre Prins (1838–1913) in 1869, she also taught (*Musik und Gender im Internet*, MUGI Hochschüle für Musik und Theater, Hamburg).

The painting is the first iteration of the subject of *The Balcony* (fig. 11), one of Manet's great compositions of the 1860s, and reveals his first thoughts on that work. However, it is no mere preliminary, unresolved study. Rather, it is a straight portrait of Clauss, accompanied on the right by Berthe Morisot (see cats 16–19), whose presence was more extensive before the right-hand side of the painting was cut (Lochard Album, vol. 1, no. 75). In the final iteration of the subject, shown at the Salon of 1869, mediated by a compositional drawing (RWII, no. 346; Private collection), Manet relocates Clauss to a secondary plane on the right and makes Morisot the principal protagonist.

The present work is a key marker in Manet's search for a new style of painting that would reflect fully his commitment to contemporary subject-matter. The composition, the limited but subtle palette and the fluid brushwork reflect his profound admiration for the art of Goya, and implicitly that of seventeenth-century Spain, most notably Velázquez. His repeated reference to these sources provided him with a potent alternative to the modelling and technique favoured by both the Salon and Courbet. However, as with other works from the later 1860s, such as *Young Man Peeling a Pear* (fig. 3), the play of light across Clauss's dress, the introduction of the subtle green of the balcony and the shutter on the left, and the careful distribution of a limited range of colours across the entire composition indicate Manet's new, exploratory visual language that privileged form over representation and was to find an even more individual voice during the early years of the 1870s. The painting was bought from Manet's studio sale in 1884 by John Singer Sargent. MAS

35
PORTRAIT OF EMILIE AMBRE AS CARMEN, 1880
Oil on canvas, 92.4 × 73.5 cm
Philadelphia Museum of Art. Gift of Edgar Scott, 1964

SELECTED EXHIBITIONS:
Baltimore 1999, no. 39; Madrid 2003, no. 104; New York 2003, no. 162; Paris 2011A, no. 146
SELECTED REFERENCES:
RWI, no. 334; Dolan 2006

Born in Algeria into a family with ties to the army, the marines and the Moroccan court, Emilie Ambre (1854–1898) abandoned these connections to pursue a career on the stage. After settling in Paris in 1878, where she made her debut in Verdi's *La Traviata* and *Aïda*, Ambre performed the title role in Bizet's *Carmen* in New York the following year. When she arrived in America, in September 1879, she had with her the final version of Manet's monumental *Execution of Maximilian* (1868–69; Stadtische Kunsthalle, Mannheim) to exhibit in New York and Boston (December 1879 – January 1880). Although Ambre and Manet were neighbours in the Parisian suburb of Bellevue in 1879, we do not know exactly how they met, although they may have been introduced through their mutual friend the opera singer Jean-Baptiste Faure. Nor do we know why Ambre, specifically, was entrusted with such a politically volatile painting.

Exactly a year later, Ambre posed for Manet at her Bellevue property, Les Montalais, in the costume of the popular Spanish heroine Carmen; at the time, Manet was once again a temporary neighbour at Bellevue. According to correspondence, the work was created under pressure: Ambre was departing for America in October (Wilson-Bareau 1991, p. 256). Manet's quick, economical brush strokes delineate the detailed and colourful costume, suggesting, with very little paint, the position of the sitter's hands and fan. Her face, the most 'finished' part of the composition, is dramatically highlighted in lambent white – an indication of the stark stage lighting beneath which Ambre was most comfortable. LL

36
PORTRAIT OF MME BRUNET, 1860–63
Oil on canvas, 132.4 × 100 cm
Signed bottom left: Manet
J. Paul Getty Museum, Los Angeles

SELECTED EXHIBITIONS:
Paris 1863, unnumbered; Paris 1867, no. 20; Paris 1983A, no. 5; Copenhagen 1989, no. 4
SELECTED REFERENCES:
RWI, no. 31

TOLEDO ONLY

The identification of the sitter has been extensively discussed. According to recent research, she is Caroline de Pène, who married on 22 October 1861 the sculptor Eugène-Cyrille Brunet (1828–1921), with whom Manet had visited Florence in 1857, rather than the wife of the writer and translator Pierre-Gustave Brunet (1805–1896), a fellow hispanophile who published a study of Goya in 1861 and a translation of William Sterling's study of Velázquez four years later (Archives de Paris, Marriages, 8th arr., 22/10/1861. VAE 878). There is a carte-de-visite photograph in Manet's family album of 'M. et Mme Brunet' (Bibliothèque Nationale de France, Paris, Fonds Moreau-Nélaton).

The composition was originally full length, but by the time of its second public exhibition in 1867 it had been cut down to its present three-quarters format. Created early in his career, the portrait summarises Manet's artistic negotiation between those Old Masters who presented radical alternatives to the academic tradition and the need to define a modern visual language. The sitter's pose within a landscape, the work's tonalities and Manet's manipulation of subtle variations of black through which Mme Brunet is defined are all characteristics that display an important debt to Spanish art, particularly that of Velázquez. However, the fashionable costume and the directness of her gaze place the sitter firmly within her period. This declaration of modernity is underscored by the figure's relationship to the generalised landscape background. While acknowledging *Philip IV as a Hunter* (Museo del Prado, Madrid), a version of which was purchased by the Louvre as a Velázquez in 1862, the landscape has affinities with such portraits as *Woman in a Riding Habit (The Amazon)* (1856; Metropolitan Museum of Art, New York) by Courbet, the leading avant-garde figure of the day, and the conventions of the newly popular photographic portrait, in which subjects were stiffly posed against painted backdrops of generalised landscapes.

It is unclear whether the portrait was commissioned, although the prominence of the wedding band suggests that it could have been made specifically to celebrate the October 1861 event. However, the sitter rejected it (Duret 1918, pp. 149–50) and it remained in Manet's studio until Théodore Duret (see cat. 29) purchased it in the 1884 studio sale under the title 'Woman of 1860', suggesting an association with *Young Lady in 1866* (fig. 10). MAS

37
THE PROMENADE (MME GAMBY), *c.* 1880
Oil on canvas, 92.3 × 70.5 cm
Tokyo Fuji Art Museum

SELECTED REFERENCES:
RWI, no. 338

Despite its title and setting (Wilson-Bareau 2011), this work was not executed in the garden of the villa at Bellevue where Manet and his wife Suzanne spent the summer of 1880 (see cat. 35), but in Manet's studio in the Rue d'Amsterdam (Leenhoff Inventory, vol. 1, p. 17; Lochard Album, vol. 2, no. 17). According to Léon Leenhoff, Mme Gamby was accompanied to the studio for the sittings by Mme Loubens, whose portrait in pastel (RWII, no. 41), purportedly made in one hour (Leenhoff Inventory, vol. 2, no. 173) as she sat on Manet's red studio couch, may have been created at the same time. Both women moved in the circles of Degas and Manet. Although Mme Gamby's identity is not clear, it is possible that she was Marie Joséphine Bullot (b. 1849), who divorced Hippolyte Gamby in 1886 and married Tiburce, the brother of Berthe Morisot, the following year. Her daughter may have been Alice Gamby, of whom portraits were made by Berthe Morisot (Higonnet 1992, pp. 75, 245, 252).

Comparison with *Portrait of Mme Brunet* (cat. 36), made two decades earlier, demonstrates the journey that Manet made towards looser brushwork and a lighter, more varied palette. However, these advances do not follow the Impressionists' goal of integrating figure and landscape through consistency of brushwork across every component of the composition; instead, Manet places Mme Gamby in front of rather than within her setting. His closed, screen-like treatment of the garden is reminiscent of his representation of Jeanne Demarsy as *Spring* (fig. 29; see cat. 56), and also possibly evokes the compositional gambits of portrait photography. However, the work's relatively ambitious scale and its representation of a woman of fashion posed in a luxuriant and richly planted man-made setting reflects the contemporary work of James Tissot and Henri Gervex, for example the latter's *Mme Valtesse de La Bigne* (1879–89; Musée d'Orsay, Paris), and possibly presages, rather than mirrors, similar treatments in the work of his Impressionist friends, notably Renoir and Caillebotte, in the early 1880s.

Mme Gamby's portrait appears to have been created at the behest of Manet rather than as a commission. As such it belongs to the extensive group of uncommissioned portraits, often in pastel (see cats 57, 58), of female friends and their acquaintances with which Manet was increasingly engaged from the second half of the 1870s (see Leah Lehmbeck in the present volume, pp. 50–57). The painting remained in his studio and was exhibited neither during his lifetime nor in his 1884 memorial exhibition, which might suggest that it was not considered fully resolved. Manet's friend and supporter Jean-Baptiste Faure purchased it from the studio sale. MAS

38
PORTRAIT OF M. BRUN, 1879
Oil on canvas, 194.3 × 126 cm
National Museum of Western Art, Tokyo. Donated by the heirs of Mr Kojiro Matsukata

SELECTED EXHIBITIONS: Copenhagen 1989, no. 34
SELECTED REFERENCES: RWI, no. 326

Much about this portrait is problematic. There are two versions (see RWI, no. 327), the present work being the larger and less resolved. It is not known why Manet made two almost identical portraits of Armand Brun, about whom little is known save that he was a friend and neighbour of Emilie Ambre, the opera singer who owned a property at Bellevue (a town between Paris and Versailles) and who sat for Manet the year after M. Brun's portrait was made (see cat. 35). The portrait was possibly made when Manet was staying at Bellevue in September and October 1879 to undergo hydrotherapy after the onset of ill health, although either or both versions may have been completed in the artist's Paris studio. It is unclear whether the work was the result of a commission or an invitation from the artist, although the smaller, more finished version was initially in M. Brun's ownership, and was probably shown at Manet's one-man exhibition at La Vie moderne in April 1880 (Copenhagen 1989, no. 34).

The present life-size version is one of the last full-length, or near full-length, portraits that Manet executed. Its outdoor setting, reminiscent of the ambitious large-scale portrait of the artist Carolus-Duran (cat. 21), firmly locates the sitter in the planned landscape of a garden, complete with gravel path. With his hands in his pockets, M. Brun is projected as a quintessentially modern man of substance, dressed in elegant town attire, surveying what appears to be his domain. Given the painting's scale it is tempting to suggest that, having completed the smaller version, already in the sitter's ownership, Manet envisaged an impressively larger version for exhibition at the Salon. Such a treatment would have been typically provocative: whereas portraits of women set within sun-dappled flower gardens and parks appeared frequently in the Salon, monumental presentations of male sitters were exceptional in a genre dominated by such artists as Léon Bonnat and Carolus-Duran himself, whose male sitters tended to be presented either in interiors or in neutral settings. MAS

39
IN THE CONSERVATORY, 1877–79
Oil on canvas, 115 × 150 cm
Signed and dated lower left: Manet 1879
Staatliche Museen zu Berlin, Alte Nationalgalerie, Berlin

SELECTED EXHIBITIONS: Paris Salon 1879, no. 2010; Paris 1884, no. 9; Paris 1983A, no. 180; Stuttgart 2002, no. 57; Madrid 2003, no. 101
SELECTED REFERENCES: RWI, no. 289; Adler 1986, p. 162

LONDON ONLY

40
MME GUILLEMET, 1880
Pastel on canvas, mounted on Masonite, 54.8 × 35.2 cm
Signed and dated lower right: Manet / 1880
Saint Louis Art Museum. Funds given by John Merrill Olin

SELECTED EXHIBITIONS: Saint Louis 1990 (no catalogue)
SELECTED REFERENCES: Wentworth 1970, no. 9; Otterlo 1972, p. 154; RWII, no. 36

TOLEDO ONLY

Mme Jules Guillemet was born Jeanne Julie Charlotte Besnier de la Pontonerie in the 10th arrondissement of Paris in 1850. She married Jules Guillemet in 1871, and may have operated a fashionable clothes boutique with him at 19 Rue du Faubourg Saint-Honoré until their divorce 17 years later. During their marriage, the Guillemets became acquainted with Manet, who captured them together in the magnificent double portrait *In the Conservatory*. Although the work has been cited as having been executed in a conservatory at the 70 Rue d'Amsterdam studio, which the artist was renting from July 1878 to April 1879 (note 1 of my essay in the present volume gives more details), the painting was described in some detail as early as December 1877 in an anonymous article in the London review *The Architect*. Even at that time, when Manet was working in his studio at 4 Rue de Saint-Pétersbourg, *In the Conservatory* was well underway: 'The background is one mass of verdure. Your first impression is a sense of open air on a spring day in a wood, when leaves of the tenderest green have but lately burst forth, but leaves of every tint of green – green everywhere – grasses, ivies, and depths of leafy woodland; against a garden bench leans a man of the world … while he speaks to his young wife seated on the bench.' The precision of flowers, leaves and costume (her dress was originally 'a violent blue') displays an attention to finish that is exceptional in Manet's career, particularly in the late 1870s. This may be a direct result of his having worked on the picture for such an extended period of time, as well as his interest in including it in the Salon in the spring of 1879. *In the Conservatory* was also the first of Manet's paintings to be purchased by a museum.

Manet's single pastel portrait of Mme Guillemet is far more typical of his stylistic approach at that time: rapid wisps of chalk define her hair, eyes and cheeks, and her piquant expression is defined with the most economical strokes of pigment. The significance of the pastel medium in the later years of Manet's career is demonstrated by the fact that out of the 25 works exhibited in his solo exhibition at La Vie moderne in April 1880, 15 were pastels, at least seven of them portraits. LL

41
PORTRAIT OF M. ARNAUD (THE RIDER), *c.* 1873–75
Oil on canvas, 218 × 136 cm
Galleria Nazionale d'Arte Moderna, Milan

SELECTED REFERENCES: RWI, no. 243

LONDON ONLY

This is a highly ambitious yet problematic portrait. Little is known either about the sitter or the circumstances in which the work was made. Arnaud appears to have been a friend of Manet's although he does not figure among those who frequented the Manets' Tuesday and Thursday soirées. The work may or may not have been commissioned, but it certainly remained unfinished (and unframed) in Manet's studio at his death (Leenhoff Inventory). Indeed, on the evidence of the photographic record in the Lochard Album (vol. 1, no. 299), the top half of the painting was relatively resolved, while the horse's legs were rapidly sketched in and the landscape background in the lower half hardly delineated, suggesting that the work was brought to its current condition by another hand, either before it was sold to Baron Vitta or when it was acquired by Durand-Ruel in 1913. A schematic pencil drawing of the overall composition exists, possibly made in advance of the painting as a means of mapping out the format of the monumental pose (RWII, no. 475).

Manet created a small group of equestrian portraits in the first half of the 1870s (see cat. 42). However, this is the only full-length treatment of the type. Manet's presentation of horse and rider within a generalised landscape suggests that he may have been making reference to English seventeenth- and eighteenth-century prototypes, as he was to do in his presentation of the artist Carolus-Duran (cat. 21). Equally, the format and the relationship between landscape and sitter parallel compositional arrangements for equestrian portrait photographs such as those by Camille de Silvy (see *Camille de Silvy: Photographer of Modern Life (1834–1910)*, exh. cat., National Portrait Gallery, London, 2010, for example 'Viscount Sydney' [1859], p. 50). MAS

42
THE AMAZON, *c.* 1875
Oil on canvas, 88 × 116 cm
Museu de São Paulo Assis Chateaubriand, São Paulo

SELECTED EXHIBITIONS: Martigny 1996, no. 43
SELECTED REFERENCES: RWI, no. 160

This work and *Portrait of M. Guillaudin* (RWI, no. 159; Private collection) were in Manet's studio on his death, and both appear to be unfinished. It is therefore assumed that they were made at his behest. While something is known of Emile Guillaudin, a landscape painter from Grenoble who made his debut at the Paris Salon in 1868, a *habitué* of the Café Guerbois, a friend of the artist Alphonse Hirsch, and a model, with Hirsch, Chabrier, Paul Roudier, Edmond André and the collector Albert Hecht, for Manet's *Masked Ball at the Opera* (1874; National Gallery of Art, Washington), about the subject of this work, Mlle Marie Lefébure, little is known.

The date of both works is uncertain. Léon Leenhoff's annotation on the photograph in the Lochard Album records that the portrait of Emile Guillaudin was painted around 1869 and bears the date of '1870'; it is noted that he posed in Alphonse Hirsch's garden at 56 Rue de Rome (Lochard Album, vol. 2, no. 88; the work is also noted as unframed). Neither date nor location is given for Mlle Marie Lefébure, the annotation in the Lochard Album (vol. 1, no. 48) being 'femme à cheval – une allée au bois'. Although Manet had engaged with paintings of horse races in the 1860s, and again in 1872, it is possible that the two portraits, and that of *Portrait of M. Arnaud (The Rider)* (cat. 41), may have been inspired by the similar, ambitiously scaled paintings of amazons – horsewomen – created in 1873 and 1874 by Manet's close associates Carolus-Duran (*On the Sea Shore [Equestrian Portrait of Mlle Croizette]*, 1873; Musée des Beaux-Arts, Tourcoing), Renoir (*Riding in the Bois de Boulogne*, 1873; Kunsthalle Hamburg, exhibited at the Salon des Refusés, 1873) and Giuseppe de Nittis (*The Amazon*, 1874; Civiche Raccolte Frugone, Genoa) (see Wilson-Bareau 2012).

The work shown here is almost identical in dimensions to *Portrait of M. Guillaudin*. They are also complementary in terms of the pose adopted by the sitters and their settings. Guillaudin, in urban apparel, is placed within a composed landscape that reveals what might possibly be a reference to buildings on the right-hand side (although evidence from the photograph in the Lochard Album suggests that this might have been 'tightened up' by another hand). Mlle Lefébure, in full amazon attire of dark riding habit and top hat (but without a veil), participates in a hunt, her mount looking back at two huntsmen galloping through the clearing on the right. The implied pairing of urban and rural scenes suggests that Manet saw the paintings as pendants, addressing a theme that he had also possibly explored in *Fishing* (cat. 3) and *Music in the Tuileries Gardens* (cat. 26), and in his portraits of Desboutin (cat. 20) and Carolus-Duran (cat. 21).

Manet recorded the fact that he did not consider himself a horse painter, but rather copied the steeds in his paintings from those who specialised in the genre (Paris 1983A, p. 339; Martigny 1996, no. 43). Indeed all his mounted sitters have the same static quality and give the viewer the impression that they are set against a painted backdrop. This may demonstrate a debt to contemporary photographic equestrian portraiture. Pickvance has noted that this work was exhibited in 1888 at an exhibition of fifteen works by Manet held at the offices of the *Revue Indépendante* (Martigny 1996, no. 43). MAS

43
THE AMAZON,
c. 1882
Oil on canvas, 73 × 52 cm
Museo Thyssen-Bornemisza, Madrid

SELECTED EXHIBITIONS:
Paris 1884, no. 114; Martigny 1996, no. 97; Paris 2011A, no. 151
SELECTED REFERENCES:
RWI, no. 394

According to Léon Leenhoff's annotations in the Lochard Album (vol. 2, no. 161), the sitter for this painting was the daughter of Mme Saguez, who was the owner of a bookshop at 46 Rue de Moscou, close to Manet's studio at 77 Rue d'Amsterdam. Her fashionable dark riding habit and top hat were lent by a fellow artist, Emmanuel Gaillard-Lépinay (1842–1885). The work was begun in the winter of 1882 in the Rue d'Amsterdam studio and was apparently intended for the Salon the following year. It is the most resolved of three extant representations of the sitter. Of the other two, the one now in the Villa Flora, Winterthur (RWI, no. 396), made on a much more ambitious scale but slashed by the artist, is closest in composition to the present work. Manet's rapidly deteriorating physical condition prevented him from completing any of the three works (Wilson-Bareau 2012). The photograph in the Lochard Album suggests that the sky in the background of the present work may have been touched in prior to its inclusion in the 1884 memorial exhibition, as was documented in the case of *Autumn* (cat. 55).

The Amazon is a representation of a type – the fashionable horsewoman either mounted or dismounted – whose appearance, notably in the Bois de Boulogne from the 1860s, had been remarked upon by Baudelaire and Zola. This type had been recorded in the popular press, in portrait photography and on the canvases of, for example, Renoir (*Riding in the Bois de Boulogne*, 1873; Kunsthalle Hamburg, exhibited at the Salon des Refusés, 1873, Carolus-Duran (*On the Sea Shore [Equestrian Portrait of Mlle Croizette]*, 1873; Musée des Beaux-Arts, Tourcoing, exhibited at the Salon, 1873) and Giuseppe de Nittis (*The Amazon*, 1874; Civiche Raccolte Frugone, Genoa) (see also Ottawa 1997, no. 13), as well as by Manet in his portrait of Mlle Lefébure (cat. 42), albeit in an overtly rural setting.

The similarity of the present work's dimensions to both *Spring* (fig. 29) and *Autumn* (cat. 55), two works commissioned by Antonin Proust in 1881 as part of a cycle of the Four Seasons, has led to the suggestion that *The Amazon* might have been conceived as the image for 'Summer' within the cycle (Paris 1983A, p. 491). If this were the case, the daughter of the bookseller of the Rue de Moscou, like Jeanne Demarsy and Méry Laurent, has also been translated into an allegorical figure.

Unlike Manet's other equestrian portraits (see cats 41, 42), this single, dismounted amazon may have been inspired by an earlier work by Courbet, *Woman in a Riding Habit (The Amazon)* (1856; Metropolitan Museum of Art, New York), which Manet could possibly have seen in Théodore Duret's collection. Whether this link represents a reconsideration of an artist who had been one of Manet's significant formative influences is open to speculation (Wilson-Bareau 2012). MAS

44
PORTRAIT OF GEORGES CLEMENCEAU,
1879–80
Oil on canvas, 115.9 × 88.2 cm
Kimbell Art Museum, Fort Worth, Texas

SELECTED EXHIBITIONS:
Paris 1983A, no. 186; Madrid 2003, no. 100; Paris 2011A, no. 180
SELECTED REFERENCES:
RWI, no. 329

Initially a journalist and the founder of the radical Republican journal *La Justice*, Georges Clemenceau (1841–1929) was elected Député of Montmartre in 1876. He went on to become a politician, twice prime minister of France and architect of French victory in the First World War. A friend and supporter of Claude Monet, he may have met Manet through the artist's brother Gustave, the Paul Meurices (see cat. 7) or Zola (cat. 28); he was listed as a regular attender at the Manets' Tuesday and Thursday soirées.

Manet made two portraits of Clemenceau, probably over the winter of 1879–80, when Clemenceau was establishing *La Justice* (Paris 1983A, nos 185–86; Copenhagen 1989, no. 35). One of these (Musée d'Orsay, Paris; RWI, no. 330) was subsequently cut down, but originally indicated the setting of the portrait – the Tribune – only very roughly with incised lines at the lower right (Lochard Album, vol. 3, no. 54); the other is the present work. Both were left unfinished, possibly due to Clemenceau's inability to attend sittings given the political demands on his time (Paris 1983A, no. 185). Indeed, similarities in pose suggest that Manet may have resorted to working from a carte de visite (fig. 59) in an attempt to complete the work. It has been suggested that the present work preceded the one in the Musée d'Orsay. However, the very sketchy indication of the Tribune in the latter, recorded in the Lochard Album (vol. 3, no. 59) but no longer visible, might suggest that the reverse was the case. Both variants appear to have been tightened up after Manet's death, the present work possibly having its background filled out, especially on the upper right-hand side.

Neither variant was exhibited during Manet's lifetime nor in the 1884 memorial exhibition, and both were given to the sitter by Mme Suzanne Manet on 11 July 1883 after the artist's death. Clemenceau also owned a pastel portrait by Manet of Mme Clemenceau (RWII, no. 33).

This is not a portrait of a private individual, but a presentation of a public figure at the Tribune of the Chambre des Députés, having just made or about to make a speech, whose text rests on the parapet to the right. The work's format reflects the presentation of early Revolutionary Députés, and reinforces by association the political affiliations of Manet's sitter. Manet's motivation to invite Clemenceau to sit for him may have come from a desire to record the launch of *La Justice*, whose political stance echoed that of the artist. MAS

45
PORTRAIT OF M. ANTONIN PROUST, 1880
Oil on canvas, 129.5 × 95.9 cm
Signed and dated bottom left: A mon ami Antonin Proust 1880
Lent by the Toledo Museum of Art. Gift of Edward Drummond Libbey

SELECTED EXHIBITIONS: Paris Salon 1880, no. 2450; Paris 1884, no. 95; Paris 1983A, no. 187; Paris 2011A, no. 182
SELECTED REFERENCES: RWI, no. 331

A childhood friend of Manet's, a fellow student at the Collège Rollin and at Couture's studio, and an anti-Imperialist like the artist, Antonin Proust (1832–1905) became a journalist, critic and politician, serving as secretary to Gambetta after the Franco-Prussian War. He was elected Député for Niort in 1876 and briefly appointed Minister of Fine Arts from November 1881 to January 1882, a position that he used to award Manet the Légion d'honneur. Unrelated to the novelist Marcel, Proust was the author of many articles and books on Manet, and these remain among the primary sources of information on the artist's life and thoughts on art.

Although Manet initially embarked upon Proust's portrait in 1877 (RWI, nos 262, 263), the present work was probably conceived at the end of 1879, at the behest of Proust himself, for exhibition at the Salon. It was probably executed in January 1880, purportedly in a single sitting, save the finishing touches to the glove. However, careful comparison between Proust's carte de visite (fig. 62) and the painted portrait suggests that certain features, such as his tie, shirt collar and tie pin, may have been derived from that photograph, which was taken some two or three years earlier in *c.* 1877. Despite the neutral space and absence of attributes other than the sitter's fashionable costume and top hat (according to the artist [Blanche 1919, p. 146], the most difficult element to realise in the whole composition), Manet succeeds in conveying all the physical, social and psychological information concerning Proust and his position in society.

Accepted for the Salon of 1880, the portrait enabled some critics immediately to grasp the modernity of Manet's presentation. Others, however, were cruelly negative, and even such valiant supporters as Zola and Huysmans could only rather grudgingly recognise that the work demonstrated Manet's leading role in the development of his younger followers, the Impressionists.

The portrait was shown with *Chez le Père Lathuille – en plein air* (cat. 60), a juxtaposition that pleased Manet's artist-friend Antoine Guillemet, who identified astutely in a letter to him the two main strands in his *oeuvre*: the portrait and the [genre] painting (RWI, p. 21). MAS

46
EUGÈNE PERTUISET, LION-HUNTER, 1881
Oil on canvas, 150 × 170 cm
Signed and dated on the tree trunk: Manet 1881
Museu de São Paulo Assis Chateaubriand, São Paulo

SELECTED EXHIBITIONS: Paris Salon 1881, no. 1517; Paris 1884, no. 104; Paris 1983A, no. 208; Martigny 1996, no. 81
SELECTED REFERENCES: RWI, no. 365

This compelling yet uncomfortable portrait presents the adventurer, big-game hunter, author and artist Eugène Pertuiset, who was a longstanding friend of Manet and an important collector of his work; they probably met in the late 1860s. He lent ten works to the 1884 memorial exhibition, including *The Smoker* (cat. 13), seven still-lifes and the present portrait. Pertuiset is shown posed in Manet's studio with the supposed attributes of his profession. His trophy behind him, he wears Bavarian hunting costume (more suited to the hunting of wild boar than lions in Africa) and holds a Devisme rifle. The bosky setting was derived either from Pertuiset's garden at 14 Passage de l'Elysée, Montmartre, or from studies made by Manet at Bellevue in 1880. However, the lack of perspectival recession and the disregard for shadows gives the scene a sense of artificiality akin to the painted backdrops used by contemporary portrait photographers (see cat. 41), which the lion, patently stuffed, reinforces. In fact the lion was already at least fifteen years old and had had a public career, having been shown at the 1878 Exposition Universelle.

It is uncertain whether the portrait was commissioned. Did Manet invite Pertuiset to pose for a painting on a monumental scale destined for the Salon, or did Pertuiset commission it, for he certainly took ownership of it? In addition it has been suggested that it was started in 1877, possibly to mark the publication of Pertuiset's memoirs, *Aventures d'un chasseur de lion* (1878), but set aside and taken up again in 1880/81 to replace *The Escape of Henri Rochefort* (Kunsthaus, Zürich) at the Salon that year (Martigny 1996, no. 81). Furthermore, did Manet intend to present an honest celebration of his sitter and his achievements, expressed in the bold pose, the tough verticality of the tree trunk, the determined glance and the large, purposeful hands? Or was he intimating a sense of the ridiculous through the overt artificiality of the setting, the reference to an outmoded genre of representations of huntsmen and the unconvincing lion? Even the palette expresses the uneasiness between the sombre tones that describe Pertuiset and the high-pitched colours used for his setting (Rubin 2010, pp. 368–69).

The painting was exhibited at the Salon of 1881 with *Portrait of Henri Rochefort* (cat. 47). It received as little praise as the other work, most notably engendering harsh words from J. K. Huysmans, a critic previously well-disposed towards Manet: 'As for Pertuiset on his knees about to level his gun in a drawing room where doubtless he sees some wild animals, with a stuffed yellow lion stretched out behind him under the trees, truly I know not what to say. The pose of this bewhiskered hunter, apparently slaying a rabbit in the wood of Cucufa, is childish' (Hamilton 1969, p. 245). MAS

47
PORTRAIT OF HENRI ROCHEFORT, 1881
Oil on canvas, 81.5 × 66.5 cm
Signed and dated right: Manet 1881
Hamburger Kunsthalle

SELECTED EXHIBITIONS:
Paris Salon 1881, no. 1516;
Paris 1884, no. 106;
Paris 1983A, no. 206;
Paris 2011A, no. 183
SELECTED REFERENCES:
RWI, no. 366

Henri Rochefort (born de Rochefort) (1830–1913) was a journalist with a controversial history. A radically outspoken critic of the Second Empire, he sided with the Paris Commune, for which he was sentenced in 1873 and interned in a penal colony on New Caledonia. He returned to Paris after the Amnesty of 21 July 1880, and established the socialist publication *L'Intransigeant*, before casting aside his left-wing beliefs and becoming an outspoken nationalist with strong anti-Semitic views.

This portrait was not the result of a commission but was made in the wake of *The Escape of Henri Rochefort* (RWI, no. 370; 1881; Kunsthaus, Zürich) at Manet's behest, when the artist had taken the decision not to present the modern-history painting to the Salon of 1881. Rochefort gave his sittings grudgingly. The two may have met in the 1870s at the salon of Nina de Callias, but were reintroduced in late 1880 by Manet's artist friend Desboutin (cat. 20) (Paris 2011A, pp. 247–48), when Manet had expressed a desire to make a re-creation of the politician's presumed dramatic escape from the penal colony.

As with his near-contemporary portrait of Clemenceau (cat. 44), Manet has posed Rochefort with his arms crossed, a trope for the man of action. Likewise, in keeping with his treatment of another politician, Antonin Proust (cat. 45), Manet has broken with convention and stripped away all attributes of professional status, suggesting that the force of Rochefort's convictions and actions is contained within his physiognomy and stance. Despite the relatively sober pose of both portraits, they quietly hint at an approach to the political portrait that had been developed by artists such as Léon Bonnat over the previous few decades.

Whereas Rochefort's pose and the treatment of his costume refer to the portraits of Frans Hals and Rembrandt, the more broken brushwork and the varied palette of his face reflect Manet's engagement with Impressionism. Indeed, this aspect of the portrait generated the intense antipathy of the young writer and critic J. K. Huysmans when it was shown at the Salon of 1881: 'This year is decidedly bad, for Manet in his turn is going to pieces … His *Portrait of Rochefort*, executed in a semi-official technique, does not hold together. You could think that these flesh tones were made of green cheese, all speckled and spotted, and that the hair is grey smoke. There is no contrast, no life' (Hamilton 1969, p. 245).

Manet sold *Portrait of Rochefort* to Jean-Baptiste Faure in 1882 with four other works, among them *Music in the Tuileries Gardens* (cat. 26) and *In the Conservatory* (cat. 39). MAS

48
PORTRAIT OF LISE CAMPINÉANU, 1878
Oil on canvas, 55.6 × 46.5 cm
The Nelson-Atkins Museum of Art, Kansas City, Missouri (Purchase: William Rockhill Nelson Trust, 36-5)

SELECTED EXHIBITIONS:
Pittsburgh 1989, no. 44;
Baltimore 1999, no. 37
SELECTED REFERENCES:
RWI, no. 284; Ward and Fidler 1993, p. 208

The commission for this portrait of the bright-eyed six-year-old Lise Campinéanu (1872–1949) was encouraged by Georges de Bellio, the sitter's great-uncle. The Romanian de Bellio was Manet's physician, a homeopath who helped the artist deal with the increasing bouts of pain he suffered in the final years of his life. De Bellio was also a major early collector of Manet's works (he owned five paintings and three pastels) and those of the Impressionists; he wrote once to Claude Monet of this picture that it expressed a 'talent with which you are familiar' (de Bellio to Monet, 31 August 1878; quoted in RWI, p. 226). De Bellio suggested to his nephew Jean Campinéanu that, while visiting Paris from Bucharest, he should go to Manet's studio to commission a portrait of his daughter.

The lively brush strokes and light palette that define the young girl's sparkling features underscore the artist's move from the influence of the Old Masters to the open engagement with the process embraced by his Impressionist contemporaries. Manet's free handling of paint and the sitter's casual pose, probably inspired by contemporary portrait photography, reveal Campinéanu's sophisticated appreciation of the artist's fresh approach to modern portraiture.

Another portrait of Lise seated frontally on a chair, which Manet left in significantly unresolved form, appears to be a first, unsuccessful attempt to capture the sitter (Spencer Museum of Art, University of Kansas; RWI, no. 283). Photographic evidence from the Lochard Album suggests that this work (which remained in Manet's studio) was scraped down and possibly pushed to a greater degree of resolution, especially in the face and on the right-hand side, after the artist's death (Lochard Album, vol. 3, no. 121). LL

49
PORTRAIT OF HENRY BERNSTEIN AS A CHILD, 1881
Oil on canvas, 135 × 97 cm
Private collection, c/o Robert Holden Ltd, London

SELECTED EXHIBITIONS:
Martigny 1996, no. 83
SELECTED REFERENCES:
RWI, no. 371

This portrait presents the young Henry Bernstein (1876–1953), future dramaturge, in naval costume (Martigny 1996, no. 83). It was made during the summer of 1881 at Versailles, where Henry's father, the businessman Marcel Bernstein d'Anvers, owned an elegant property. Marcel Bernstein frequented the Manets' Tuesday soirées, had a carte de visite mounted in Manet's family carte-de-visite album (Bibliothèque Nationale de France, Paris, Fonds Moreau-Nélaton) and contributed to the purchase of *Olympia* (fig. 9) by the French State in 1890. It was he who encouraged Manet to spend from June or July to late September 1881 at 20 Avenue Villeneuve l'Etang, Versailles, a villa set within what Manet described as 'quite the most hideous of gardens' (Wilson-Bareau 1991, p. 262).

This apparently simple and direct representation of a five-year-old boy, devoid of the sentimentality that Renoir brought to his portraits of children, contains a number of complex, loaded references that suggest Manet is revisiting earlier artistic procedures and works. Despite the modernity of his outfit and his relaxed naturalness, the boy's pose is a direct reference back to the *commedia dell'arte* figure of Pierrot in *Pierrot*, formerly known as *Gilles* (Musée du Louvre, Paris) by the eighteenth-century French master Watteau. Not only did Manet quote this figure in *The Old Musician* (RWI, no. 52; 1862; National Gallery of Art, Washington), but he also used it for the pose in *Portrait of a Child (The Little Lange)* (fig. 8). Its reuse after Manet's move from the early 1870s beyond specific references to the Old Masters may say more about his on-going engagement with the art of the eighteenth century in the closing years of his life – an engagement manifested most immediately in his increasing involvement with the medium of pastel – than his need to assert at this stage in his career the legitimacy of his innovative artistic procedures by referring to examples of the great art of the past. Marcel Bernstein owned a further three works by Manet, and Henry subsequently acquired a seascape made at Berck-sur-Mer in 1873 (RWI, no. 198), the pastel *On the Bench* (fig. 28) and two other pastels. MAS

50
VICTORINE MEURENT, *c.* 1862
Oil on canvas, 42.9 × 43.8 cm
Museum of Fine Arts, Boston. Gift of Richard C. Paine in memory of his father, Robert Treat Paine 2nd

SELECTED EXHIBITIONS:
Paris 1983A, no. 31; Baltimore 1999, no. 34; Madrid 2003, no. 37; Paris 2011A, no. 55
SELECTED REFERENCES:
RWI, no. 57

Victorine Louise Meurent (1844–1927) came from an artisan family. Titian-haired and petite, she began modelling for Couture's studio in 1862, the year in which she apparently met Manet. She had an affair with Alfred Stevens (see cat. 54), travelled to America in *c.* 1870 as a result of an amorous liaison, had ambitions to be a professional painter (she had work accepted by the Salon from 1876), and suffered a decline into alcoholism and poverty in later life (Tabarant Archive). Known for her lively manner and witty conversation, she was also a competent musician (see Clark 1985; Fried 1996; Armstrong 2002; Sidlauskas, in Dolan 2012, pp. 29–48).

Meurent was one of Manet's favourite models. She posed for seven major works (see cats 51–53) between 1862 and 1873 in which, through subject-matter and pictorial treatment, Manet asserted a new language of art to meet the demands of the modern age. In this straight portrait, Meurent makes her debut in Manet's art by confronting the viewer with a directness of gaze and a visual force that the dramatic lighting illuminating her face seems to reinforce. The treatment of the flesh tones of her face and the indication of highlight and shadow in the folds of her dress are handled with the broad sweep of a heavily loaded brush and with minimum application of half tones, technical characteristics that Manet had reinterpreted from the Dutch and Spanish seventeenth-century masters. He was also applying these in more formal portraits, such as that of Mme Brunet (cat. 36), at this time. However, as with the majority of his other representations of Meurent, Manet undermines the apparently immediate realism of the portrait by projecting a certain blankness of stare, an indifference that dehumanises her and forces the viewer to focus more directly upon the formal qualities of the work.

The rapid, overlaid brush strokes that define Meurent's chin and the collar and folds of her dress reveal that the portrait was made directly in front of the subject. The almost sculptural build-up of the structure of her face presages both Manet's later procedures (see cat. 47) and Cézanne's application of slabs of constructive brushwork in his sequence of portraits of Uncle Dominique made in 1866. MAS

51
STREET SINGER, *c.* 1862
Oil on canvas, 171.1 × 105.8 cm
Signed bottom left: éd Manet
Museum of Fine Arts, Boston. Bequest of Sarah Choate Sears in memory of her husband, Joshua Montgomery Sears

SELECTED EXHIBITIONS:
Paris 1863, no. 65; Paris 1867, no. 19; Paris 1884, no. 10; Paris 1983A, no. 32; Madrid 2003, no. 38; Paris 2011A, no. 56
SELECTED REFERENCES:
RWI, no. 50

Probably the second large-scale subject painting for which Victorine Meurent posed, after Manet had made her portrait (cat. 50) and executed *Mlle V… in the Costume of an Espada* (1862; Metropolitan Museum of Art, New York), *Street Singer* is one of a series of ambitious single-figure paintings of 'types' made in the 1860s that mediate between the portrait and the subject painting. These include *The Tragic Actor* (cat. 33), *Young Lady in 1866* (fig. 10, another representation of Victorine Meurent) and the two paintings of philosophers (Art Institute of Chicago). Although he uses a model to act out the role, Manet's translation of sitter to actor demonstrates succinctly his need to underpin his scenes from contemporary life with knowledge of his sitters who populate his real world.

There is a certain incongruity, even a contradiction, about the presentation and execution of the subject. A fashionably dressed young woman plays the role of an itinerant street musician, a category of entertainer who inhabited the margins of modern Paris. According to Proust's account of the genesis of the work, she has just left a low bar in the area close to Manet's studio in the Rue Guyot (Proust 1996, p. 28). She clutches her guitar, but provocatively holds a cluster of fruit to her lips and hitches up her skirt to reveal her petticoat. Although her dress could have been sourced in contemporary fashion plates, and the sharpness of its outline and the artist's harsh differentiation between light and shadow may reflect both the visual effects of contemporary portrait photography and the novelty of Japanese *ukiyo-e* prints, Manet is reported to have admitted that his primary artistic references were 'the Madrid masters' and Frans Hals (Wilson-Bareau 1991, p. 29).

The contemporaneity of the subject is underscored by Victorine's costume, and hence echoes Baudelaire's analysis of fashion as an expression of contemporary beauty (Dolan 1997), but the degree to which Manet's representation was seen to be truthful to reality generated conflicting views. In 1863 critics dismissed the work for its distortion of reality, whereas when Zola came to address the painting in 1867 he celebrated it for being the product of 'nature which seems to me to have been analysed with extreme simplicity and exactitude … [one] senses in it an acute search for the truth, the conscientious work of a man who wants, above all, to state frankly what he sees' (Zola 1974, p. 86). MAS

52
DÉJEUNER SUR L'HERBE, *c.* 1863–68
Oil on canvas, 89.5 × 116.5 cm
The Samuel Courtauld Trust. The Courtauld Gallery, London

SELECTED EXHIBITIONS: Paris 1983A, no. 62
SELECTED REFERENCES: RWI, no. 66

LONDON ONLY

The present work is a reduced version of the painting of the same title in the Musée d'Orsay, Paris. Victorine Meurent sat for both this multi-figure painting and its near-contemporary work *Olympia* (fig. 9). Both elicited critical outcry and deep consternation when they were shown at the Salon des Refusés in 1863 and the Salon of 1865 respectively.

The painting was made in the Rue Guyot studio, against a backdrop derived from a landscape on the Ile Saint-Ouen, near the Manet family's property at Gennevilliers, on the Seine to the west of Paris (see cat. 3). Victorine Meurent has undressed and sits with two men, the one in the centre modelled by Ferdinand (Karl Adolph Constantin) Leenhoff (1841–1914), the sculptor brother of Suzanne Leenhoff (whom Manet married in 1863), and the one on the right posed by a composite of Manet's two younger brothers, Eugène (1833–1892), who married Berthe Morisot in 1874 (see cats 16–19), and Gustave (1835–1884), a lawyer who became a politician and friend of Georges Clemenceau (see cat. 44). In uniting these members of his immediate and extended families, Manet is in some sense making a 'family portrait' (Paris 1983A, no. 62; Locke 2001).

The composition demonstrates the processes through which Manet went in order to create an image of modernity endowed with a legitimacy derived from reference to the great art of the past. The figures – naked and clad – seated in a landscape look back to Titian's *Fête Champêtre* (Musée du Louvre, Paris), Giorgione's *La Tempesta* (Gallerie dell'Accademia, Venice) and Marcantonio Raimondi's engraving after Raphael's lost *Judgement of Paris*, while the subject owes much to the eighteenth-century French artist Watteau. However, Manet's concern to give his subject absolute contemporaneity has led him to refer to the work of the arch-Realist Gustave Courbet, notably his *Young Ladies on the Banks of the Seine (Summer)* (1856–57; Musée du Petit Palais, Paris), and treatments of similar subjects by lesser early nineteenth-century French artists and engravers (Fried 1996).

Despite its bolder brushwork and its lesser focus on detail, the work shown here is now considered not to be a preparatory sketch but instead to have been made subsequently, possibly on commission. A watercolour drawing in the Ashmolean Museum, Oxford, which records the first exhibited version, probably lies between the two (Wilson-Bareau 1986). MAS

53
THE RAILWAY, 1873
Oil on canvas, 93.3 × 111.5 cm
Signed and dated bottom right: Manet 1873
National Gallery of Art, Washington.
Gift of Horace Havemeyer in memory of his mother, Louisine W. Havemeyer, 1956.10.1

SELECTED EXHIBITIONS: Paris Salon 1874, no. 1260; Paris 1884, no. 68; Paris 1983A, no. 133; Madrid 2003, no. 91; Paris 2011A, no. 103
SELECTED REFERENCES: RWI, no. 207

Victorine Meurent, who had apparently recently returned from an amorous escapade in America, posed for *The Railway* in the autumn of 1872, a few months after Manet's move to his new studio at 4 Rue de Saint-Pétersbourg. The work was generally thought to have been painted out of doors in the garden of Manet's friend Alphonse Hirsch's studio at 58 Rue du Rome, but Wilson-Bareau has demonstrated that it was probably made in Manet's studio (Wilson-Bareau 1998, pp. 41–63; Mayo Roos 2012, pp. 86–89). The background, however, records the view from Hirsch's studio: the railings of his small garden, the railway cutting, a stone pier from which the ambitiously engineered six-armed cast-iron Pont de l'Europe (seen on the extreme right) sprang, and, to the left of Victorine's bonnet, the entrance to the building in which Manet's own new studio was located. The identity of the model for Victorine's youthful companion is uncertain, although it has been suggested that she was Hirsch's daughter.

In this painting, Victorine acts as an agent in an uncompromising essay in modernity, whose title proclaims its direct association with a new mode of transport and whose realism is underscored by the identifiable sitter and location. Manet's composition permits no conventional spatial recession, being severely divided into two parallel planes demarcated by the iron railings. Beyond lie manifestations of modernising Paris: a glimpse of the Quartier de l'Europe, an area of Paris laid out in the later 1860s in the Haussmann era, the railway tracks from the Gare Saint-Lazare, initially laid in 1835, the new Pont de l'Europe, opened in 1868, and clouds of steam rising from the railway cutting where a locomotive is passing. In front of the railings, set within an uncomfortably narrow and immediate foreground plane, sits Victorine sporting the latest autumn fashion, confronting but not engaging with the viewer, accompanied by an equally smartly attired girl.

The operatic baritone Jean-Baptiste Faure purchased the painting on its completion in 1873. It was one of two works out of four by Manet to be accepted at the Salon of 1874 (see cat. 8), where it provoked the usual array of hostile criticism, ranging from ridicule to incomprehension, one critic identifying, perceptively, the apparent confusion of genres in Manet's subject paintings: 'Is Manet's *Railway* a double portrait or a subject picture? … We lack information to solve this problem; we hesitate all the more concerning the young girl which at least might be a portrait seen from the rear' (Duvergier de Hauranne, quoted in Hamilton 1969, p. 179). However, *The Railway* also drew the first praise for the artist's work from the poet Stéphane Mallarmé (see cat. 30). MAS

54
A GAME OF CROQUET, 1873
Oil on canvas, 72.5 × 106 cm
Städel Museum, Frankfurt am Main.
Property of the Städelscher Museums-Verein e.V.

SELECTED EXHIBITIONS: Paris 2011A, no. 104
SELECTED REFERENCES: RWI, no. 211

LONDON ONLY

Although it has been suggested (Rubin 2010, pp. 290–98) that this painting was made in Manet's studio, the modest format, the broken brushwork and the focus on light and shade are all hallmarks of the Impressionists' approach to capturing a scene from contemporary life out of doors, directly in front of the motif. The scene is apparently set in the garden of the studio of Manet's friend the Belgian painter Alfred Stevens in the Rue des Martyrs. The painting was made in late summer 1873, after Manet's return from Etaples (see cat. 8). It uses as models, from left to right, probably Alfred Stevens himself, Victorine Meurent (see cats 50–53), Alice Legouvé (Alfred Stevens's mistress-model and the model for Manet's later *The Laundry* [1875; Am Römerholz, Winterthur]) and, in the background, bathed in sunlight, Manet's close friend Paul Roudier.

The subject is a reprise of a painting of the same title that Manet had made at Boulogne-sur-Mer in 1871 (Nelson-Atkins Museum of Art, Kansas City), and for which Paul Roudier, Léon Leenhoff and Jeanne Gonzalès served as models. The two paintings record the recent arrival from England of the modern version of croquet, which had been developed in the 1860s from a seventeenth-century French model. Both demonstrate Manet's fascination with a thoroughly up-to-date bourgeois leisure pursuit (see cat. 11), but the brushwork of the present canvas, which seeks to integrate the figures with their surrounding space, its lighter palette and its capture of dappled areas of light and shade place it within the trajectory of Manet's consideration of Impressionism, linking it to such paintings as *The Swallows* (cat. 8), made earlier that summer near Berck-sur-Mer, and *The Monet Family in Their Garden at Argenteuil* (cat. 25), which was made the following summer. Their modest formats and their subject-matter qualify these works as genre paintings recording aspects of contemporary life, while Manet's use of identifiable models underscores the veracity of each scene. MAS

55
AUTUMN (PORTRAIT OF MÉRY LAURENT), 1881
Oil on canvas, 72 × 51.5 cm
Musée des beaux-arts, Nancy

SELECTED EXHIBITIONS: Paris 1884, no. 113; Paris 1983A, no. 215; Copenhagen 1989, no. 48; Martigny 1996, no. 95; Paris 2011A, no. 150
SELECTED REFERENCES: RWI, no. 393

One of four portraits of beautiful young women commissioned from Manet by Antonin Proust in 1881 to serve as allegories of the Seasons, *Autumn (Portrait of Méry Laurent)* is the second of the possible three that were eventually executed. Of the other two, one used Jeanne Demarsy as the model for 'Spring' (fig. 29; see cat. 56) (Paris 1983A, no. 215), and the other the daughter of a bookseller, possibly for the representation of 'Summer' (cat. 43). Whereas *Spring* was exhibited at the Salon of 1882, *Autumn (Portrait of Méry Laurent)* remained in Manet's studio, and, according to Léon Leenhoff, was 'finished' by another hand prior to its inclusion in the memorial exhibition of 1884 (Copenhagen 1989, no. 48). Comparison with the photograph in the Lochard Album reveals, for example, a heightened definition of the model's facial features, completion of the muff and a sharpening of details of the decorative background.

Méry Laurent (Anne Rose Suzanne Louviot, 1849–1900) was a minor actress, a witty conversationalist, a brilliant courtesan and a loyal friend to Manet during his last illness. The long-time mistress of Thomas William Evans (1823–1897), the wealthy, highly sought-after American dentist to the Imperial family and a modest collector of works by Manet (RWI, nos 165, 169 and 251), Laurent moved in literary, musical and artistic circles that encompassed Mallarmé (cat. 30), Huysmans, Verlaine, George Moore (cat. 32), Chabrier, Reynaldo Hahn, Whistler and Manet (Proust 1996, p. 41). She inspired Marcel Proust's Odette de Crécy in *A la Recherche du temps perdu*. A resident of the Rue de Rome, she was introduced to Manet by Alphonse Hirsch (see cat. 53) at the 1876 studio exhibition of Manet's two rejected Salon paintings and other works. She became a close friend of his, a favourite model in his last years (she posed for at least eleven works, seven of which were pastel portraits), and a supporter who both collected works by the artist, including the sketch for *The Execution of Maximilian* (1867; Ny Carlsberg Glyptotek, Copenhagen), and acted as his 'agent' with other collectors.

Laurent purchased a new outfit from the British-born Parisian fashion designer Worth especially to pose for *Autumn (Portrait of Méry Laurent)* (Proust 1996, p. 59). With its brown, autumnal pelisse trimmed with fur, and a black muff, it represented the height of fashion in Paris in the early 1880s. Despite the pose's suggestion of Italian quattrocento profile portraits or Japanese *ukiyo-e* prints, the undeniably contemporary costume that Laurent wears in this modern representation of a timeless, allegorical subject aligns Manet's work with similar treatments by Morisot and Alfred Stevens, and with Baudelaire's aesthetic for the new art, which proclaimed the superiority of modern dress over classical or historical costume. MAS

56
JEANNE (SPRING), 1882; printed 1890
Etching with aquatint
Signed lower left: Manet
Bibliothèque nationale de France, Paris

SELECTED EXHIBITIONS:
Paris 2011A, no. 152
SELECTED REFERENCES:
Harris 1970, no. 88

57
GIRL IN A SUMMER BONNET (JEANNE DEMARSY), *c.* 1879
Pastel on canvas, 56 × 35 cm
Collection of Diane B. Wilsey

SELECTED EXHIBITIONS:
Paris 1884, no. 141;
Martigny 1996, no. 60
SELECTED REFERENCES:
RWII, no. 18

LONDON ONLY

Jeanne Demarsy (Anne Darlaud, 1865–1937) had already posed as a model for both Manet and Renoir (*Portrait of Mlle de Marsy*, 1882; Private collection) before making her name as a successful and popular actress on the Paris stage during the 1880s and 1890s (Lehmbeck 2007, pp. 60–61, 239–40). She posed in Manet's Rue d'Amsterdam studio in 1881 for the painting *Spring* (fig. 29), one of four allegories of the Seasons commissioned by Antonin Proust in that year (see cat. 55). *Spring* was the only work of the four to be completed and enjoyed great critical acclaim at the Salon of 1882.

In contrast to the implied role-playing in *Spring*, Manet's other two images of Jeanne Demarsy were intended as straightforward representations. Her beauty ensured that she was among the sitters for the 62 pastel portraits of identified and unidentified women that he made in the closing years of his life. Whereas the background of the present pastel portrait only sketchily implies the presence of plants, the example in the Pola Museum of Art in Japan (fig. 28) clearly defines the space in which both portraits were posed: the conservatory attached to the studio of the Swedish painter Otto Rosen at 70 Rue d'Amsterdam, which Manet rented from July 1878 to April 1879 (see also cats 6, 39).

In keeping with Manet's enthusiasm for haute couture, Demarsy sports extravagant, fashionable hats in *Spring* and both her pastel portraits. The elegant hat in the painting and the etching was apparently supplied by the celebrated milliner Mme Virot, and it is possible that the straw bonnet in the present pastel might also have come from the same source (Proust 1996, p. 58). MAS

58
MLLE SUZETTE LEMAIRE, FULL FACE, *c.* 1880/81
Pastel on canvas, 53 × 33 cm
Signed right: Manet
Private collection. On long-term loan to the Ashmolean Museum, Oxford

SELECTED EXHIBITIONS:
Paris 1884?
SELECTED REFERENCES:
RWII, no. 43

LONDON ONLY

This pastel represents Suzette, the daughter of Madeleine Lemaire (*née* Coll; 1845–1928), a talented artist and a founder member of both the Société des Aquarellistes and the Société des Pastellistes. Madeleine Lemaire was the hostess of a celebrated musical and theatrical salon at her home, 31 Rue de Monceau, which was attended by artists, politicians, composers, musicians, actresses and writers, including Marcel Proust. Suzette generated the admiration of her mother's guests, not least that of Proust, who corresponded with her, dedicated the second section of his translation of Ruskin's *Sesame and Lilies* (1906) to her, and wrote a short story about her and her mother (now lost).

The present work is the second of Manet's two pastel portraits of Suzette. It was made for the collector Charles Ephrussi in gratitude for the generous sum that he had paid in commissioning the first pastel portrait of Suzette, *Portrait of Mlle Suzette Lemaire in Profile*, in *c.* 1880 (Private collection; RWII, no. 42). Manet had given that pastel to Madeleine Lemaire, who, in a letter addressed to Manet dated '1881' records her admiration for the work: 'I was counting on going to see you these last few days in order to tell you about the great success that your ravishing portrait has had… It is charming, a very good likeness, and I think that you can hear the echo of all the compliments which I have received' (Tabarant Archive; Tabarant 1947, p. 429). The pastel was lent by Mme Lemaire to the 1884 memorial exhibition at the Ecole des Beaux-Arts (no. 126).

With the onset of serious illness, Manet engaged increasingly with pastel. Indeed, in his solo exhibition in 1880 at the gallery of the review *La Vie moderne*, of the 25 works exhibited, 15 were pastels. The medium attracted the artist for its speed of execution, for the freshness with which it could capture an immediate likeness without demanding multiple sittings, and for its direct reference to eighteenth-century practice. Indeed, in the present pastel, the near-frontal presentation of Suzette, with a white fichu around her neck, suggests that she is as much a product of the revival of interest in the eighteenth century, promulgated by the Empress Eugénie and such leading cultural figures as the de Goncourt brothers, as a citizen of the Third Republic. MAS

59
PORTRAIT OF M. GAUTHIER-LATHUILLE FILS, *c.* 1879
Pastel on canvas, 56 × 46 cm
Private collection

SELECTED EXHIBITIONS:
SELECTED REFERENCES:
RWII, no. 12

NOT EXHIBITED

Louis Gauthier-Lathuille (b. 1857) was the eldest son of the restaurant proprietor of the same name. Probably made at the same time as the genre painting *Chez le Père Lathuille – en plein air* (cat. 60), in which he played the role of the amorous young man, Gauthier-Lathuille *fils* is presented in this pastel as a smartly dressed professional in his father's business. He stands in the interior of his father's restaurant at 7 Avenue de Clichy, a grand, panelled establishment, with the reflection of his back caught in the mirror behind him; to the right can be glimpsed the fronds of a potted plant. Given that *Chez le Père Lathuille – en plein air* is set in the garden of the restaurant, it is interesting to speculate whether this is an example, not necessarily explicit, of Manet making two images of complementary environments, such as he had already done earlier in his career, where he contrasted the urban with the rural (see cats 3 and 26, and 20 and 21). The portrait of Louis Gauthier-Lathuille's younger sister Marguerite (Musée des Beaux-Arts, Lyons; RWI, no. 292), a reluctant sitter to Manet, was probably made at the same time.

Unlike Manet's other representations of figures in café interiors, such as *Portrait of Alphonse Maureau* (cat. 22) or *The Café-Concert* (1879; National Gallery, London), the image is firmly static and formal, giving no hint of the lively atmosphere of such establishments. Its composition has an affinity with such works as Gustave Caillebotte's *In a Café* (1880; Musée des Beaux-Arts, Rouen), although it communicates none of the latter's air of leisurely bonhomie. MAS

60
CHEZ LE PÈRE LATHUILLE – EN PLEIN AIR, 1879
Oil on canvas, 92 × 112 cm
Signed and dated bottom left: Manet 1879
Musée des Beaux-Arts, Tournai

SELECTED EXHIBITIONS: Paris Salon 1880, no. 2451; Ghent 1880, no. 571; Paris 1884, no. 94; Martigny 1996, no. 56; Paris 2011A, no. 129
SELECTED REFERENCES: RWI, no. 291

The models for this intimate scene of modern life were Louis (b. 1857) (cat. 59), eldest son of the restaurant proprietor Louis Gauthier-Lathuille, and, initially, the actress Ellen Andrée (1857–1925), the sought-after model of Degas, Renoir and Manet in the later 1870s. Andrée made her debut on the stage of the Théâtre du Palais-Royal in 1879 and subsequently gave up modelling for a successful stage career in vaudeville and pantomime, where her skill in mimicry was celebrated. Her theatrical commitments meant that her place as model for the painting had to be taken by Judith French, a cousin of the composer Jacques Offenbach (see cat. 26). Manet also made a pastel portrait of Louis Gauthier-Lathuille *fils* (cat. 59) in 1879, and Ellen Andrée was the model for *At the Café* (1878; Am Römersholz, Winterthur) and possibly the sitter for *Profile of a Young Girl* (1880; Private collection, RWI, no. 339). Some doubt has been cast on her being the model in Manet's monumental depiction of a fashionable Parisienne (1875; Nationalmuseum, Stockholm) (Lehmbeck 2007 and forthcoming).

The setting for this amorous encounter in socially neutral territory is the terrace of the restaurant Chez le Père Lathuille at 7 Avenue de Clichy, close to the Café Guerbois. Run by Louis Gauthier-Lathuille, who owned a few works by Manet, it was to be the venue for the Manet memorial banquet on 5 January 1885. The composition was initially to have featured Louis Gauthier-Lathuille in army uniform, engaged in an amorous encounter, but Manet exchanged the uniform for his own coat: 'Take off your tunic … Put on my jacket!' (Wilson-Bareau 1991, p. 246).

The painting takes its place among a group of café and café-cabaret scenes recorded over the previous few years both by Manet and artists such as Degas and Renoir and by writers including Zola and Huysmans, which was to culminate in Manet's great *Bar at the Folies-Bergère* of 1882 (Courtauld Gallery, London) (Reff 1982, pp. 73–75). According to Proust, and as its title proclaims, the work was executed according to Impressionist principles: out of doors in front of the motif (Proust 1996, pp. 55–56). The open brushwork, the bold interweaving of colour and the intense areas of light and shade give the work a vitality and sense of movement absent in such earlier outdoor genre scenes as *The Railway* (cat. 53) and *Argenteuil* (1874; Musée des Beaux-Arts, Tournai). The intimate engagement of the two principal figures brings to the painting the animated quality of an eighteenth-century conversation piece, as does the waiter on the right, whose complicit invitation to the viewer to participate in this private scene is worthy of Watteau or Boucher (Paris 2011A, p. 222).

Chez le Père Lathuille – en plein air was exhibited at the Salon of 1880 with *Portrait of M. Antonin Proust* (cat. 45). The critic Paul Mantz was shocked by the fact that it was a 'scene in the "open air"', and concluded that 'to lunch with a woman so badly turned out is punishment beyond the horrors of the imagination … Let us forget this nightmare' (Hamilton 1969, p. 232). Manet had his defenders, however. Théophile Silvestre clearly identified the painting as a record of modernity: 'All is brightness and joy in this corner of a restaurant … There is truly extraordinary vitality in this little scene of everyday life' (Hamilton 1969, p. 233). In a letter dated 7 April 1880 Antoine Guillemet responds to Manet's two Salon exhibits – portrait and genre painting – eliding them as if they naturally expressed the two dominant, interrelated facets of Manet's art: he found the portrait 'really very beautiful. As for the painting ("tableau"), it has amazing luminosity' (RWI, p. 21). MAS

61
ISABELLE LEMONNIER WITH A MUFF, *c.* 1879
Oil on canvas, 91.4 × 73 cm
Dallas Museum of Art.
Gift of Mr and Mrs Algur H. Meadows and the Meadows Foundation Incorporated

SELECTED EXHIBITIONS: Paris 1983A, no. 190; Dallas 1989, no. 51; Atlanta 2007, no. 58
SELECTED REFERENCES: RWI, no. 302; Kostenevich 1995, p. 57

62
ISABELLE LEMONNIER WITH A WHITE COLLAR, *c.* 1879–82
Oil on canvas, 86.5 × 63.5 cm
Ny Carlsberg Glyptotek, Copenhagen

SELECTED EXHIBITIONS: Tokyo 1986, no. 27; Copenhagen 1989, no. 33; London 2004A, no. 163
SELECTED REFERENCES: RWI, no. 299; Munk 1993, no. 20

In the years following Manet's 1879 move to what was to be his final Paris studio at 77 Rue d'Amsterdam, he painted six oil portraits and several watercolour sketches of the charming, sophisticated and well-connected Isabelle Lemonnier (1857–1926). Born to the jeweller of the imperial court of Napoleon III, Lemonnier was sister-in-law to the publisher Georges Charpentier, an early supporter of the Impressionist painters. Charpentier's publications, in particular the journal *La Vie moderne* (founded in April 1879), as well as a gallery of the same name, advocated this new style of painting, and Manet's was the first solo exhibition to be held in the space, in April 1880. Lemonnier's older sister and Charpentier's wife, Marguerite-Louise, hosted a celebrated salon at their home on the Rue de Grenelle and Georges Charpentier was a regular at the Manets' Tuesday soirées; it is likely that Manet met Isabelle in one of these two settings. Together with Méry Laurent (see cat. 55), Isabelle was to become one of Manet's most favoured models, and a close friend, during the closing years of his life.

The earliest mention of a portrait of Isabelle is made in a letter from Manet to his friend Emile Zola (see cat. 28), who was spending his holiday with the Charpentiers in late July and August 1876 (Wilson-Bareau 1991, p. 180). Manet states that he was about to begin a portrait of Isabelle the following Friday. It is impossible to determine which portrait (if any at all) was begun at that time; indeed, the dating of the six oils is difficult to pinpoint. Lemonnier recalled that five three-quarter-length portraits, which include the present works, were executed in Manet's final studio (a sixth, showing her seated in a domestic setting, was created in his apartment), but no indication is given of the order of their execution.

In both the present portraits, Manet has painted Lemonnier as if she has just arrived. She wears a double-breasted jacket in one and a fur-lined coat with a muff in the other, and both portraits are delineated in quick brush strokes of thinned oil paint. Likewise, in both pictures, the sitter's face, in contrast to her costume, has far greater texture. The confident strokes remain, but instead Lemonnier's plain features are presented in creamy layers of browns, reds, whites and greens. An X-ray of the Copenhagen picture suggests that there were few changes in the overall composition, although there appears to be evidence of a muff that was ultimately removed. A close examination of both pictures, however, reveals the rapidity with which the figure was laid out, despite Lemonnier's insistence that Manet was unable to draw (Robida 1958, p. 119). LL

Endnotes

Manet: Portraying Life. Themes and Variations

MARYANNE STEVENS

1 Noted by Antonin Proust; see Wilson-Bareau 1991, p. 187.
2 Paris 1983b, no. 73.
3 Otto Scholderer, German artist, critic and admirer of Courbet and his followers; the civil servant Edmond Maistre, musician, friend of the recently deceased poet Charles Baudelaire and supporter of the Impressionists; Auguste Renoir, Frédéric Bazille and Claude Monet, three younger artists who were to go on to become Impressionists; and their supporter Emile Zola, the author and critic who had first come to Manet's defence in 1866. See also Colin B. Bailey in the present volume, p. 63.
4 Quoted in Hamilton 1969, p. 144.
5 The percentage of portraits relative to all categories of works accepted by the Salon fell from 30% in 1833 to 24% in 1853 and 16% in 1866, whereafter it appears to have stabilised. See McCauley 1985.
6 See the excellent map in Paris 1983a, pp. 502–03.
7 Manet to Zacharie Astruc, Bellevue, undated [5 July 1880], in Wilson-Bareau 1991, p. 250.
8 Other literary and artistic friends included Astruc, Silvestre, Burty and G. E. Moore, and Fantin-Latour, Bracquemond, Legros and Nadar.
9 See Paris 1983a, pp. 502–03.
10 Mme Meurice to Charles Baudelaire, 5 [January] 1865: 'Manet, discouraged, rips up his studies', in Paris 1983a, p. 508.
11 For example *The Amazon* (1882; Hahnloser Stiftung, Villa Flora, Winterthur; RWI, no. 396).
12 For example *The Velocipede* (cat. 11), *Portrait of Fanny Clauss* (cat. 34), *The Execution of Maximilian* (1867; National Gallery, London; RWI, no. 126). See also Laurence des Cars, 'Painting in *Morceaux*', in Paris 2011a, pp. 45–54.
13 Albert Wolff, *Le Figaro*, 2 May 1880, in Hamilton 1969, p. 230.
14 See, for example, Bertall (Charles-Albert d'Arnoux), *Paris-Journal*, 2 May 1880, in Hamilton 1969, p. 230.
15 Mallarmé in 1876, quoted in Wilson-Bareau 1991, p. 305.
16 See notably Fried 1996; Paris 2002; Madrid 2003.
17 See Madeline 2011; Mayo Roos 2012; and Colin B. Bailey in the present volume (pp. 58–65).
18 Proust 1996, p. 101.
19 1859, 1863 (*Young Man in the Costume of a Majo* [RWI, no. 70], *Mlle V… as an Espada* [RWI, no. 58], *Le Déjeuner sur l'herbe* [RWI, no. 67]), 1866 (*The Tragic Actor* [cat. 33], *The Fifer* [RWI, no. 113]) and 1876 (*The Artist* [cat. 20], *The Laundry* [1875; Am Römerholz, Winterthur]).
20 1874 (*The Swallows* [cat. 8], *The Opera Ball* [RWI, no. 216]).
21 St Petersburg, 1861; Brussels, 1863, 1869 and 1872; Bordeaux, 1866; Le Havre, 1868; Marseilles, 1868, 1880; London, 1872, 1873 and 1874; New York and Boston, 1879–80; Lyons, 1883.
22 Louis Martinet (1814–1895) housed the Galerie Martinet in a pavilion erected in the garden of Richard Wallace's property. Both the gallery and the Société Nationale des Beaux-Arts were disbanded on the death of Martinet's financial backer, the Duc de Morny, in 1865.
23 Frédéric Chevalier, 'Impressionnisme au Salon', *L'Artiste*, 1 July 1877, in Hamilton 1969, p. 206.
24 Mallarmé in 1876, quoted in Wilson-Bareau 1991, p. 305.
25 Callen 2000, p. 173.
26 A spare compositional study (RWII, no. 475) exists for this work. Two drawings claim to be related to *The Luncheon* (cat. 10): RWII, no. 347, is a record of the painting before certain compositional changes were made, and RWII, no. 465, apparently a study of Léon, although it may not be by Manet.
27 RWI, nos 262, 263.
28 RWI, nos 389, 390.
29 Proust 1996, p. 53; Wilson-Bareau 1991, p. 184.
30 Rouart 1987, pp. 44–45.
31 *Le Figaro*, 4 January 1884, quoted in Hamilton 1969, p. 268.
32 Proust 1913, p. 49.
33 Proust 1996, p. 53.
34 Wilson-Bareau 1991, p. 252.
35 Proust 1996, p. 59.
36 Wilson-Bareau 1991, p. 181.
37 Photographers whom he used included Nadar, Reutlinger, Mulvier and Chardin.
38 Bibliothèque Nationale de France, Paris (Collection Moreau-Nélaton; NA 115).
39 For example, the etching of Edgar Allan Poe (1860–62) and the two etched portraits of Charles Baudelaire (1862–69).
40 Morgan Library, New York.
41 See McCauley 1985; Ligo 2007.
42 See for example Claudet, in McCauley 1985.
43 Linda Nochlin, in Ottawa 1997, p. 54.
44 See, for example, Klaus Albrecht Schröder, Walter Feilchenfeldt et al. (eds), *Cézanne, Finished/Unfinished*, exh. cat., Kunstforum, Vienna; Kunsthaus, Zürich, 2000.
45 For example, *The Amazon* (cat. 42), recorded in Leenhoff Inventory, vol. 1, p. 48.
46 'La main qui tient le manchon a été terminée par le peintre de chez Kievert', Leenhoff Inventory, vol. 1, p. 20.
47 See photograph in the Lochard Album, vol. 4, Tabarant Archive, Morgan Library, New York (MA3950).
48 *Le Temps*, 24 May 1873, quoted in Hamilton 1969, p. 169.
49 *Revue des deux mondes*, 1 June 1873, quoted in Hamilton 1969, pp. 165–66.
50 Reff 1975.
51 Paris 2002; Madrid 2003; Guégan 2011c.
52 Fried 1996.
53 Wilson-Bareau 1991, p. 183.
54 Paris 2000, pp. 83–84.
55 Hamilton 1969.
56 Quoted Hamilton 1969, p. 211.
57 Manet to Charles Baudelaire, undated [early May 1865], in Wilson-Bareau 1991, p. 33.
58 Proust 1996, p. 101.
59 See notably Fried 1996.
60 'Letter to Young Artist', *Le Courier de dimanche*, 29 December 1861.
61 Edmond Duranty, 'Réalisme', *Réalisme*, 15 November 1861, p. 1.
62 Proust 1996, p. 21.
63 Wilson-Bareau 2012.
64 Proust 1996, p. 51; Wilson-Bareau 1991, p. 183.
65 Ottawa 1997, p. 55.

Théophile Gautier, Militant of Modernity

STÉPHANE GUÉGAN

1 Gautier 1859: 'L'école romantique contenait dans son sein quelques adeptes, partisans de la vérité absolue, qui rejetaient le vers comme peu ou point naturel … Etre de son temps, rien ne paraît plus simple et rien n'est plus malaisé!'
2 On Manet's career and his presence at the Salon, see Guégan 2011a, pp. 26–43.
3 Both close to Baudelaire, Banville and de la Fizelière were to play a major role in converting romanticism into modernity during the Second Empire. The former became a strong supporter of Manet in the 1870s. On de la Fizelière, see Guégan 2011b, pp. 86–101.
4 For more on Gautier, see Guégan 2011c.
5 Gautier 1861, pp. 264–65: 'Caramba! voilà un *Guitarrero* qui ne vient pas de l'Opéra-Comique, et qui ferait mauvaise figure sur une lithographie de romance; mais Velázquez le saluerait d'un petit clignement d'œil amical, et Goya lui demanderait du feu pour allumer son papelito. – Comme il braille de bon courage en râclant le jambon! – Il nous semble l'entendre. – Ce brave Espagnol au *sombrero calañés*, à la veste marseillaise, a un pantalon. Hélas! la culotte courte de Figaro n'est plus portée que par les *espadas* et les *banderilleros*. Mais cette concession aux modes civilisées, les alpargates le rachètent. Il y a beaucoup de talent dans cette figure de grandeur naturelle, peinte en pleine pâte, d'une brosse vaillante et d'une couleur très vraie.' It is worth noting that Manet's *Mademoiselle V. in the Costume of an Espada* (Metropolitan Museum of Art, New York), shown at the 1863 Salon des Réfusés, did present herself wearing Figaro's knee-breeches.
6 See Guégan 2011c, pp. 114–65, and Guégan 2003.
7 Gautier 1836: 'Il faut bon gré mal gré nous enfermer tous dans de vilains suaires noirs, où nous avons l'air de porter le deuil de notre gaieté.' On Baudelaire's debt to Gautier, see Guégan 1997.
8 Gautier 1847, p. 108: 'M. Vidal … a l'élégance, le goût, la délicate compréhension de la beauté moderne, égale pour le moins à la beauté antique, mais dont nos artistes, trop préoccupés de la Grèce et de Rome, ne savent pas dégager l'idéal.'
9 See Guégan 2011c, pp. 363–67. After the 1850–51 Salon, Gautier made it clear that he felt Courbet deserved an award from the Republic for his crucial contribution to the exhibition; see Gautier 1851.
10 See Guégan 2008.
11 Gautier 1852a: 'On sent bien qu'il y a quelque chose à faire – mais quoi? Est-ce une blanchisseuse ou une dryade, une cuvette ou un héros, un taudis ou l'Olympe?'
12 Gautier 1852b: 'On a tort selon nous d'affecter une certain répugnance ou du moins un certain dédain pour les types purement actuels. Nous croyons, pour notre part, qu'il y a des effets neufs, des aspects inattendus dans la représentation intelligente et fidèle de ce que nous nommerons la modernité … Plus que tout autre, un portraitiste doit donner le sens de son époque et signer sa peinture à un millésime exact.'
13 Gautier 1855, p. 19: 'le caractère de la peinture anglaise est … la modernité. Le substantif existe-t-il? Le sentiment qu'il exprime est si récent que le mot pourrait bien ne pas se trouver dans les dictionnaires.' See also Compiègne 2008.
14 See Guégan 2011c, pp. 453–61.
15 See Gautier 1857a and Gautier 1857c. See also Gautier 1857b, in which he mentioned a realistic print by Félix Bracquemond that actually included a female figure by Paul Gavarni. There is much evidence that Manet was himself receptive to Gavarni's prints. As for *Young Lady in 1866*, see Reed 2003, pp. 137–39.
16 See Guégan 2011c, pp. 511–16.
17 Gautier 1864: '…une certaine puissance, une certaine action sur la peinture contemporaine, dont il représente les tendances les plus outrées.'
18 See Reed 2003, pp. 116–45.
19 Gautier 1869: 'Très peu restent indifférents à cette peinture étrange qui semble la négation de l'art et qui pourtant s'y rattache.'
20 Gautier 1869: 'L'exposition de M. Manet est relativement sage et ne fera pas scandale. S'il voulait s'en donner la peine, il pourrait devenir un bon peintre. Il en a le tempérament.'
21 Gautier 1870: 'Aucune des promesses du début n'a été réalisée, et chaque exposition semble prouver que M. Manet a résolu de mourir dans l'impénitence finale, égaré par une fausse doctrine et d'imprudents éloges.'

Manet at the Intersection of Portraits and Personalities

CAROL M. ARMSTRONG

1 Daumier's lithographic cartoon was published in *Le Boulevard* in 1862. As fellow caricaturists of a similar age, Daumier and Nadar moved in the same circles. Moreover, as caricaturists, they were both adept at the so-called *portrait-charge*, the caricatural study of specific, recognisable individuals, so they also shared a stake in the transformations being made in portraiture by the photograph during Manet's career. (Nadar's own record of *portrait-charge*-making is summarised in his well-known lithograph of 1854, *Panthéon Nadar*.)

Moreover, some time between 1856 and 1858, Nadar's studio made at least four portraits of Daumier. On nineteenth-century caricature, see Wechsler 1982. On Nadar, Daumier and their shared circle, see Paris 1994B, in particular Françoise Heilbrun, 'Nadar and the Art of Portrait Photography', pp. 35–58, and Philippe Néagu, 'Nadar and the Artistic Life of His Time', pp. 59–76.

2 On the proliferation of photographic businesses in nineteenth-century Paris, see McCauley 1994.

3 In addition to etching and drawing him, Degas also painted Manet listening to his wife play the piano in the late 1860s. Meanwhile Bracquemond etched a standard bust-length portrait of Manet in 1867 (a portrait that strongly suggests a photographic derivation), and at the same time spoofed Manet's reputation in a print entitled *Manet manebit*, by placing the artist's head on a tall pedestal from which sprout, roughly at groin-level, a palette and a set of erect brushes. For his part, Fantin-Latour also painted Manet seated at the centre of a gathering of the artists who were to become the Impressionist painters in his *Atelier in Les Batignolles* (fig. 1).

4 The Nadar portraits of Manet were taken between 1863 and 1864, after Nadar had moved to the Boulevard des Capucines, having made numerous concessions to contemporary taste, and announced his boredom with portrait-photography. Much of the work of this period was probably not done by Nadar himself, but by one of his 'operators'. Nevertheless, photographs such as those of Manet retain the strength of personality that marked the earlier work, and were very possibly overseen by Nadar himself. On this period, see Françoise Heilbrun, in Paris 1994B, pp. 50ff.

5 McCauley 1985, pp. 172–95; Worth 2007. See also Ligo 2007.

6 On the work of Charles Aubry, see McCauley 1994, 'Aubry's Dream for Industry', pp. 233–64.

7 On the etching revival, and the discourse on the autographic dimension of etching and aquatint versus the mechanical qualities of photography and reproductive engraving, see Armstrong 2002, 'Reproducing Originality: The Cadart Portfolio', pp. 71–98. Manet not only undertook etchings after his own works (as well as after works believed to be by Velázquez), but also had some of his paintings photographed: witness the photograph of *Olympia* that he re-reproduces on the bulletin board on the wall behind Zola in his 1868 portrait of the critic (cat. 28). None of the remarks from Manet's time address the resemblance of the aquatint's tonal language to that of the photograph. On the aquatint, see Benson 2008, pp. 40–43.

8 Baudelaire's sole published remarks on Manet's work are to be found in his 'Peintres et aquafortistes', *Le Boulevard*, 37, 14 September 1862; reprinted in Bailly 1986, pp. 414–19.

9 See Charles Baudelaire, 'Le Public moderne et la photographie', in 'Le Salon de 1859', *La Revue française*, 10 June – 20 July 1859, reprinted in Bailly 1986, pp. 285–91, and Baudelaire 1868, pp. 254–63: '…A partir de ce moment, la société immonde se rua, comme un seul Narcisse, pour contempler sa triviale image sur le metal. Une folie, un fanatisme extraordinaire s'empara de tous ces mouveaux adorateurs du soleil. D'étranges abominations se produisirent. En associant et en groupant des drôles et des drôlesses, attifés comme les bouchers et les blanchisseuses dans le carnival, en priant des héros de vouloir bien continuer, pour le temps nécessaire à l'opération, leur grimace de circonstance, on se flatta de rendre les scenes, tragiques ou gracieuses, de l'histoire ancienne. Quelque écrivain démocrate a dû voir là le moyen, à bon marché, de répandre dans le peuple le dégoût de l'histoire et de la peinture, commettant ainsi un double sacrilége et insultant à la fois la divine peinture et l'art sublime du comedién…' (p. 259).

10 See McCauley 1994, 'Nadar and the Selling of Bohemia', pp. 105–48.

11 'Puis, coup decisive, l'apparition de Disdéri et de la carte de visite qui donnait pour quelque vingt francs douze portraits quand on avait payé jusque-là cinquante ou cent francs pour un seul. / Ce fout la déroute. Il fallait se soumettre, c'est-à-dire suivre le mouvement, ou se démettre…', Nadar 1900, p. 206 (republished as a small, abridged volume in 1998). In his long disquisition 'Les Primitifs de la photographie' (pp. 208–13), Nadar includes a rather more generous account of the rise and fall of Disdéri than his acerbic words might suggest possible.

12 On the concept of the 'punctum', see Barthes 1980. It is not by chance that Barthes chooses Nadar as his nineteenth-century portrait-photographer par excellence; beneath the photograph of Nadar's wife (which Barthes, preferring to see it as a portrait of the photographer's mother, nominates as 'l'une des plus belles photos au monde'), he remarked that Nadar was 'le plus grand photographe du monde' (pp. 108–09).

13 See Clement Greenberg, 'Avant-garde and Kitsch', in Greenberg 1986, vol. 1, pp. 5–22.

14 On Courbet's retrospective of 1855 and the place and meaning of *The Studio: A Real Allegory of Seven Years of My Life as a Painter* within it, and on Manet's retrospective of 1867 and the concept of 'individuality' offered up in it, see Armstrong 2002, 'Two Retrospectives: Courbet in 1855 and Manet in 1867', pp. 3–30.

15 I believe, however, that it is unlikely that Manet worked much from photographs, for he required the person to be there in the flesh. The difference in vivacity between his pastel of Méry Laurent and the carte de visite by Disdéri suggests that Laurent was there before him when he sketched her.

16 Here Manet possibly also looked back to an earlier pictorial dialogue between Degas and Courbet, witnessed in Degas's *Self-portrait Saluting* (1865; Museu Calouste Gulbenkian, Lisbon), which in turn looks back to Courbet's *Bonjour Monsieur Courbet* (1854; Musée Fabre, Montpellier).

17 On the pictorial dialogue between Manet's portrait of Antonin Proust and Fantin-Latour's top-hatted portrait of Manet of 1867, see Armstrong 2002, 'To You, Edouard Manet', pp. 303–17.

'L'Esprit de l'atelier': Manet's Late Portraits of Women, 1878–1883

LEAH LEHMBECK

1 There is some debate over the nature of Rosen's studio, the artist from whom Manet was renting the space. Adolphe Tabarant, Manet's primary biographer, notes that the studio belonged to Otto Rosen, and had a conservatory, which explains the indoor garden setting. Recently, Juliet Wilson-Bareau has discovered that the temporary studio may have belonged to Jean Rosen, a Polish painter whose address was listed at 77 Rue d'Amsterdam during those years, suggesting that, instead of number 70, Manet was already at number 77, awaiting the move to his final, larger studio in the same building. Furthermore, some of these portraits were started before Manet rented the temporary space. For more detailed information, see the entries for *In the Conservatory* (cat. 39) and *Mme Manet in the Conservatory* (cat. 6) in the present catalogue and Juliet Wilson-Bareau, 'Edouard Manet dans ses ateliers', in Tokyo 2010, pp. 304–12.

2 These two symbolic portraits may have been a commission for the four seasons requested by Antonin Proust, one of Manet's constant supporters. Paris 1983A, pp. 490–91, note 8.

3 Maurice Du Seigneur, *L'Artiste*, 1 June 1882, cited in Hamilton 1954, p. 249.

4 Emile Zola, *Une Nouvelle Manière de peindre: Edouard Manet*, Paris, 1867, cited in Rubin 1994, p. 121.

5 Jacques-Emile Blanche, *Manet*, Paris, 1924, cited in Courthion and Cailler 1960, p. 200.

6 My count from RW.

7 René Maizeroy, *Gil Blas*, January 1882, cited in Brombert 1996, p. 405.

8 Paul Sebillot, *L'Artiste*, 1 May 1880, in a review of Manet's solo exhibition at *La Vie moderne* in 1880, cited in Hamilton 1954, pp. 229–30.

9 Her salon is recounted in Robida 1958.

10 Over a dozen illustrated letters to Isabelle survive, written when Manet was undergoing hydrotherapy treatments at Bellevue from July to September or October 1880. They are all in the Cabinet des Dessins at the Musée du Louvre.

11 Interestingly, this work was owned by Berthe Morisot, another of Manet's favourite portrait subjects, and was included in the background of the portrait of her daughter Julie entitled *Violin Practice* (1893; Private collection); Higonnet 1992, p. 243.

12 For more on the performative relationship between sitter and artist, see Berger 1994.

13 The painting could not be shown in France for political reasons. It is not known why Ambre was entrusted with it. See Brennecke 2004 for a consideration of the relationship between Manet's painting and Ambre's trip to America.

14 Tabarant 1947, p. 365.

15 New York 2003, pp. 503–04, note 5.

16 Therese Dolan's article on Manet's portrait of Ambre notes that 'Carmen provided Manet with an occasion to foreground what [she perceives] are mutual concerns shared by the musician and the artist regarding the performative aspects of their respective mediums'. See Dolan 2006.

17 RWII, pastels, no. 89.

Manet and Renoir: An Unexamined Dialogue

COLIN B. BAILEY

It is a pleasure to thank Shannon Victoria, Nicholas Wise and Maude Bass-Krueger for their assistance in the research and writing of this essay. I am grateful to Augustin de Butler for his unstinting generosity and to Judy Sund and Alan Wintermute for their encouragement, and for their enthusiasm for this topic.

1 Manet 1979, p. 61 (23 August 1895).

2 Vollard (1938, pp. 171–72) expressed surprise at Renoir's enthusiasm for Manet's early work, 'his first canvases, so directly inspired by the museums'.

3 Manet 1979, pp. 191–92, 248. 'In the works of a great painter who knows to give them the appropriate place, how beautiful and simple the whites are; look at Titian's whites, Manet's whites, Corot's whites' (2 October 1898). 'Titian said that a great painter was one who knows how to use black … Manet's blacks are so beautiful, always done in one stroke' (7 August 1899).

4 Vollard 1919, pp. 22–23. 'Not content with having painted one of the most recognisable subjects of the great Venetian School, he even imitated one of Raphael's figures for his nude woman.'

5 Vollard 1938, p. 172.

6 Renoir 1981, p. 117. Jean Renoir attributed this remark to Bazille.

7 Distel 2006, pp. 144, 149. Renoir paid 200 francs for the *Port of Bordeaux* (1871) and 150 francs for *Small Boats* (*c.* 1873); see RWII, nos 234, 249. The former was hanging in the dining room of his apartment on the Boulevard Rochechouart in December 1915.

8 Vollard 1938, p. 137.

9 Ottawa 1997, p. 238.

10 RWI, p. 26; Ottawa 1997, pp. 100, 270.

11 Vollard 1919, p. 52.

12 Bazire (1884, p. 74) noted that Manet was a generous promoter of his younger colleagues. 'To any visitor who came to him, he would say: 'Ah! Look at this Degas! Look at this Renoir! Look at this Monet! What talent my friends have.' This is confirmed in a somewhat bitter letter that Manet wrote to Théodore Duret on 13 July 1879: 'I would appreciate it if my friends would find buyers for my work. I've sold enough pictures for other people' (Wilson-Bareau 1991, p. 251).

13 Wilson-Bareau 1991, p. 181, where, following Moreau-Nélaton, the letter is incorrectly dated to 1877. Rewald (1973, p. 395, note 10) noted that the letter must date to 1875, since the first Impressionist auction took place on 24 March 1875 (the second was held on 28 May 1877).

14 Renoir's letter to Manet is partially published in Moreau-Nélaton 1926, vol. 2, p. 88; it is in the collection of the Louvre's Cabinet des Dessins (see Chillaz 1997, Aut. 3642). Manet's unpublished response is known from a virtually illegible photocopy in the Jean Renoir Papers at the Young Research Library, Special Collections, UCLA, Los Angeles, Box 20, Folder 15. The letter itself appeared in *Pierre-Auguste Renoir (1841–1919): Personal Artifacts and Archives Collection*, Hantmann's Auctioneers, May 2005, p. 52, no. 71. For their assistance in verifying my transcriptions of both letters, I am extremely grateful to Augustin de Butler and Samuel Rodary, who, respectively – the latter in collaboration with Juliet Wilson-Bareau – are preparing editions of Renoir's and Manet's correspondence.

15 On this reforming ministry, see Green 1987.

16 Moreau-Nélaton 1926, vol. 2, p. 88.

17 See Appendix, p. 207.

18 Manet to Renoir, 31 December 1881, see the Young Research Library, Special Collections, UCLA, Los Angeles, Jean Renoir Papers, Box 20, Folder 15, and Appendix, p. 207.

19 'And in all things that live there are certain irregularities and deficiencies which are not only signs of life, but sources of beauty.' Quoted in Herbert 2000, p. 27.

20 Ibid., pp. 1–16.

21 Proust 1996, p. 53.

22 Herbert 2000, p. 123.
23 Renoir sent Léon Leenhoff his payment of 20 francs for the banquet at Père Lathuille's on 23 December 1884; see Medeiros 2002, 'Memorial Banquet Correspondence; Renoir'.
24 On 11 August 1899 Renoir informed Monet that he would be unable to participate, 'Impossible de trouver l'argent… Manet ira au Louvre sans moi, je l'espère,' Geffroy 1924, vol. 1, p. 245. For Monet's leadership in this undertaking, see Paris 1983A, p. 183.
25 'Chronique Parisienne', *La Vie moderne*, 12 January 1884, p. 859. For Renoir's drawing, first illustrated in Meier-Graefe 1929, p. 85, and now in the Schlossberg Collection, Atlanta, see Atlanta 1994, pp. 35, 67 (no. 70).
26 Tabarant 1947, p. 252.
27 Rewald 1945, p. 181.
28 Ottawa 1997, p. 16.
29 Moffett in Paris 1983A, p. 29.
30 Paris 1998, p. 182.
31 As Monet noted to Pissarro on 22 April 1873 of the proposal to launch the first group exhibition, 'Without a doubt, everyone is finding it to be a good idea; only Manet is against it' (Wildenstein 1974–91, vol. 1, p. 428, letter 64). Renoir was not to become involved in these discussions until the autumn of 1873; see Bailey 2007, p. 55.
32 Washington 1986, pp. 121, 164. Manet lent Morisot's *Hide and Seek* (1873; Private collection, New York) in 1874 and Renoir's *Frédéric Bazille* (see fig. 33) in 1876.
33 The appearance of twenty-five of Renoir's paintings in the Seventh Impressionist Exhibition in April 1882 was due entirely to Durand-Ruel, who lent them from his stock. He was bitterly opposed in this by Renoir. See Bailey 2007, p. 66.
34 House 1986, and House 2004, especially Chapters 1 and 2. On Renoir's Salon strategy, see Bailey 2012, Chapter 1.
35 Wollheim 1987, p. 161.
36 Bazire 1884, p. 116.
37 Reff 1964, p. 556.
38 Vollard 1938, p. 144.
39 Manet began his copy of the *Portrait of Helena Fourment and Her Children* on 21 August 1857; see Reff 1964, p. 566. Renoir's copy of the central portion of the composition dates to the early 1860s; see White 1984, pp. 13–14. In the second half of the 1850s Manet made two copies after Delacroix's *Barque of Dante* (1822; Musée du Louvre, Paris); Renoir, a more profound admirer of Delacroix, was commissioned in 1875 to make a to-scale copy of his *Jewish Wedding* (1876; Worcester Art Museum). See Paris 1983A, pp. 45–46, and Dauberville 2007–10, vol. 1, no. 231.
40 Fried 1996, p. 3.
41 Moore 1906, p. 38; Moore 1914, p. 163.
42 The term 'tache colorante' – the touch or patch of colour – was coined by the liberal critic Jules Castagnary in his review of the Salon of 1869; see House 2004, p. 11. In the 1880s Renoir's advanced coloristic handling was routinely characterised as 'du tricotage' – a piece of knitting; see Ottawa 1997, p. 189.
43 House (2004, p. 122) elegantly summarised the difference between Renoir's enduring Bohemian vision and Manet's relentlessly patrician one: 'Renoir domesticates class markers, Manet parades them.'
44 For a summary introduction to one side of this relationship, see Gurley 1973.
45 House 2004, p. 6.
46 Paris 1983B, pp. 208–14.
47 See Fantin-Latour's preparatory compositional drawings in the graphic collection of the Musée du Louvre, Paris, RF 12551 (dated 15 October [1869]), RF 12687 (16 October [1869], RF 12501 (9 November [1869]).
48 Paris 1983B, pp. 205–07. As Druick pointed out, the heavily bearded and heavy-set figure behind Manet was most probably the critic Edmond Duranty. This drawing must date to before 20 February 1870, when Manet challenged Duranty to a duel; not surprisingly, Fantin excised him from the composition.
49 Jullien 1909, p. 71, quoting from Fantin's letter to Edwards, 1 March 1870.
50 In April 1875 Fantin lamented Manet's decision to send *Argenteuil* (1874; Musée des Beaux-Arts, Tournai) to the Salon, which he felt was indicative of the direction Manet's art had now taken: 'I don't like it at all, it was done under Monet's influence, who was by his side at Argenteuil and who is seducing Manet a great deal at the moment. He is thoroughly enchanted with that world, Monet, Sisley, Renoir, Pizarro [*sic*] and Melle Morizot (Berthe).' Arnoux, Gaehtgens and Tempelaere-Panzani 2011, p. 230: Fantin to Scholderer, 4 April 1875. Thanks to Augustin de Butler for bringing this letter to my attention.
51 Tabarant 1947, p. 175.
52 And whose 'modest likeness', in turn, 'is transformed into the portrait of a master'; Paris 1994A, p. 384.
53 London 1985, pp. 58, 198; Distel 2009, pp. 89–93.
54 Manet showed it at the Salon des refusés in 1863, at his one-man exhibition at the Pont d'Alma in 1867 and at the Salon of 1869. In the last two venues mentioned, the etching was accompanied by Manet's painted copy.
55 'Having been marked by Edouard Manet's *Olympia*, he was no longer admitted to the Salon.' P. Burty, 'Les Peintures de M. P. Renoir,' *La République française*, 15 April 1883, p. 1.
56 Faison 1973.
57 Ottawa 1997, pp. 114–15; Renoir inscribed the date 'Avril 71' after his signature on his *Portrait of Rapha Maître*, which allows us to date the *Still-life with Bouquet* to that month.
58 Paris 1983A, pp. 347–49; Wildenstein 1996, vol. 2, p. 159, no. 387.
59 Ottawa 1997, pp. 130–31, 282.
60 Elder 1924, p. 70.
61 Wildenstein 1996, vol. 2, p. 142, no. 342.
62 Ottawa 1997, p. 130.
63 'To return to the Rue Saint-Georges, among the paintings that I executed in this studio, I remember… finally *The Monet Family en Plein Air*, in Monet's garden at Argenteuil.' Vollard 1919, p. 67.
64 Tabarant 1947, pp. 252–57. The source of the story seems to have been the ageing Monet, who, in retirement at Giverny, told it to Vollard and Marc Elder. The latter published the fullest version in 1924 in *A Giverny, Chez Claude Monet*.

Manet and Hals: Two Geniuses, One Vision

LAWRENCE W. NICHOLS

I am grateful to Pieter Biesboer, Edwin Buijsen, Quentin Buvelot, Stéphane Guégan, Alison Huftalen, Brian Kennedy, Michiel Plomp, Seymour Slive and Anna Tummers for their kind assistance in my research for this essay.

1 Wilson-Bareau 2004, p. 204. (Originally published in Proust 1897, p. 180: 'Ce qui a toujours fait mon désespoir, ce sont les musées. J'éprouve un grande tristesse quand j'y entre, en constatant combien la peinture est misérable. Les visiteurs, les gardiens, tout grouille. Les portraits ne vivent pas. Et cependant, dans ces portraits, il y en a (ici un claquement de langue), les Velasquez, les Goya, les Hals … car il ne faut pas blaguer, c'étaient des bonshommes, ces mâtins-là. Trop d'arrangement, mais ils ne perdaient pas de vue la nature.')
2 Wilson-Bareau 2004, p. 42.
3 For Manet's copy, see RWI, no. 103. Wilson-Bareau 2004, p. 41. A considerable body of literature examines the influence of Spanish painting on Manet, the catalogues accompanying the exhibitions mounted in New York and in Madrid in 2003 being foremost.
4 RWI, no. 32; Wilson-Bareau 2004, p. 35.
5 Jowell 2007, pp. 84–89; Atkins 2012, pp. 218–24.
6 The far-reaching impact of seventeenth-century Dutch art on nineteenth-century French painting as a whole has of course received significant attention; see Doesschate Chu 1974; Epstein 2007; as well as Jowell 2007. For the influence of Dutch art on Manet specifically, see also Fried 1996, pp. 107–09; Hecht 1997; and DeWitt 2003.
7 Slive 1970–74, no. 30; see also Jowell 1989, pp. 66–67 and notes 58 and 59.
8 Slive 1970–74, no. 185; published by Thoré-Bürger (Bürger 1864). See Jowell 1989, p. 66.
9 Bürger 1868; see Jowell 1989, pp. 64–70.
10 Slive 1970–74, nos 62 and 171 respectively. *Gypsy Girl* was also on public view in the 1866 Exposition Rétrospective in the Champs-Elysées; see Jowell 1989, p. 67.
11 RWI, no. 17, a copy of a work that was then thought to be a self-portrait by Brouwer and is now recognised to be by Joos van Craesbeeck (Musée du Louvre, Paris, M.I. 906). See Doesschate Chu 1974, p. 43 and note 3. The Louvre also had in its possession from its founding a portrait of Descartes (inv. no. 1317), rejected as the work of Hals by most modern scholars; Slive 1970–74, no. 175-1.
12 Due to an ambiguous statement made by Proust (1913, p. 31) – 'Manet laissa l'atelier Couture in 1856 … Il visita le Belgique, la Hollande, l'Allemagne et l'Italie. Chaque fois qu'il revenait à Paris il risquait un apparition chez Couture pour lui montrer les copies qu'il avait faites dans les musées ou les impressions qu'il avait fixées sur le papier ou sur la toile' – it is sometimes claimed that Manet also visited Holland in 1856, but there is no evidence for this. Doesschate Chu (1974, p. 43) notes that Bazire, Manet's first biographer, stated in 1884 that the painter travelled to Kassel, Dresden, Prague, Vienna and Munich in the mid-1850s (Bazire 1884, p. 10).
13 The Rijksmuseum's works were then installed in the Trippenhuis, at Kloveniersburgwal 29 (the collection was moved to the present building in 1885). Noord-Hollands Archief, Haarlem, #476, Rijksmuseum en rechtsvoorgangers te Amsterdam 1807–1945, Registers van bezoekers, 1844–1878, inv. 125 (May 1844 – 4 July 1853); Verbeek 1958, p. 64 (with facsimile of signature), and Doesschate Chu 1974, p. 43, notes 1 and 3.
14 Slive 1970–74, no. 17.
15 Slive 1970–74, no. 63.
16 Slive 1970–74, no. 80.
17 RWI, no. 8; Sotheby's, London, 4 February 2003, lot 10; Verbeek 1958, p. 64. Often dated 1856, this work seems more likely to have been executed in Holland in 1852.
18 As communicated in a letter of this date from Baudelaire to his fellow writer Etienne Carjat; RWI, p. 12.
19 New York 1994, p. 301.
20 The collection was moved in 1913 to what had been the Old Men's Alms House, whose name was changed to the Frans Hals Museum at the same time.
21 Noord-Hollands Archief, Haarlem, #1374, Haarlem Municipal Museum, Registers van bezoekers, 1862–1872, inv. 102; Doesschate Chu, p. 45 and note 4. Presumably he did not visit the Teylers Museum as his name does not appear in the visitors' register of that institution.
22 Slive 1970–74, nos 7, 45, 46, 79, 124, 140, 221 and 222.
23 Noord-Hollands Archief, Haarlem, #476, Rijksmuseum en rechtsvoorgangers te Amsterdam 1807–1945, Registers van bezoekers, 1844–1878, inv. 133 (15 March 1870 – 2 July 1872); Verbeek 1958, p. 64 (with facsimile of signature), and Doesschate Chu 1974, p. 45, note 4.
24 RWI, no. 185; Chicago 2003, no. 56.
25 Slive 1970–74, no. 222. Pieter Biesboer, former curator at the Frans Hals Museum, kindly informed me that a letter and a photograph were sent to Haarlem before November 1976, and again in the early 1990s, from a private collector in Rome offering for sale a purported copy by Manet of Hals's *Regentesses*. Unfortunately it has not been possible to locate these communications in the records of the Frans Hals Museum, nor is this alleged Manet copy known at the Musée d'Orsay or by Seymour Slive.
26 Proust 1901, p. 230; see Jowell 1989, p. 71, Fried 1996, p. 108, and Jowell 2007, p. 86–89.
27 RWI, nos 19, 32 and 30; Proust 1901, p. 230.
28 RWI, no. 186.
29 Duret 1923, p. 122.
30 Wilson-Bareau 2004, p. 132.
31 Proust 1901, p. 235 (the English translation used here is by Bridget McDonald and was published in Fried 1996, p. 433).
32 Wilson-Bareau 2004, p. 119.
33 Slive 1970–74, no. 15. Hals's original composition was cut down at some point prior to the end of the eighteenth century. A section with three children belongs to the Musée des Beaux-Arts, Brussels (gift 1928, inv. no. 4732); the larger portion seen in fig. 44, with the parents and seven children, was acquired by the Toledo Museum of Art in 2011. The painting will be the subject of a forthcoming article by Pieter Biesboer.
34 Proust 1913, pp. 102–03 (English translation from Armstrong 2002, p. 312).
35 Proust 1901, p. 235.

COLIN B. BAILEY

Manet and Renoir: An Unexamined Dialogue

Appendix: An Exchange of Letters by Renoir and Manet in December 1881

Renoir to Manet, 28 December 1881
Musée du Louvre, Paris. Cabinet des Dessins, Aut. 3642

À Édouard Manet / Capri, 28 décembre [18]81

Mon cher Manet,
Il y a longtemps que je voulais vous écrire à propos de la nomination de Proust, et je ne l'ai pas fait. Cependant il vient de me tomber sous la main un vieux Petit Journal, qui parle avec transport des achats des tableaux du maître Courbet, ce qui m'a fait un plaisir extrême. Non pas pour Courbet, ce pauvre vieux, qui ne peut pas jouir de son triomphe, mais pour l'art français. Il y a donc enfin un ministre qui se doute que l'on fait de la peinture en France, et j'attendais dans le numéro suivant du même Petit Journal, votre nomination de Chevalier, ce qui m'eût fait applaudir de mon île lointaine. Mais j'espère que ce n'est que retardé et qu'à mon entrée dans la capitale j'aurai à saluer en vous le peintre aimé de tout le monde reconnu officiellement. Car je suppose que ce ministre, intelligent et brave comme il me paraît, doit savoir que son portrait est fait pour le Louvre, et non pas pour lui.

Vous ne supposez pas, je crois, qu'il entre dans ma correspondance un seul mot de compliment.

Vous êtes le lutteur joyeux, sans haine pour personne, comme un vieux Gaulois, et je vous aime à cause de cette gaîté même dans l'injustice.

Je suis dans un joli pays, mais sans beaucoup de nouvelles. Quand la mer est grosse je n'ai aucuns journaux [*sic*], et pas français [*sic*], et je ne sais comment le Petit Journal est venu s'égarer à Capri où je suis [le] seul Français.

Vous ne vous doutez pas que je vous écris pour vous souhaiter la bonne année. Eh bien si, je le fais, et avec joie.

Quand je reviendrai, vous me ferez bien plaisir en venant voir ce que j'ai rapporté, mais nous n'en sommes pas là.

Je ne sais quand vous recevrez cette lettre car le courrier est irrégulier. Voilà déjà quatre jours de tempête et plus de 6 jours que je n'ai reçu aucune lettre de Paris. Le temps se remet, j'espère que cette lettre arrivera bientôt.

Ah, mon cher Manet, j'oubliais [le] nouveau ministère. Pensez donc à ce pauvre Lestringuez. 34 ans, connaissant bien son service, ce serait un rude sous-chef aux Beaux-Arts. Qu'en pensez-vous? Êtes-vous de mon avis? Dites-le moi dans un mot. Je vous serais bien reconnaissant. C'est une idée qui me pousse avec ma plume. Vous me pardonnerez car je n'ai pas oublié que vous avez été déjà bon camarade, comme toujours.

À bientôt, et mille amitiés et une longue santé, Renoir.

Albergo La Trinacria, piazzetta Principessa Margherita, Napoli. C'est de là qu'on m'envoie les lettres à Capri.

Manet to Renoir, Paris, 31 December 1881
Photocopy at the Young Research Library, Special Collections, UCLA, Los Angeles, Jean Renoir Papers, Box 20, Folder 15

Paris 31 Xbre [1881] Mon cher Renoir, Votre lettre me fait grand plaisir – vous avez de la chance d'être au soleil ici il y a un affreux brouillard et vous allez sans doute nous rapporter une masse d'études toutes personnelles et intéressantes. En effet le nouveau ministre vient de donner leurs tristes jours à Cabanel et autres professeurs de l'école, il ferme les ateliers et renvoie dans la désolation les jeunes paresseux qui les fréquentaient aux frais de l'état [*Two lines illegible*] Il vient pour le jour de l'an de décorer Bracquemont [*sic*], moi et d'autres. Faure aussi et j'espère qu'il restera assez longtemps pour vous donner le complément indispensable aux peintres de nos [*word illegible*]. J'ai pensé au brave Lestringuez et je ne lui en ai pas parlé cependant mais si on réussit il l'apprendra et n'aura pas eu les inquiétudes de la réussite ni les déboires de la défaite. J'ai eu de vos nouvelles par Deudon toujours si aimable et qui avait reçu une lettre de vous. Mille amitiés mon cher Renoir et rapportez beaucoup de toiles. Ed. Manet.

Bibliography

Adler 1986
Kathleen Adler, *Manet*, Oxford, 1986

Armstrong 2002
Carol M. Armstrong, *Manet Manette*, New Haven and London, 2002

Arnoux, Gaehtgens and Tempelaere-Panzani 2011
Mathilde Arnoux, Thomas W. Gaehtgens and Anne Tempelaere-Panzani, *Passages, No. 24: Correspondance entre Henri Fantin-Latour et Otto Scholderer, 1858–1902*, Paris, 2011

Atkins 2012
Christopher D. M. Atkins, *The Signature Style of Frans Hals: Painting, Subjectivity, and the Market in Early Modernity*, 2012

Atlanta 1994
Eric M. Zafran and Paula Marlais Hancock, *Nineteenth- and Twentieth-century European Drawings and Sculpture from the Schlossberg Collection*, exh. cat., High Museum of Art, Atlanta, 1994

Atlanta 2007
Ann Dumas (ed.), *Inspiring Impressionism: The Impressionists and the Art of the Past*, exh. cat., High Museum of Art, Atlanta; Denver Art Museum; Seattle Art Museum, 2007–08

Bailey 2007
Colin B. Bailey, '"The Greatest Luminosity, Colour and Harmony": Renoir's Landscapes, 1862–1883', in Colin B. Bailey and Christopher Riopelle (eds), *Renoir Landscapes: 1865–1883*, exh. cat., National Gallery, London, 2007, pp. 50–81

Bailey 2012
Colin B. Bailey, *Renoir, Impressionism, and Full-length Painting*, New York, 2012

Bailly 1986
Jean-Christophe Bailly (ed.), *Ecrits esthétiques par Charles Baudelaire*, Paris, 1986

Baltimore 1999
Sona Johnston, with Susan Bollendorf, *Faces of Impressionism: Portraits from American Collections*, exh. cat., Baltimore Museum of Art; Museum of Fine Arts, Houston; Cleveland Museum of Art, 1999–2000

Barthes 1980
Roland Barthes, *La Chambre claire: Note sur la photographie*, Paris, 1980

Basel 1999
Manet, Zola, Cézanne: das Porträt des Anderen Literaten, exh. cat., Kunstmuseum, Basel, 1999

Baudelaire 1868
Curiosités esthétiques par Charles Baudelaire (Oeuvres complètes de Charles Baudelaire, vol. 2), Paris, 1868

Baudelaire 1973
Charles Baudelaire, *Correspondance de Baudelaire*, 2 vols, Paris, 1973

Bazire 1884
Edmond Bazire, *Manet*, Paris, 1884

Benson 2008
Richard Benson, *The Printed Picture*, New York, 2008

Berger 1994
Harry Berger, 'Fictions of the Pose: Facing the Gaze of Early Modern Portraiture', *Representations*, 46, Spring 1994, pp. 87–120

Berson 1996
Ruth Berson, *The New Painting, 1874–1886*, 2 vols, San Francisco, 1996

Blanche 1919
J. E. Blanche, *Propos de peintre, de David à Degas*, Paris, 1919

Blanche 1924
Jacques-Emile Blanche, *Manet*, Paris, 1924

Bonnet 2007
Alain Bonnet, *Artistes en groupe. La Représentation de la communauté des artistes dans la peinture au XIXe siècle*, Rennes, 2007

Bremen 2005
Monet und Camille, exh. cat., Kunsthalle, Bremen, 2005–06

Brennecke 2004
Mishoe Brennecke, 'Double Début: Edouard Manet and *The Execution of Maximilian* in New York and Boston, 1879–80', *Nineteenth-century Art Worldwide*, 3, Autumn 2004, http://19thc-artworldwide.org

Brombert 1996
Beth Archer Brombert, *Rebel in a Frock Coat*, Chicago, 1996

Brussels 1869
Exposition des Beaux-Arts, Brussels, 1869

Bürger 1864
W. Bürger, 'Galerie de MM. Pereire', *Gazette des Beaux-Arts*, 16, 1864, pp. 193–213, 297–317

Bürger 1868
W. Bürger, 'Frans Hals', *Gazette des Beaux-Arts*, 24, 1868, pp. 219–30, 431–48

Callen 2000
Anthea Callen, *The Art of Impressionism: Painting Technique and the Making of Modernity*, New Haven and London, 2000

Chesnau 1864
Ernest Chesnau, *L'Art et les artistes en France et en Angleterre*, Paris, 1864

Chicago 2003
Juliet Wilson-Bareau and David Degener (eds), *Manet and the Sea*, exh. cat., Art Institute of Chicago; Philadelphia Museum of Art; Van Gogh Museum, Amsterdam, 2003–04

Chillaz 1997
Valentine de Chillaz, *Inventaire général des autographes*, Musée du Louvre, Département des arts graphiques, Paris, 1997

Clark 1985
T. J. Clark, *The Painting of Modern Life: Paris in the Art of Manet and His Followers*, New York, 1985

Compiègne 2008
Napoléon III et la Reine Victoria, exh. cat., Musées et Domaine Nationaux du Palais, Compiègne, 2008

Copenhagen 1989
Mikael Wivel, *Manet*, exh. cat., Ordrupgaardsamlingen, Copenhagen, 1989

Copenhagen 2006
Women in Impressionism: From Mythical Feminine to Modern Woman, exh. cat., Ny Carlsberg Glyptotek, Copenhagen, 2006

Courthion and Cailler 1960
Pierre Courthion and Pierre Cailler (eds), *Portrait of Manet by Himself and His Contemporaries*, London, 1960

Dallas 1989
Richard Brettell, *Impressionist and Modern Masters in Dallas: Monet to Mondrian*, exh. cat., Dallas Museum of Art, 1989

Dauberville 2007–10
Guy-Patrice Dauberville and Michel Dauberville, *Renoir: Catalogue Raisonné des Tableaux, Pastels, Dessins et Aquarelles*, 3 vols, Paris, 2007–10

DeWitt 2003
Lloyd DeWitt, 'Manet and the Dutch Marine Tradition', in Chicago 2003, pp. 1–15

Distel 2006
Anne Distel, 'Vollard and the Impressionists: The Case of Renoir', in Rebecca A. Rabinow (ed.), *Cézanne to Picasso: Ambroise Vollard, Patron of the Avant-Garde*, exh. cat., Metropolitan Museum of Art, New York; Art Institute of Chicago; Musée d'Orsay, Paris, 2006, pp. 142–49

Distel 2009
Anne Distel, *Renoir*, Paris, 2009; English translation published as *Renoir*, New York, 2010

Doesschate Chu 1974
Petra ten Doesschate Chu, *French Realism and the Dutch Masters: The Influence of Dutch Painting between 1830 and 1870*, Utrecht, 1974

Dolan 1997
Therese Dolan, 'Skirting the Issues: Manet's Portrait of "Baudelaire's Mistress, Reclining"', *Art Bulletin*, 79, December 1997, pp. 611–29

Dolan 2006
Therese Dolan, '*En garde*: Manet's Portrait of Emilie Ambre in the Role of Bizet's *Carmen*', *Nineteenth-century Art Worldwide*, 5, 1, Spring 2006, www.19thc-artworldwide.org

Dolan 2012
Therese Dolan (ed.), *Perspectives on Manet*, Farnham, 2012

Duret 1885
Théodore Duret, *Critiques d'Art*, Paris, 1885

Duret 1902
Théodore Duret, *Histoire de Edouard Manet et son oeuvre, avec un catalogue des peintures et des pastels*, Paris, 1902

Duret 1918
Théodore Duret, *Courbet*, Paris, 1918

Duret 1923
Théodore Duret, 'Le Bon Bock', *La Renaissance de l'art français et les industries de luxe*, March 1923, pp. 121–22

Elder 1924
Marc Elder, *A Giverny, Chez Claude Monet*, Paris, 1924

Epstein 2007
Johanna Ruth Epstein, *The Impassioned Brush: Perceptions of Seventeenth-century Dutch Art in France, 1848–1890*, PhD dissertation, New York University, 2007

Faison 1973
Samson Lane Faison, 'Renoir's hommage à Manet', in *Intuition und Kunstwissenschaft: Festschrift für Hanns Swarzenski*, Berlin, 1973, pp. 571–78

Frazier 2000
Adrian Frazier, *George Moore, 1852–1933*, London, 2000

Fried 1996
Michael Fried, *Manet's Modernism, or The Face of Painting in the 1860s*, Chicago, 1996

Gautier 1836
Théophile Gautier, 'Beaux-Arts', *La Presse*, 6 December 1836

Gautier 1847
Théophile Gautier, *Salon de 1847*, Paris, 1847

Gautier 1851
Théophile Gautier, 'Salon de 1850–1851. 23e article. Distribution des récompenses aux artistes', *La Presse*, 7 May 1851

Gautier 1852A
Théophile Gautier, 'Salon de 1852. Premier article', *La Presse*, 4 May 1852

Gautier 1852B
Théophile Gautier, 'Salon de 1852. 10e article', *La Presse*, 27 May 1852

Gautier 1855
Théophile Gautier, *Les Beaux-Arts en Europe*, Paris, 1855, Première série

Gautier 1857A
Théophile Gautier, 'Paul Gavarni', *L'Artiste*, 1 January 1857

Gautier 1857B
Théophile Gautier, 'Le Bois de Boulogne', *L'Artiste*, 17 May 1857

Gautier 1857C
Théophile Gautier, 'Gustave Doré', *L'Artiste*, 20 December 1857

Gautier 1859
Théophile Gautier, *Balzac*, Paris, 1859; Jean-Luc Steinmetz (ed.), Mayenne, 1999

Gautier 1861
Théophile Gautier, *Abécédaire du Salon de 1861*, Paris, 1861

Gautier 1862
Théophile Gautier, *Les Dieux et les Demis-dieux de la peinture*, Paris, 1862

Gautier 1864
Théophile Gautier, 'Salon de 1864', *Moniteur universel*, 25 June 1864

Gautier 1869
Théophile Gautier, 'Salon de 1869', *L'Illustration*, 15 May 1869

Gautier 1870
Théophile Gautier, 'Salon de 1870', *Le Journal officiel*, 18 July 1870

Gautier 1874
Théophile Gautier, *Histoire du Romantisme suivie de Notes romantiques 1830–1868*, Paris, 1874

Geffroy 1924
Gustave Geffroy, *Claude Monet: Sa vie, son oeuvre*, 2 vols, Paris, 1924

Ghent 1880
Exposition Triennale, Ghent, 1880

Green 1987
Nicholas Green, '"All the Flowers of the Field": The State, Liberalism and Art in France under the Early Third Republic', *Oxford Art Journal*, 10, 1, 1987, pp. 71–84

Greenberg 1986
John O'Brian (ed.), *Clement Greenberg: The Collected Essays and Criticism*, Chicago, 1986

Guégan 1997
Stéphane Guégan, 'Naïveté et modernité autour de 1846. Baudelaire lecteur de Gautier?', *L'Année Baudelaire*, 3, 1997, pp. 103–21

Guégan 2003
Stéphane Guégan, 'From Ziegler to Courbet: Painting, Art Criticism, and the Spanish Trope under Louis-Philippe', in New York 2003, pp. 190–201

Guégan 2008
Stéphane Guégan, 'Note sur les Goncourt au Salon de 1852: Notre réalisme à nous', *La Revue du Musée d'Orsay*, 26, 2008, pp. 6–15

Guégan 2011A
Stéphane Guégan, 'Manet en vue, Manet à vue', in Paris 2011A, pp. 26–43

Guégan 2011B
Stéphane Guégan, 'Captation d'héritage? Retour sur un tableau noir', in Paris 2011B, pp. 86–101

Guégan 2011C
Stéphane Guégan, *Théophile Gautier*, Paris, 2011

Gurley 1973
Elizabeth Ryan Gurley, 'Renoir a beaucoup puisé chez Manet', *Connaissance des arts*, 255, May 1973, pp. 132–39

Hamilton 1954
George Heard Hamilton, *Manet and His Critics*, New Haven, 1954 (see also Hamilton 1969)

Hamilton 1969
George Heard Hamilton, *Manet and His Critics*, New York, 1969 (first edition, 1954)

Harris 1970
Jean C. Harris, *Edouard Manet, Graphic Works: A Definitive Catalogue Raisonné*, New York, 1970; reissued San Francisco, 1990

Hecht 1997
Peter Hecht, 'Over Rembrandt, Manet, en het tweede leven van de kunst', Openingskollege, Faculteit der Letteren, Utrecht University, 2 September 1997 (published by Brouwer Uithof, Utrecht)

Heilbrun 1994
Françoise Heilbrun, 'Nadar and the Art of Portrait Photography', in Paris 1994B, pp. 35–58

Herbert 2000
Robert L. Herbert, *Nature's Workshop: Renoir's Writings on the Decorative Arts*, New Haven, 2000

Higonnet 1992
Anne Higonnet, *Berthe Morisot's Images of Women*, Cambridge, Mass., 1992

Hoog 1987
Michel Hoog, *Musée de l'Orangerie: Catalogue of the Jean Walter and Paul Guillaume Collection*, Paris, 1987

House 1986
John House, 'Manet's Naïveté', in London 1986, pp. 1–19

House 2004
John House, *Impressionism: Paint and Politics*, New Haven and London, 2004

Jeanniot 1907
Georges Jeanniot, 'En Souvenir de Manet', *La Grande Revue*, 46, 1907

Jowell 1989
Frances Suzman Jowell, 'The Rediscovery of Frans Hals', in Seymour Slive (ed.), *Frans Hals*, exh. cat., National Gallery of Art, Washington; Royal Academy of Arts, London; Frans Hals Museum, Haarlem, 1989–90, pp. 61–86

Jowell 2007
Frances Suzman Jowell, 'Impressionism and the Golden Age of Dutch Art', in Atlanta 2007, pp. 79–109

Jullien 1909
Adolphe Jullien, *Fantin-Latour, sa vie et ses amitiés: Lettres inédites et souvenirs personnels*, Paris, 1909

Kostenevich 1995
A. G. Kostenevich, *Hidden Treasures Revealed: Impressionist Masterpieces and Other Important French Paintings Preserved by The State Hermitage Museum, St Petersburg*, New York, 1995

Leenhoff Inventory
Léon Leenhoff, *Inventory of the Paintings, Pastels, Drawings and Prints in Manet's Studio at the Time of His Death*, 3 vols, Bibliothèque Nationale de France, Paris (Département des Arts Graphiques)

Lehmbeck 2007
Leah Lehmbeck, 'Edouard Manet's Portraits of Women', doctoral dissertation, New York University, 2007

Ligo 2007
Larry Leroy Ligo, *Manet, Baudelaire and Photography*, 2 vols, Lewiston, New York, 2007

Lille 2002
Berthe Morisot, 1841–1895, exh. cat., Palais des Beaux-Arts, Lille; Fondation Pierre Gianadda, Martigny, 2002

Lochard Album
Lochard Album of archive photographs, 3 vols, Pierpont Morgan Library, New York

Locke 2001
Nancy Locke, *Manet and the Family Romance*, Princeton, 2001

London 1983
Manet at Work, exh. cat., National Gallery, London, 1983

London 1985
John House and Anne Distel, *Renoir*, exh. cat., Hayward Gallery, London; Galeries Nationales du Grand Palais, Paris; Museum of Fine Arts, Boston, 1985

London 1986
Juliet Wilson-Bareau (ed.), *The Hidden Face of Manet: An Investigation of the Artist's Working Processes*, exh. cat., Courtauld Gallery, London, 1986

London 1994
James McNeill Whistler, exh. cat., Tate Gallery, London, 1994

London 2004A
Ancient Art to Post Impressionism: Masterpieces from the Ny Carlsberg Glyptotek, Copenhagen, exh. cat., Royal Academy of Arts, London, 2004

London 2004B
Face to Face, exh. cat., Courtauld Institute of Art Gallery, London; Neue Pinakothek, Munich, 2004–05

Loyrette 2002
Henri Loyrette, 'Manet pour Duret, Duret pour Manet', in *Mélanges en hommage à Françoise Cachin*, Paris, 2002, pp. 119–25

Madeline 2011
Laurence Madeline, 'C'était l'été 74. Manet face à Monet', *La Revue du Musée d'Orsay*, 31, Spring 2011, pp. 54–65

Madrid 2003
Manuela B. Mena Marqués (ed.), *Manet en el Prado*, exh. cat., Museo Nacional del Prado, Madrid, 2003–04

Mallarmé 1874
Stéphane Mallarmé, 'Le Jury de peinture pour 1874 et M. Manet', *La Renaissance littéraire et artistique*, 12 April 1874, in Stéphane Mallarmé, *Oeuvres complètes*, Paris, 1970, pp. 695–700

Manet 1979
Julie Manet, *Journal, 1893–1899: Sa jeunesse parmi les peintres impressionnistes et les hommes de letters*, Paris, 1979

Martigny 1996
Ronald Pickvance (ed.), *Manet*, exh. cat., Fondation Pierre Gianadda, Martigny, 1996

Mayo Roos 2012
Jane Mayo Roos, 'Manet and the Impressionist Moment', in Dolan 2012, pp. 73–96

McCauley 1985
Elizabeth Anne McCauley, *A. A. E. Disdéri and the Carte de Visite Portrait Photograph*, New Haven, 1985

McCauley 1994
Elizabeth Anne McCauley, *Industrial Madness: Commercial Photography in Paris 1848–1871*, New Haven and London, 1994

Medeiros 2002
Melissa De Medeiros, *The Document as Voice: The Manet Archive of the Pierpont Morgan Library*, Masters thesis, Hunter College, City University of New York, 2002

Meier-Graefe 1929
Julius Meier-Graefe, *Renoir, mit 407 Text-abbildungen und 10 Tafeln in farbigen Lichtdrucken und Heliogravüren*, Leipzig, 1929

Menard 1875
René Joseph Menard, *Entretiens sur la peinture*, Paris, 1875

Mexico 1998
Alexandra Pena, *Maestros del Impressionismo*, exh. cat., Instituto Nacional de Bellas Artes and Museu del Palacio de Bellas Artes, Mexico, 1998

Monti 1859
Raffaele Monti, 'Correspondences particulaires', *Gazette des Beaux-Arts*, 1, January–March 1859, pp. 117–19

Moore 1906
George Moore, *Reminiscences of the Impressionist Painters*, Dublin, 1906

Moore 1914
George Moore, *Hail and Farewell: Vale*, New York, 1914

Moreau-Nélaton 1926
Etienne Moreau-Nélaton, *Manet raconté par lui-même*, 2 vols, Paris, 1926

Munk 1993
Jens Peter Munk, *Ny Carlsberg Glyptotek Catalogue: French Impressionism*, Copenhagen, 1993

Nadar 1900
Nadar, *Quand j'étais photographe*, Paris, 1900 (republished 1998)

Néagu 1994
Philippe Néagu, 'Nadar and the Artistic Life of His Time', in Paris 1994B, pp. 59–76

New York 1988
Show and Tell: Artist's Illustrated Letters, exh. cat., Grey Art Gallery and Study Center, New York University, 1988

New York 1994
Gary Tinterow and Henri Loyrette (eds), *Origins of Impressionism*, exh. cat., Metropolitan Museum of Art, New York; Galeries Nationales du Grand Palais, Paris, 1994–95

New York 2003
Gary Tinterow and Geneviève Lacambre with Deborah L. Roldán and Juliet Wilson-Bareau, *Manet/Velázquez: The French Taste for Spanish Painting*, exh. cat., Metropolitan Museum of Art, New York, 2003 (see Paris 2002 for abridged French edition)

Oshima 1981
Seiji Oshima (ed.), *Manet (25 Great Masters of Modern Art)*, Tokyo, 1981

Ottawa 1997
Colin B. Bailey, with the assistance of John B. Collins, *Renoir's Portraits: Impressions of an Age*, exh. cat., National Gallery of Canada, Ottawa; Art Institute of Chicago; Kimbell Art Museum, Fort Worth, 1997–98

Otterlo 1972
Anna Barskaya et al., *From Van Gogh to Picasso*, exh. cat., Kröller-Müller Museum, Otterlo, 1972

Paris 1863
Manet, exh., Galerie Martinet, 26 Boulevard des Italiens, Paris, 1863

Paris 1865
Société Nationale des Beaux-Arts, exh., Galerie Martinet, 26 Boulevard des Italiens, Paris, 1865

Paris 1867
Manet, exh., Avenue de l'Alma, Paris, 1867

Paris 1876
Atelier de Manet, exh., 4 Rue de Saint-Pétersbourg, Paris, 1876

Paris 1883
Portraits du siècle, exh. cat.,
Ecole des Beaux-Arts, Paris, 1883

Paris 1884
Exposition posthumes Manet, exh.,
Ecole Nationale des Beaux-Arts, Paris, 1884

Paris 1932
Retrospective Manet, exh. cat.,
Orangerie des Tuileries, Paris, 1932

Paris 1950
Cent portraits des femmes, exh. cat.,
Galerie Charpentier, Paris, 1950

Paris 1983A
Françoise Cachin (ed.), *Manet, 1832–1883*,
exh. cat., Galeries Nationales du Grand Palais,
Paris; Metropolitan Museum of Art, New York,
1983–84

Paris 1983B
Douglas W. Druick and Michel Hoog,
Fantin-Latour, exh. cat., Galeries Nationales du
Grand Palais, Paris; National Gallery of Canada,
Ottawa; California Palace of the Legion of
Honor, San Francisco, 1983

Paris 1994A
Gary Tinterow and Henri Loyrette,
Impressionisme: Les Origines, 1859–69, exh. cat.,
Galeries Nationales du Grand Palais, Paris;
Metropolitan Museum of Art, New York, 1994

Paris 1994B
Maria Morris Hambourg, Françoise Heilbrun
and Philippe Néagu, *Nadar*, exh. cat., Musée
d'Orsay, Paris; Metropolitan Museum of Art,
New York, 1994–95

Paris 1998
Juliet Wilson-Bareau, *Manet, Monet, and the Gare
Saint-Lazare*, exh. cat., Musée d'Orsay, Paris;
National Gallery of Art, Washington, 1998

Paris 2000
*La Dame aux éventails: Nina de Callias, modèle
de Manet*, exh. cat., Musée d'Orsay, Paris, 2000

Paris 2002
Jeannine Baticle, Stéphane Guégan, Geneviève
Lacambre et al., *Manet/Velázquez: La manière
espagnole au XIXème siècle*, exh. cat., Musée
d'Orsay, Paris, 2002 (see New York 2003
for fuller American edition)

Paris 2011A
Stéphane Guégan (ed.), *Manet, inventeur du
Moderne*, exh. cat., Musée d'Orsay, Paris, 2011

Paris 2011B
*Fantin-Latour, Manet, Baudelaire: L'Hommage à
Delacroix*, exh. cat., Musée Delacroix, Paris, 2011

Philadelphia 1966
Anne Coffin Hanson, *Edouard Manet 1832–1883*,
exh. cat. Philadelphia Museum of Art;
Art Institute of Chicago, 1966

Philadelphia 1985
Suzanne G. Lindsay, *Mary Cassatt and
Philadelphia*, exh. cat., Philadelphia Museum
of Art, 1985

Pittsburgh 1989
*Impressionism: Selections from Five American
Museums*, exh. cat., Carnegie Museum of Art,
Pittsburgh; Minneapolis Institute of Arts; Nelson-
Atkins Museum of Art, Kansas City; Saint Louis
Art Museum; Toledo Museum of Art, 1989

Proust 1897
Antonin Proust, 'Edouard Manet: Souvenirs',
La Revue blanche, February–May 1897,
pp. 125–35, 168–80, 201–07, 306–15 and 413–24

Proust 1901
Antonin Proust, 'The Art of Edouard Manet',
The Studio, 21, 94, January 1901, pp. 227–36

Proust 1913
Antonin Proust, *Edouard Manet: souvenirs*,
Paris, 1913

Proust 1996
Antonin Proust, *Edouard Manet: souvenirs*,
first published in *La Revue blanche*,
February–May 1897; reprinted Paris, 1996

Reed 2003
Arden Reed, *Manet, Flaubert, and the Emergence
of Modernism. Blurring Genre Boundaries*,
Cambridge, 2003

Reff 1964
Theodore Reff, 'Copyists in the Louvre,
1850–1870', *The Art Bulletin*, 46, 4, December
1964, pp. 552–57

Reff 1975
Theodore Reff, *Manet and Modern Paris*,
Washington, 1975

Reff 1982
Theodore Reff, *Manet and Modern Paris:
One Hundred Paintings, Drawings, Prints and
Photographs by Manet and His Contemporaries*,
Washington, 1982

Renoir 1981
Jean Renoir, *Pierre-Auguste Renoir, mon père*,
Paris, 1981; English translation published as
Renoir, My Father, London, 1962

Rewald 1945
John Rewald, 'Auguste Renoir and His Brother',
Gazette des Beaux-Arts, 27, 3, March 1945,
pp. 171–88

Rewald 1947
John Rewald, *Edouard Manet: Pastels*,
Oxford, 1947

Rewald 1973
John Rewald, *The History of Impressionism*,
revised and enlarged edition, New York, 1973

Robida 1958
Michel Robida, *Le Salon Charpentier
et les Impressionistes*, Paris, 1958

Rouart 1987
Denis Rouart (ed.), *Berthe Morisot:
The Correspondence*, translated by
Betty W. Hubbard, London, 1987

Rubin 1994
James H. Rubin, *Manet's Silence and the Poetics
of Bouquets*, London, 1994

Rubin 2010
James H. Rubin, *Manet: Initial M, Hand and Eye*,
Paris, 2010

RWI, RWII
Denis Rouart and Daniel Wildenstein,
Edouard Manet: Catalogue raisonné, 2 vols,
Lausanne, 1975

Serena 1879
E. Serena, 'Chronique mondaine',
La Comedie parisienne, 1879, 92, p. 2

Singletary 2012
Suzanne Singletary, 'Manet and Whistler:
Baudelairean Voyage', in Dolan 2012, pp. 55–61

Slive 1970–74
Seymour Slive, *Frans Hals*, 3 vols,
New York and London, 1970–74

Stuttgart 2002
Ina Conzen (ed.), *Edouard Manet und die
Impressionisten*, exh. cat., Staatsgalerie,
Stuttgart, 2002

Tabarant 1947
Adolphe Tabarant, *Manet et ses oeuvres*,
Paris, 1947

Tabarant Archive
Tabarant Archive, Morgan Library, New York

Tate 1991
Concise Catalogue of the Tate Gallery Collection,
ninth edition, London, 1991

Tokyo 1986
Edouard Manet, exh. cat., Isetan Museum of Art,
Tokyo; Fukuoka Art Museum; Osaka Municipal
Museum of Art, 1986

Tokyo 2010
Manet et le Paris Moderne, exh. cat., Musée
Mitsubishi Ichigokan, Tokyo, 2010

Toledo 1964
The Collection of Mrs C. Lockhart McKelvy,
exh. cat., Toledo Museum of Art, 1964

Verbeek 1958
J. Verbeek, 'Bezoekers van het Rijksmuseum
in hit Trippenhuis 1844–1885', *Gedenkboek
uitgegeven ter gelegenheid van het
honderdvijftigjarig bestaan van het Rijksmuseum*,
special issue of the *Bulletin van het Rijksmuseum,
1808–1958*, 6, 1958, pp. 59–72

Vollard 1919
Ambroise Vollard, *La Vie et l'oeuvre de
Pierre-Auguste Renoir*, Paris, 1919

Vollard 1938
Ambroise Vollard, *En écoutant Cézanne, Degas,
Renoir*, Paris, 1938

Ward and Fidler 1993
Roger Ward and Patricia J. Fidler (eds),
*The Nelson-Atkins Museum of Art: A Handbook
of the Collections*, New York, 1993

Washington 1986
Charles S. Moffett, with the assistance of Ruth
Berson, Barbara Lee Williams and Fronia E.
Wissman, *The New Painting: Impressionism,
1874–1886*, exh. cat., National Gallery of Art,
Washington; M. H. de Young Memorial Museum,
Fine Arts Museums of San Francisco, 1986

Washington 1989
Seymour Slive (ed.), *Frans Hals*, exh. cat.,
National Gallery of Art, Washington;
Royal Academy of Arts, London;
Frans Hals Museum, Haarlem, 1989–90

Wechsler 1982
Judith Wechsler, *Human Comedy: Physiognomy
and Caricature in Nineteenth-century Paris*,
Chicago, 1982

Wentworth 1970
Michael Wentworth, 'Tissot's *La Dormeuse*',
The Currier Gallery of Art Bulletin,
January–March 1970

White 1984
Barbara Ehrlich White, *Renoir: His Life, Art,
and Letters*, New York, 1984; reprinted 2010

Wildenstein 1974–91
Daniel Wildenstein, *Claude Monet: Biographie
et catalogue raisonné*, 5 vols, Lausanne and Paris,
1974–91

Wildenstein 1996
Daniel Wildenstein, *Monet: Catalogue raisonné*,
4 vols, Cologne, 1996

Wilson-Bareau 1986
Juliet Wilson-Bareau, 'The Hidden Face of
Manet: An Investigation of the Artist's Working
Processes', *Burlington Magazine*, April 1986,
supplement

Wilson-Bareau 1991
Juliet Wilson-Bareau (ed.), *Manet by Himself:
Correspondence and Conversation, Paintings,
Pastels, Prints and Drawings*, London and Sydney,
1991 (see also Wilson-Bareau 2004)

Wilson-Bareau 1998
Juliet Wilson-Bareau, *Manet, Monet and
the Gare Saint-Lazare*, Washington, 1998

Wilson-Bareau 2004
Juliet Wilson-Bareau (ed.), *Manet by Himself:
Correspondence and Conversation, Paintings, Pastels,
Prints and Drawings*, 2004 (first edition, 1991)

Wilson-Bareau 2011
Juliet Wilson-Bareau, 'The Manet Exhibition
in Paris, 2011', *Burlington Magazine*,
December 2011, pp. 815–24

Wilson-Bareau 2012
Juliet Wilson-Bareau, 'Manet's "Amazon":
A Final Salon Painting', *Burlington Magazine*,
April 2012, pp. 256–59

Wollheim 1987
Richard Wollheim, *Painting as an Art*,
London, 1987

Worth 2007
Alexi Worth, 'The Lost Photographs of Edouard
Manet', *Art in America*, January 2007, pp. 59–64

Zola 1974
Emile Zola, *Le Bon Combat: De Combat
aux Impressionistes*, Jean-Paul Bouillon (ed.),
Paris, 1974

Zola 1996
Emile Zola, *Le Bon Combat: De Courbet
aux Impressionnistes*, Paris, 1996

Lenders to the Exhibition

BERLIN
Alte Nationalgalerie

BIRMINGHAM
Barber Institute of Fine Arts, University of Birmingham

BOSTON
Museum of Fine Arts

BREMEN
Kunsthalle

BUDAPEST
Szépművészeti Múzeum

CHICAGO
Art Institute of Chicago

CLEVELAND
Cleveland Museum of Art

COPENHAGEN
Ny Carlsberg Glyptotek

DALLAS
Dallas Museum of Art

FORT WORTH
Kimbell Art Museum

FRANKFURT AM MAIN
Städel Museum

HAMBURG
Hamburger Kunsthalle

KANSAS CITY
Nelson-Atkins Museum of Art

LISBON
Calouste Gulbenkian Foundation

LONDON
National Gallery
Royal Academy of Arts
Samuel Courtauld Trust
Tate

LOS ANGELES
J. Paul Getty Museum

MADRID
Museo Thyssen-Bornemisza

MILAN
Galleria Nazionale d'Arte Moderna

MINNEAPOLIS
Minneapolis Institute of Arts

MUNICH
Neue Pinakothek

NANCY
Musée des beaux-arts

NEW YORK
Metropolitan Museum of Art
Morgan Library and Museum (Pierpont Morgan Library)

OSLO
National Museum of Art, Architecture and Design

PARIS
Bibliothèque nationale de France
Musée Clemenceau
Musée d'Orsay
Petit Palais, Musée des Beaux-Arts de la Ville de Paris

PHILADELPHIA
Philadelphia Museum of Art

PROVIDENCE
Museum of Art, Rhode Island School of Design

SAINT LOUIS
Saint Louis Art Museum

SÃO PAULO
Museu de São Paulo Assis Chateaubriand

SHELBURNE, VERMONT
Shelburne Museum

TOKYO
Bridgestone Museum of Art, Ishibashi Foundation
National Museum of Western Art
Tokyo Fuji Art Museum

TOLEDO, OHIO
Toledo Museum of Art

TOURNAI
Musée des Beaux-Arts

WASHINGTON DC
National Gallery of Art

WILLIAMSTOWN, MASS.
Sterling and Francine Clark Art Institute

Diane B. Wilsey

ZÜRICH
Foundation E. G. Bührle

and others who wish to remain anonymous

Photographic Acknowledgements

All works of art are reproduced by kind permission of their owners. Every effort has been made to trace photographers of works reproduced. Specific acknowledgements are as follows:

Atlanta, image courtesy of the Oglethorpe University Museum of Art: fig. 34
Berlin, © bpk/Nationalgalerie, SMB/Jörg P. Anders: cat. 39
Karen Blindow: cat. 27
Boston, courtesy Museum of Fine Arts: cats 50, 51
Budapest, © Museum of Fine Arts: cat. 31
© The Cleveland Museum of Art: cat. 19
Florence, © Scala 2012: cat. 60; fig. 17 (bpk, Berlin/Hermann Buresch/Art Resource, NY); fig. 22 (Digital Image Museum Associates/LACMA/Art Resource, NY); cats 3, 25, figs 5, 10, 15, 18, 37 (© The Metropolitan Museum of Art/Art Resource, NY); cat. 7, fig. 39 (White Images)
Frankfurt, © U. Edelmann/Städel Museum/ARTOTHEK: cat. 54
Haarlem, © Noord-Hollands Archief: figs 41–43
Hamburg, © bpk/Hamburger Kunsthalle/Elke Walford: cat. 47
Børre Høstland: cat. 6
London, akg-images: figs 4, 8, 16
London, The Bridgeman Art Library: cats 1, 23, 54; figs 23, 78, 81 (Archives Charmet); figs 21, 30 (© Christie's Images); figs 51, 52 (Musée Marmottan Monet); fig. 33 (Musée d'Orsay, Paris); fig. 71 (Musée de la Ville de Paris, Musée Carnavalet, Paris/Giraudon); cat. 29 (© Musée de la Ville de Paris, Musée du Petit Palais/Giraudon); fig. 39 (Museum of Fine Arts, Houston/Robert Lee Blaffer Memorial Collection. Gift of Sarah Campbell Blaffer); cat. 38 (© The National Museum of Western Art, Tokyo); figs 72, 88 (Private collection); fig. 28 (Suzuki Collection, Tokyo/Peter Willi); cat. 37 (© Tokyo Fuji Art Museum)
London, © Christie's Images Limited: cats 14, 57
London, Corbis/Francis G. Mayer: fig. 29
London, The Library of Nineteenth-century Photography: figs 25, 26
London, © Royal Academy of Arts/J. Hammond: fig. 48
London, © Tate, 2011: cat. 5
Madrid, © 2012 Museo Nacional del Prado: fig. 40
Madrid, © Museo Thyssen-Bornemisza: cat. 43
Milan, © Comune di Milano, Galleria d'Arte Moderna, Collezione Grassi/Fabio Saporetti: cat. 41
Jamison Miller: cat. 48
Munich, © bpk/Bayerische Staatsgemäldesammlungen: cat. 10
Nancy, © Cliché P. Mignot: cat. 55
New York, Richard Goodbody: cat. 4
New York, © The Pierpont Morgan Library. MA 3950: fig. 69 (Graham Haber); fig. 80
Paris, Bibliothèque des Arts décoratifs, Paris/Suzanne Nagy: fig. 32
Paris, © Bibliothèque nationale de France: cat. 56, figs 35, 45, 47, 49, 53–59, 61–67, 70, 74–76, 85
Paris, collection du Musée Clemenceau: fig. 60
Paris, RMN/Musée d'Orsay: figs 31, 84, 87 (Michèle Bellot); fig. 9 (Jean-Gilles Berizzi); fig. 13 (Philipp Bernard); fig. 83 (Gérard Blot); fig. 12 (Gérard Blot/Hervé Lewandowski); cats 16, 28, figs 1, 2, 11, 14, 24 (Hervé Lewandowski); fig. 36 (Stéphane Maréchalle); cat. 30, figs 19, 73 (Patrice Schmidt)
Providence, Erik Gould, by courtesy of the Museum of Art, Rhode Island School of Design: cat. 18, fig. 50
Oliver Rheindorf: cat. 11
Rochester (New York), courtesy of George Eastman House, International Museum of Photography and Film: fig. 27
São Paolo, © Museu de São Paolo Assis Chateaubriand: cats 20, 42, 46
Stockholm, Nationalmuseum: fig. 3
© Toledo Museum of Art. Photo: Richard Goodbody, New York: fig. 44
Toledo, © Photography Incorporated: cat. 45
Vermont, © Shelburne Museum: cat. 24
Vulaines-sur-Seine, Musée départemental Stéphane Mallarmé: fig. 82
Washington DC, © 2012 National Gallery of Art: cats 32, 33, 53, figs 7, 20, 77
Williamstown, © Sterling and Francine Clark Art Institute/Michael Agee: cat. 12
© 2012 Kunsthaus Zürich: fig. 6

Index

All references are to page numbers;
those in **bold** type indicate catalogue plates,
and those in *italic* type indicate essay illustrations

Royal Academy Trust

MAJOR BENEFACTORS
The Trustees of the Royal Academy Trust are grateful to all its donors for their continued loyalty and generosity. They would like to extend their thanks to all those who have made a significant commitment, past and present, to the galleries, the exhibitions, the conservation of the Permanent Collection, the Library collections, the Royal Academy Schools, the Learning programme and other specific appeals.

HM The Queen
Her Majesty's Government
The 29th May 1961 Charitable Trust
The Aldama Foundation
The American Associates of the Royal Academy Trust
The Annenberg Foundation
Barclays Bank
BAT Industries plc
Sir David and Lady Bell
The late Tom Bendhem
The late Brenda M Benwell-Lejeune
John Frye Bourne
British Telecom
The Brown Foundation
John and Susan Burns
Mr Raymond M Burton CBE
Sir Trevor Chinn CVO and Lady Chinn
The Trustees of the Clore Foundation
John S Cohen Foundation
Sir Harry and Lady Djangoly
The Dulverton Trust
Alfred Dunhill Limited
John Ellerman Foundation
Ernst & Young
Esso UK plc
Esmée Fairbairn Charitable Trust
The Fidelity UK Foundation
The Foundation for Sports and the Arts
Friends of the Royal Academy
Jacqueline and Michael Gee
The Getty Grant Programme
Mr Thomas Gibson
Glaxo Holdings plc
Diane and Guilford Glazer
Mr and Mrs Jack Goldhill
Maurice and Laurence Goldman
The Horace W Goldsmith Foundation
HRH Princess Marie-Chantal of Greece
Mr and Mrs Jocelin Harris
The Philip and Pauline Harris Charitable Trust
Heritage Lottery Fund
IBM United Kingdom Limited
The Idlewild Trust
Lord and Lady Jacobs
The JP Jacobs Charitable Trust
The Japan Foundation
Gabrielle Jungels-Winkler Foundation
Mr and Mrs Donald Kahn
The Lillian Jean Kaplan Foundation
The Kresge Foundation
The Samuel H Kress Foundation
The Kirby Laing Foundation
The Lankelly Foundation
The late Mr John S Latsis
The David Lean Foundation
The Lennox and Wyfold Foundation
Lord Leverhulme's Charitable Trust
Lex Service plc
The Linbury Trust
Sir Sydney Lipworth QC and Lady Lipworth CBE
John Lyons Charity
Ronald and Rita McAulay
McKinsey and Company Inc
John Madejski OBE DL
The Manifold Trust
Marks and Spencer
The Paul Mellon Estate
The Monument Trust
The Moorgate Trust Fund
Mr Minoru Mori HON KBE and Mrs Mori
Robin Heller Moss
Museums and Galleries Improvement Fund
National Westminster Bank
Stavros S Niarchos
Simon and Midge Palley
The Pilgrim Trust
PF Charitable Trust
The Edith and Ferdinand Porjes Trust
The Porter Foundation
John Porter Charitable Trust
Rio Tinto
John A Roberts FRIBA
Sir Simon and Lady Robertson
The Ronson Foundation
Rothmans International plc
RTZ Corporation Plc
Dame Jillian Sackler DBE
Jillian and Arthur M Sackler
Mr Wafic Rida Saïd
Mrs Jean Sainsbury
The Saison Foundation
The Sammermar Trust
The Basil Samuel Charitable Trust
Mrs Coral Samuel CBE
Sea Containers Ltd
Shell UK Limited
Miss Dasha Shenkman
William and Maureen Shenkman
The late Pauline Sitwell
The Starr Foundation
The Swire Charitable Trust
Sir Hugh Sykes DL
Alfred Taubman
Sir Anthony and Lady Tennant
Ware and Edythe Travelstead
The Trusthouse Charitable Foundation
The Douglas Turner Trust
Unilever plc
The Weldon UK Charitable Trust
The Welton Foundation
The Weston Family
The Malcolm Hewitt Wiener Foundation
The Maurice Wohl Charitable Foundation
The Wolfson Foundation

And others who wish to remain anonymous

PATRONS
The Royal Academy is extremely grateful to all its Patrons, who generously support every aspect of its work.

Chair
Mr Robert Suss

Platinum
Mrs Celia Atkin
Mr Edward Atkin CBE
Genevieve and Peter Davies
Mr and Mrs Patrick Doherty
Ms Ghizlan El Glaoui
Mr Denis Korotkov-Koganovich
Mr and Mrs Jake Shafran
David and Sophie Shalit

Gold
Ms Linda Cooper
Lord and Lady Davies of Abersoch
Ms Angela Farrugia
Mr and Mrs Andrew Higginson
Mrs Elizabeth Hosking
Sir Sydney Lipworth QC and Lady Lipworth CBE
Mr and Mrs Ronald Lubner
Mr Scott Mead
Sir Keith and Lady Mills
Lady Rayne
Mrs Stella Shawzin
Jane Spack
David Stileman

Silver
Lady Agnew
Mrs Nancy Al Zain
Miss H J C Anstruther
Lord Ashburton
Edgar Astaire
Mr and Mrs Simon Bamber
Jane Barker
Ms Catherine Baxendale
The Duke of Beaufort
Mrs Gary Brass
Mr and Mrs Richard Briggs OBE
Mrs Elie Brihi
Mrs Marcia Brocklebank
Sir Francis Brooke Bt
Jeremy Brown
Lady Brown
Lord Browne of Madingley
Mr Martin Burton
Mr F A A Carnwath CBE
Jean and Eric Cass
Sir Charles and Lady Chadwyck-Healey
Mr David Cheyne
Sir Trevor Chinn CVO and Lady Chinn
Mr and Mrs George Coelho
Denise Cohen Charitable Trust
Sir Ronald Cohen
Mrs Jennifer Cooke
Mark and Cathy Corbett
Mr and Mrs Ken Costa
Julian Darley and Helga Sands
The Countess of Dartmouth
Mr Daniel Davies
Melanie Deanfield
Anita Dinkin
Dr Anne Dornhorst
Lord Douro
Ms Noreen Doyle
Janet and Maurice Dwek
Mrs Sheila Earles
Lord and Lady Egremont
Benita and Gerald Fogel
Mrs Rosamund Fokschaner
Mrs Joscelyn Fox
Mrs Anthony Foyle
Mr and Mrs Eric Franck
Mr Simon Freakley
Arnold Fulton
Mr and Mrs Spencer Fung
The Lord Gavron CBE
Mrs Mina Gerowin
Jacqueline and Jonathan Gestetner
Lady Getty
Mr Mark Glatman
Lady Gosling
Mr Stephen Gosztony
Piers Gough CBE RA
Mr Gavin Graham
Mrs Mary Graves
HRH Princess Marie-Chantal of Greece
Mrs Margaret Guitar
Peter and Andrea De Haan
Mr James Hambro
Sir Ewan and Lady Harper
Mrs Melanie Harris
Sir John Hegarty and Miss Philippa Crane
Michael and Morven Heller
Mr Mark Hendriksen
Lady Heseltine
Mr and Mrs Alan Hobart
Mr Patrick Holmes
Mr Philip Hudson
Mr and Mrs Jon Hunt
Mrs Pauline Hyde
Mrs Deanna Ibrahim
S Isern-Feliu
Mrs Caroline Jackson
Mr Derek Jacobson
Mr Michael Jacobson
Sir Martin and Lady Jacomb
Mrs Raymonde Jay
Mr and Mrs Sidney Jefcoate
Fiona Johnstone
Mr Nicholas Jones
Mrs Ghislaine Kane
Miss Joanna Kaye
Dr Elisabeth Kehoe
Mr Duncan Kenworthy OBE
Princess Jeet Khemka
Mr and Mrs Naguib Kheraj
Mr Gerald Kidd
Mr D H Killick
Mr and Mrs James Kirkman
Mrs Aboudi Kosta
Mr and Mrs Herbert Kretzmer
Norman A Kurland and Deborah A David
The de Laszlo Foundation
Joan H Lavender
Mrs Rachel Laxer
Mr George Lengvari and Mrs Inez Lengvari
Lady Lever of Manchester
Mr Peter Lloyd
Miss R Lomax-Simpson
The Marquess of Lothian
The Hon Mrs Virginia Lovell
Mr and Mrs Henry Lumley
Mrs Josephine Lumley
Mrs Sally Lykiardopulo
Gillian McIntosh
Andrew and Judith McKinna
Mr Nicholas Maclean
Sir John Mactaggart
Sally and Donald Main
Mrs Inge Margulies
Mr and Mrs Richard Martin
Zvi and Ofra Meitar Family Fund
Professor Anthony Mellows OBE TD and Mrs Anthony Mellows
Mrs Ann Miller
Mrs Joy Moss
Mr Michael Moszynski
Mrs Carole Myers
Marion and Guy Naggar
Dr Ann Naylor
Mr Stuart C Nelson
Ann Norman-Butler
North Street Trust
Mr Michael Palin
John H Pattisson
Nicholas B Paumgarten
Mr and Mrs D J Peacock
Mr and Mrs A Perloff
Mr Philip Perry
David Pike
Mr and Mrs Anthony Pitt-Rivers
Mr and Mrs Stuart Popham
Mr Basil Postan
John and Anne Raisman
Lady Renwick
Lord Rothschild
Miss Elaine Rowley
Mr and Mrs K M Rubie
Roland and Sophie Rudd
The Lady Henrietta St George
Mr Adrian Sassoon
H M Sassoon Charitable Trust
Mr and Mrs Christopher Satterthwaite
The Schneer Foundation
Carol Sellars
Mr and Mrs Kevin Senior
Dr Lewis Sevitt
Christina Countess of Shaftesbury
Mr Robert N Shapiro
Mrs Victoria Sharp
Major General and Mrs Jonathan Shaw
Richard and Veronica Simmons
Mr and Mrs Alan K Simpson
Brian D Smith
Summers Art Gallery/Mrs J K M Bentley
Sir Hugh Sykes DL
The Tavolozza Foundation
Mr Anthony J Todd
Mr and Mrs David Turner
Miss M L Ulfane
John and Carol Wates
Mrs Angela Webb
Edna and Willard Weiss
Anthony and Rachel Williams
Dr Yvonne von Egidy-Winkler and Mr Peter Philip Winkler
Mr William Winters
Ms Clare Woodman

Patron Donors
Stephen Barry Charitable Settlement
J Birr
Bryan Ferry
Mrs Bianca Roden
The Michael H Sacher Charitable Trust

And others who wish to remain anonymous

Benjamin West Group Patrons
Chair
Lady Judge CBE

Platinum
Charles and Kaaren Hale
Mr Christian Levett
Ms Dambisa Moyo
Mr and Mrs John R Olsen

Gold
Marco and Francesca Assetto
Lady Judge CBE
Ms Alessandra Morra

Silver
Lady J Lloyd Adamson
Mr Dimitry Afanasiev
Mrs Spindrift Al Swaidi
Ms Ruth Anderson
Ms Sol Anitua
Mr Andy Ash
Mr Stefano Aversa
Mrs Leslie Bacon
Naomi and Ted Berk
Mrs Michal Berkner Jenrick
Micaela and Christopher Boas
Mrs Adrian Bowden
Mr Simon Brocklebank-Fowler
Mrs Olga But-Gusaim
Mrs Sophie Cahu
Brian and Melinda Carroll
Mr and Mrs Paul Collins
Dr Sorca Conroy-Sherman
Ms Karla Dorsch
Mr and Mrs Jeff Eldredge
Cyril and Christine Freedman
Ms Moya Greene
Mr and Mrs Timothy Hart
Mr Michael Hatchard
Mr Andrew Hawkins
Ms Alexandra Hess
Mr Rashid Hoosenally
Katie Jackson
Suzanne and Michael Johnson
Syrie Johnson
Lord and Lady Leitch
Mrs Stephanie Léouzon
Mrs Valerie Nataliya Levine
Mrs Rose-Marie Lieberman
Mr Guido Lombardo
Charles G Lubar
Ted and Patricia Madara
Mr and Mrs Michael Malone
Cornelius Medvei
Mrs Victoria Mills
Mr and Mrs Frank Moretti
Scott and Christine Morrissey
Neil Osborn and Holly Smith
Lady Purves
Mr James B Sherwood
Mr and Mrs Scott and Kathleen Simpson
Mrs Sahim Sliwinski-Hong
Mr Stuart Southall

Mr Ian Taylor
Mr and Mrs Julian Treger
Frederick and Kathryn Uhde
Mr and Mrs Edouard Ullmo
Mr Martin Waller
Mr Craig D Weaver
Prof Peter Whiteman QC
Mr and Mrs John Winter
Mrs Deborah Woodbury

Patron Donor
Mr John C Harvey

And others who wish to remain anonymous

Schools Patrons
Chair
Clare Flanagan

Platinum
Mrs Sarah Chenevix-Trench
Mark and Samantha Mifsud
Matthew and Sian Westerman

Gold
Sam and Rosie Berwick
Christopher Kneale
Mr William Loschert
Mr Keir McGuinness

Silver
Lord and Lady Aldington
Mrs Elizabeth Alston
Mr Nicholas Andrew
Dr Anne Ashmore-Hudson
Mr and Mrs Jonathan and Sarah Bayliss
Mrs Gemma Billington
Mrs Inge Borg Scott
Mrs Jeanne Callanan
Tatiana Cherkasova
Rosalind Clayton
Mr Richard Clothier
Ms Davina Dickson
Mrs Dominic Dowley
John Entwistle OBE
Mark and Sarah Evans
Mrs Catherine Farquharson
Ian and Catherine Ferguson
Ms Clare Flanagan
Mr Mark Garthwaite
Mrs Michael Green
Ms Louise Hallett
Mr Lindsay Hamilton
Mrs Lesley Haynes
Rosalyn Henderson
The Hon Tom Hewlett
Ken Howard OBE RA and Mrs Howard
Mark and Fiona Hutchinson
Mrs Susan Johns
Ms Karen Jones
Mrs Marcelle Joseph
Mr Paul Kempe
Ms Nicolette Kwok
Mr and Mrs Mark Loveday
Mr David Low
Mr Philip Marsden
The Mulberry Trust
Lord and Lady Myners
Mrs Yelena Oosting
Peter Rice Esq
Anthony and Sally Salz
Christopher and Anne Saul
Brian D Smith
Mr Simon Thorley QC
Mr Ray Treen
Mrs Carol Wates
Mrs Diana Wilkinson
Mr and Mrs Maurice Wolridge

And others who wish to remain anonymous

Contemporary Circle Patrons
Chair
Susie Allen-Huxley

Platinum
Robert and Simone Suss

Gold
Mr Jeremy Coller
Helen and Colin David
Mrs Alison Deighton
Matthew and Monika McLennan
Richard Sharp
Ms Rebecca Wang

Silver
Joan and Robin Alvarez
Mrs Charlotte Artus
Jeremy Asher
Mrs Miel de Botton
Viscountess Bridgeman
Dr Elaine C Buck
Ms Debra Burt
Jenny Christensson
Nadia Crandall
Georgina David
Mollie Dent-Brocklehurst
Chris and Angie Drake
Mrs Jennifer Duke
Mr Stephen Garrett
Belinda de Gaudemar
Simon Gillespie
George Goldsmith
and Ekaterina Malievskaia
Mrs Selima Gürtler
Stefa Hart
Mrs Susan Hayden
Margaret A Jackson
Mr David Kempton
Anna Lapshina
Mrs Sarah Macken
Mrs Chantal Maljers-van Erven Dorens
Mrs Penelope Mather
Mrs Sophie Mirman
Victoria Miro
Mrs Tessa Nicholson
Mrs Yelena Oosting
Veronique Parke
Mrs Tineke Pugh
Mr Andres Recoder
and Mrs Isabelle Schiavi
Mrs Catherine Rees
Mrs Karen Santi
Edwina Sassoon
Richard and Susan Shoylekov
Jeffery C Sugarman
and Alan D H Newham
Anna Watkins
Cathy Wills
Manuela and Iwan Wirth
Mr and Mrs Maurice Wolridge
Ms Cynthia Wu

Patron Donors
Lord and Lady Aldington

And others who wish to remain anonymous

Young Patrons
Lily Arad
Rosanna Bossom
May Calil
Mr and Mrs Tom Davies
Mr Rollo Gabb
Laura Graham
Soliana Habte
Kalita al Swaidi
LinLi Teh

Library and Collections Circle
Mr Loyd Grossman
Miss Jo Hannah Hoehn
Mr and Mrs Robert Hoehn
Lowell Libson
Mr John Schaeffer
Pam and Scott Schafler
Mr and Mrs Bart Tiernan
Mr Andrew Williams

And others who wish to remain anonymous

TRUSTS AND FOUNDATIONS
Artists Collecting Society
The Atlas Fund
The Albert Van den Bergh Charitable Trust
The Bomonty Charitable Trust
The Charlotte Bonham-Carter
Charitable Trust
William Brake Charitable Trust
R M Burton 1998 Charitable Trust
C H K Charities Limited
P H G Cadbury Charitable Trust
The Evan Cornish Foundation
The Sidney and Elizabeth Corob
Charitable Trust
The Dovehouse Trust
The Gilbert and Eileen Edgar Foundation
The Eranda Foundation
Lucy Mary Ewing Charitable Trust
The Lord Faringdon Charitable Trust
The Margery Fish Charity
The Flow Foundation
The Garfield Weston Foundation
Gatsby Charitable Foundation
The Golden Bottle Trust
The Gordon Foundation
Sue Hammerson Charitable Trust
The Charles Hayward Foundation
Hiscox
Holbeck Charitable Trust
The Harold Hyam Wingate Foundation
The Ironmongers' Company
The Emmanuel Kaye Foundation
The Kindersley Foundation
The de Laszlo Foundation
The Leche Trust
The Leverhulme Trust
The Maccabaeans
The McCorquodale Charitable Trust
The Paul Mellon Centre
The Mercers' Company
Margaret and Richard Merrell Foundation
The Millichope Foundation
The Mondriaan Foundation
The Henry Moore Foundation
The Mulberry Trust
The J Y Nelson Charitable Trust
Newby Trust Limited
The Old Broad Street Charity Trust
The Peacock Charitable Trust
The Pennycress Trust
The Stanley Picker Charitable Trust
The Pidem Fund
The Edith and Ferdinand Porjes
Charitable Trust
Gilberto Pozzi
Mr and Mrs J A Pye's Charitable Settlement
Rayne Foundation
The Reed Foundation
T Rippon & Sons (Holdings) Ltd
Rootstein Hopkins Foundation
The Rose Foundation
The Rothschild Foundation
Schroder Charity Trust
The Sellars Charitable Trust
The Archie Sherman Charitable Trust
Paul Smith
The South Square Trust
Spencer Charitable Trust
Oliver Stanley Charitable Trust
Peter Storrs Trust
Strand Parishes Trust
The Joseph Strong Frazer Trust
The Swan Trust
Thaw Charitable Trust
Sir Jules Thorn Charitable Trust
The Bruce Wake Charity
Celia Walker Art Foundation
Warburg Pincus International LLC
Weinstock Fund
Wilkinson Eyre Architects
The Spencer Wills Trust
The Worshipful Company
of Painter-Stainers

AMERICAN ASSOCIATES OF THE ROYAL ACADEMY TRUST
Burlington House Trust
Mrs James C Slaughter

Benjamin West Society
Mrs Deborah Loeb Brice
Mrs Nancy B Negley

Benefactors
Mr Michael Moritz and Ms Harriet Heyman
Mrs Edmond J Safra
The Hon John C Whitehead

Sponsors
Mrs Drue Heinz HON DBE
David Hockney OM CH RA
Mr Arthur L Loeb
Mr and Mrs Hamish Maxwell
Mr and Mrs Richard J Miller Jr
Diane A Nixon
Ms Joan Stern
Dr and Mrs Robert D Wickham

Patrons
Mr and Mrs Steven Ausnit
Mr and Mrs E William Aylward
Mr Donald A Best
Mrs Mildred C Brinn
Mrs Benjamin Coates
Lois M Collier
Mr and Mrs Stanley De Forest Scott
Mr and Mrs Lawrence S Friedland
Mr and Mrs Leslie Garfield
Ms Helen Harting Abell
Dr Bruce C Horten
Mr William W Karatz
The Hon Eugene A Ludwig
and Dr Carol Ludwig
Miss Lucy F McGrath
Mr and Mrs Wilson Nolen
Mrs Mary Sharp Cronson
Ms Louisa Stude Sarofim
Martin J Sullivan OBE
Ms Britt Tidelius
Mr Robert W Wilson

Donors
Mr James C Armstrong
Ms Naja Armstrong
Mr Constantin R Boden
Dr and Mrs Robert Bookchin
Laura Christman and William Rothacker
Ms Alyce Faye Cleese
The Hon Anne Collins
Mr Richard C Colyear
Mr and Mrs Howard Davis
Ms Zita Davisson
Mr Gerry Dolezar
Ms Maria Garvey Dowd
Mrs Beverley C Duer
Mrs June Dyson
Mr Robert H Enslow
Mrs Katherine D Findlay
Mr and Mrs J Winston Fowlkes
Mr and Mrs Gordon P Getty
Mr and Mrs Ellis Goodman
Mrs Oliver R Grace
Sir Jeremy and Lady Greenstock
Mr and Mrs Gustave M Hauser
Mrs Judith Heath
Ms Elaine Kend
Mr and Mrs Nicholas L S Kirkbride
Ms Jeanne K Lawrence
The Hon Samuel K Lessey Jr
Mr Henry S Lynn Jr
Ms Clare E McKeon
Ms Christine Mainwaring-Samwell
Ms Barbara T Missett
The Hon and Mrs William A Nitze
Mrs Charles W Olson III
Ms Jennifer Pellegrino
Cynthia Hazen Polsky and
Leon B Polsky
Ms Wendy Reilly
Mr and Mrs Daniel Rose
Mrs Nanette Ross
Dr Michael Schmerin
Mrs Martin Slifka
Mr Albert H Small
Mr and Mrs Morton I Sosland
Mrs Frederick M Stafford
Mr and Mrs Alfred Taubman
Ms Evelyn Tompkins
Mr Peter Trippi
Mrs Judith Villard
Ms Lucy Waring

Corporate and Foundation Support
American Express Foundation
The Blackstone Charitable Foundation
British Airways PLC
The Brown Foundation
Crankstart Foundation
Fortnum & Mason
Gibson, Dunn & Crutcher
The Horace W Goldsmith Foundation
Hauser Foundation
Kress Foundation
Lasalle Fund
Leon Levy Foundation
Loeb Foundation
Henry Luce Foundation
Lynberg & Watkins
Edmond J Safra Philanthropic
Foundation
Siezen Foundation
Sony Corporation of America
Starr Foundation
Thaw Charitable Trust

CORPORATE MEMBERS OF THE ROYAL ACADEMY
Launched in 1988, the Royal Academy's Corporate Membership Scheme has proved highly successful. Corporate membership offers benefits for staff, clients and community partners and access to the Academy's facilities and resources. The outstanding support we receive from companies via the scheme is vital to the continuing success of the Academy and we thank all members for their valuable support and continued enthusiasm.

Premier Level Members
A T Kearney Limited
Barclays plc
Bird & Bird
British Airways
Catlin Group Limited
CBRE
Christie's
Deutsche Bank AG
FTI Consulting
GlaxoSmithKline plc
Insight Investment
JM Finn & Co
Jones Lang LaSalle
JTI
KPMG
Linklaters
Neptune Investment Management
Schroders Private Banking
Smith and Williamson

Corporate Members
All Nippon Airways
Bank of America Merrill Lynch
BGC Partners
Bloomberg LP
BNP Paribas
Bonhams 1793 Ltd
The Boston Consulting Group
UK LLP
British American Tobacco
Brunswick
BUPA
Capital International Limited
Clifford Chance LLP
Coca Cola Retail Research Council
Crédit Agricole CIB
Ernst & Young
Essex Court
F & C Asset Management plc
GAM
Generation Investment Management LLP
GKN Aerospace
Heidrick & Struggles
Hermès GB
Jefferies International
John Lewis Partnership
J P Morgan
La Mania
Lazard
Lend Lease Limited
Lindsell Train
Lloyds TSB Private Banking
Lubbock Fine Chartered Accountants
Marie Curie
Moelis & Co
Morgan Stanley
Pentland Group plc
Realty Insurances Limited
Rio Tinto London
The Royal Society of Chemistry
Savills
Slaughter and May
Sotheby's
Tiffany & Co
Timothy Sammons Fine Art Agents
Trowers & Hamlins
UBS
Vision Capital Limited
Weil, Gotshal & Manges

Supporters of Past Exhibitions
The President and Council of the Royal Academy would like to thank the following supporters and benefactors for their generous contributions towards major exhibitions in the last ten years:

2012
Mariko Mori
Supported by JTI
Bronze
Christian Levett and Mougins Museum of Classical Art
Daniel Katz Gallery
Baron Lorne Thyssen-Bornemisza
John and Fausta Eskenazi
The Ruddock Foundation for the Arts
Tomasso Brothers Fine Art
Jon and Barbara Landau
Janine and J. Tomilson Hill
Embassy of the Kingdom of the Netherlands
Eskenazi Limited
Lisson Gallery
Alexis Gregory
Alan and Mary Hobart
Richard de Unger and Adeela Qureshi
Rossi & Rossi Ltd
Embassy of Israel
244th Summer Exhibition
Insight Investment
From Paris: A Taste for Impressionism – Paintings from the Clark
2009–2013 Season supported by JTI
Edwards Wildman
The Annenberg Foundation
Premiums, RA Schools Annual Dinner and Auction and *RA Schools Show 2012*
Newton Investment Management
Johan Zoffany RA: Society Observed
2009–2013 Season supported by JTI
Cox & Kings
Building the Revolution: Soviet Art and Architecture 1915–1935
2009–2013 Season supported by JTI
The Ove Arup Foundation
The Norman Foster Foundation
Richard and Ruth Rogers
David Hockney RA: A Bigger Picture
BNP Paribas
Welcome to Yorkshire: Tourism Partner
Visit Hull & East Yorkshire: Supporting Tourism Partner
NEC

2011
Degas and the Ballet: Picturing Movement
BNY Mellon
Region Holdings
Blavatnik Family Foundation
Eyewitness: Hungarian Photography in the Twentieth Century. Brassaï, Capa, Kertész, Moholy-Nagy, Munkácsi
2009–2013 Season supported by JTI
Hungarofest
OTP Bank
243rd Summer Exhibition
Insight Investment
Premiums, RA Schools Annual Dinner and Auction and *RA Schools Show 2011*
Newton Investment Management
Watteau: The Drawings
2009–2013 Season supported by JTI
Region Holdings
Modern British Sculpture
American Express Foundation
The Henry Moore Foundation
Hauser & Wirth
Art Mentor Foundation Lucerne
Sotheby's
Blain Southern
Welcome to Yorkshire: Tourism Partner

2010
GSK Contemporary – Aware: Art Fashion Identity
GlaxoSmithKline
Pioneering Painters: The Glasgow Boys 1880–1900
2009–2013 Season supported by JTI
Glasgow Museums
Treasures from Budapest: European Masterpieces from Leonardo to Schiele
OTP Bank
Villa Budapest
Daniel Katz Gallery, London
Cox & Kings: Travel Partner
Sargent and the Sea
2009–2013 Season supported by JTI
242nd Summer Exhibition
Insight Investment
Paul Sandby RA: Picturing Britain, A Bicentenary Exhibition
2009–2013 Season supported by JTI
The Real Van Gogh: The Artist and His Letters
BNY Mellon
Hiscox
Heath Lambert
Cox & Kings: Travel Partner
RA Outreach Programme
Deutsche Bank AG

2009
GSK Contemporary
GlaxoSmithKline
Wild Thing: Epstein, Gaudier-Brzeska, Gill
2009–2013 Season supported by JTI
BNP Paribas
The Henry Moore Foundation
Anish Kapoor
JTI
Richard Chang
Richard and Victoria Sharp
Louis Vuitton
The Henry Moore Foundation
J W Waterhouse: The Modern Pre-Raphaelite
2009–2013 Season supported by JTI
Champagne Perrier-Jouët
GasTerra
Gasunie
241st Summer Exhibition
Insight Investment
Kuniyoshi. From the Arthur R. Miller Collection
2009–2013 Season supported by JTI
Canon
Cox & Kings: Travel Partner
Premiums and *RA Schools Show*
Mizuho International plc
RA Outreach Programme
Deutsche Bank AG

2008
GSK Contemporary
GlaxoSmithKline
Byzantium 330–1453
J F Costopoulos Foundation
A G Leventis Foundation
Stavros Niarchos Foundation
Cox & Kings: Travel Partner
Miró, Calder, Giacometti, Braque: Aimé Maeght and His Artists
BNP Paribas
Vilhelm Hammershøi: The Poetry of Silence
OAK Foundation Denmark
Novo Nordisk
240th Summer Exhibition
Insight Investment
Premiums and *RA Schools Show*
Mizuho International plc
RA Outreach Programme
Deutsche Bank AG
From Russia: French and Russian Master Paintings 1870–1925 from Moscow and St Petersburg
E.ON
2008 Season supported by Sotheby's

2007
Paul Mellon's Legacy: A Passion for British Art
The Bank of New York Mellon
Georg Baselitz
Eurohypo AG
239th Summer Exhibition
Insight Investment
Impressionists by the Sea
Farrow & Ball
Premiums and *RA Schools Show*
Mizuho International plc
RA Outreach Programme
Deutsche Bank AG
The Unknown Monet
Bank of America

2006
238th Summer Exhibition
Insight Investment
Chola: Sacred Bronzes of Southern India
Cox & Kings: Travel Partner
Premiums and *RA Schools Show*
Mizuho International plc
RA Outreach Programme
Deutsche Bank AG
Rodin
Ernst & Young

2005
China: The Three Emperors, 1662–1795
Goldman Sachs International
Impressionism Abroad: Boston and French Painting
Fidelity Foundation
Matisse, His Art and His Textiles: The Fabric of Dreams
Farrow & Ball
Premiums and *RA Schools Show*
The Guardian
Mizuho International plc
Turks: A Journey of a Thousand Years, 600–1600
Akkök Group of Companies
Aygaz
Corus
Garanti Bank
Lassa Tyres

2004
236th Summer Exhibition
A T Kearney
Ancient Art to Post-Impressionism: Masterpieces from the Ny Carlsberg Glyptotek, Copenhagen
Carlsberg UK Ltd
Danske Bank
Novo Nordisk
The Art of Philip Guston (1913–1980)
American Associates of the Royal Academy Trust
The Art of William Nicholson
RA Exhibition Patrons Group
Vuillard: From Post-Impressionist to Modern Master
RA Exhibition Patrons Group

2003
235th Summer Exhibition
A T Kearney
Ernst Ludwig Kirchner: The Dresden and Berlin Years
RA Exhibition Patrons Group
Giorgio Armani: A Retrospective
American Express
Mercedes-Benz
Illuminating the Renaissance: The Triumph of Flemish Manuscript Painting in Europe
American Associates of the Royal Academy Trust
Virginia and Simon Robertson
Masterpieces from Dresden
ABN AMRO
Classic FM
Premiums and *RA Schools Show*
Walker Morris
Pre-Raphaelite and Other Masters: The Andrew Lloyd Webber Collection
Christie's
Classic FM
UBS Wealth Management

Other Supporters
Sponsors of events, publications and other items in the past five years:

Carlisle Group plc
Castello di Reschio
Cecilia Chan
Country Life
Guy Dawson
Derwent Valley Holdings plc
Dresdner Kleinwort Wasserstein
Lucy Flemming McGrath
Fosters and Partners
Goldman Sachs International
Gome International
Gucci Group
Hines
IBJ International plc
John Doyle Construction
Harvey and Allison McGrath
Martin Krajewski
Marks & Spencer
Michael Hopkins & Partners
Morgan Stanley Dean Witter
The National Trust
Prada
Radisson Edwardian Hotels
Richard and Ruth Rogers
Rob van Helden
The Wine Studio